ISRAEL

JORDAN

DEAD SEA

Hebron

El Falouja

Eilath

GULF OF AQABA

SINAI PENINSULA

BEN-GURION

The Armed Prophet

MICHAEL BAR-ZOHAR

Translated from the French by Len Ortzen

Prentice-Hall, Inc.   Englewood Cliffs, N. J.

Ben-Gurion: The Armed Prophet
by Michael Bar-Zohar

© 1966 by Librairie Arthème Fayard
© 1967 by Arthur Barker Limited for this translation

Published in France by Librairie Arthème Fayard
under the title *Ben-Gourion Le Prophète Armé*

First American Edition published by
Prentice-Hall, Inc., 1968

Library of Congress Catalog Card Number: 68–13398

Printed in the United States of America • T

Publisher's Note: For purposes of this edition, the
French form of certain proper nouns has been retained.

FOREWORD

In the week beginning June 5, 1967, the world was startled by a lightning war which threw the Middle East into a turmoil—the Six-Day War. Six vital days which saw the birth of a new Middle East, altered the map of this part of the world, alarmed the Great Powers, humbled the Soviet Union and demonstrated the power of Israel.

In the aftermath of this astounding victory, few thought about the crucial weeks which Israel lived through immediately preceding the war. Incited by Syrian extremists, Nasser was determined to show that he was the supreme leader of the Arab world. Obsessed by memories of the defeats inflicted upon him by Israel in 1948 and 1956, he launched into an unreasonable undertaking. It seemed an opportune time to wipe Israel from the map. Events succeeded each other with frightening speed—troop movements towards Sinai involving a 100,000 men, thousands of vehicles, hundreds of tanks and planes; the closing of the Straits of Tiran to Israeli shipping; the signing of military pacts with Jordan and Iraq . . .

Israel was taken by surprise, and for help and support turned to the Great Powers and the international organizations—but to no avail. Yet David Ben-Gurion, the first prime minister of the State of Israel, had stated repeatedly over the years his belief that the country could rely only on her own strength. International guarantees, the promises of heads of state and the resolutions of the United Nations would never insure the security and the survival of Israel. The State had to be master of its fate.

On June 1, 1967, General Moshe Dayan, disciple and confidant of Ben-Gurion, was appointed Minister of Defense. He shared Ben-Gurion's views on the manner in which Israel should meet any threat to her existence. He was appointed to this key post despite the fact that he belonged to a small opposition party, RAFI. Popular feeling forced the Government to entrust him with the

iii

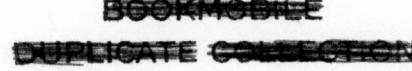

gravest of responsibilities—the safety and, indeed, existence of the State.

Six days after the outbreak of war, Israel emerged from battle as a power in the Middle East, having destroyed the Arab air forces and armor, crushed the armies of three countries and conquered great expanses of territory. Israeli forces were on the Suez Canal and in possession of all of the Sinai Peninsula. They had captured the grim Syrian heights, cleared the area east of the Jordan and freed Jerusalem, the eternal capital of Jewish independence.

Israel's victory had proved that she could not be destroyed. Would it lead the Arabs to open peace talks with their neighbor? At the time of this writing, it is impossible to predict what the outcome will be.

But one conclusion that Israel and the world draw from this war is that Ben-Gurion had been right. By creating the Israeli Army, by impressing upon its soldiers the need for integrity and devotion to the people, by stressing that the Army was the one and only guarantee of Israel's continuing existence, and by tirelessly repeating to the two and a half million Jews that, opposed by one hundred million Arabs, they must count only on their own strength —by all this, Ben-Gurion had forged the weapons of victory.

And Dayan, by his lightning victory, showed himself worthy of the torch handed on to the younger generation of Israelis by the man who had laid the foundations of the State of Israel.

MICHAEL BAR-ZOHAR
Tel Aviv

PREFACE

I spent eighteen months in the company of David Ben-Gurion, and for eighteen months I tried to discover the secret of his drive and energy, of the magical force which has enabled him to overcome insuperable obstacles and to wave the blue-and-white flag of the Jewish people's independence after two thousand years of exile.

I accompanied him on his long silent journeys about the country. I interviewed him for long periods in his kibbutz at Sde Boker, in his office in Tel Aviv and while riding with him in the car along the sun-drenched roads of the Promised Land. I saw Ben-Gurion at moments of dramatic decision, on the platform at huge gatherings, during bitter arguments, in private council, and at meetings with visitors from abroad and with the ordinary people of Israel. I came to know him very well and to love him, he and his loyal companion, Paula, who is modest and frank and devoted body and soul to the man who symbolizes the rebirth of Israel.

He answered all the questions I put to him without ever trying to evade a point or to avoid a painful subject. He gave me full use of his personal documents and papers, and told me his closest secrets.

I have consulted dozens of books in Hebrew and in European languages, have examined thousands of documents, read Ben-Gurion's diaries with great interest, and gone through files of newspaper articles and reports. I had the great privilege of being allowed the use of Ben-Gurion's notebooks, containing his ideas and thoughts from day to day. I interviewed his supporters and his opponents, and noted what they had to say about minor details as well as decisive events, big moments and major situations.

During those eighteen months I thought of nothing but Ben-Gurion, of his life and the trying times he has gone through, of his assets and his defects. I had never before been as passionately and completely interested in a subject.

This book is the result. I have tried to be impartial, but like all those who write the lives of great men, I have found it very difficult. No ordinary criterion can be applied to Ben-Gurion. And his colleagues and associates seem small, pale figures beside this David who is a Goliath.

Other writers have covered the ground before me, and the day will come when other biographers, protected by time against the passions and feelings of the moment, will be able to bring impartial minds to the examination. They probably will have more sources and documents to draw upon, and in any case will know what has succeeded the Ben-Gurion period and how the State of Israel further develops. But one question will still remain difficult to answer—what sort of man was he? What was his charm, and whence came his hold over great crowds, How did he succeed in convincing others, in carving out a career, attaining his aims and drawing everyone in his wake? My Ben-Gurion is not the impersonal figure of official documents, nor the man who emerges from factual reports. He is a fiery, impetuous, passionate man, ever striving for his goal, a man capable of the impossible.

It is David Ben-Gurion, the fighter, the builder and the soldier, a man who is still very much with us, of whom I write.

And this book can only be dedicated to one person—the man who is the subject of it.

CONTENTS

I
THE
VISIONARY

ONE

THE STREET OF THE GOATS

Towards the end of the nineteenth century, having been hated for many centuries, the Jews in most parts of Europe were made hopeful by the French Revolution. The Declaration of the Rights of Man had brought them equality, and then Napoleon's armies had swept into Italy and Poland and had blithely broken down the solid gates of the ghettos. Once under way, the emancipation of the Jews had developed amazingly fast. In Western Europe they discarded their traditional garments and were soon found in the highest scientific and intellectual circles, on the benches of Parliament and other national assemblies, and even in ministerial office. In Britain, Benjamin Disraeli became Prime Minister. The prosperity of Jewish communities soared. Small moneylenders became powerful merchant bankers, one-shop tailors became heads of the clothing trade, and whole districts of the big towns and cities were populated by Jewish artisans and shopkeepers. Such progress was much too rapid in the eyes of some people. The reaction was not long in coming.

In 1879, Wilhelm Merr added a new expression to the international vocabulary—anti-Semitism. Europe had to teach a lesson to these Jews who had made such great strides in a mere half-century.

In Russia, the era of pogroms began on the evening of April 27, 1881, just before Easter. The pretext was the assassination of the Czar, Alexander II. A number of terrorists were arrested in the days following, and among them was a young Jewess, Hesia Helfman. She was a very minor figure in the plot on the Czar's life, but this was enough for the semiofficial paper *Novoye Vremya* to accuse the Jews of the assassination. And the new Czar, Alexander III, was only too ready to accept this version.

Then, on April 27, an excited crowd attacked an inn at Elizabethgrad belonging to a Jew. They invaded the cellars, got drunk, and made for the Jewish quarter of the town. The mob broke into synagogues, looted shops, and then turned on the inhabitants. Thirty Jewish women were raped, and the men who tried to save them were massacred. For three days the mob looted, killed and raped, broke up shops and set fire to whole streets of the wooden shacks which housed the poor. On the third day, Czarist troops intervened. Until then, the military had been indifferent or had even been drawn into the mass hysteria. Now orders were issued to put a stop to the riot. Russia could indulge in the luxury of a pogrom, but it could not be allowed to degenerate into a riot which might turn against the authorities.

Elizabethgrad was only the start. On May 8 the terror struck Kiev. By May 15 it had reached Odessa, which was the scene of violence for four days, and then it spread to ten, twenty, fifty towns and villages. By Christmas, when the pogrom virus was at work in Warsaw, more than 150 Jewish communities in southern Russia had been laid waste.

Was this outbreak the prelude to a "final solution" of the Jewish problem? Certainly Alexander III's chief counselor and "Gray Eminence," Constantin Petrovitch Pobyedonostzev, did not hide his attitude: "One third of Russian Jews will become converts, one third will emigrate, and the remainder will be exterminated."

Hundreds of thousands of terrified Jews were already making for the frontiers, swarming along the roads, or boarding ships, for other continents. Was that the way to salvation, the right solution?

The Jews had been seeking a solution for two thousand years. Scattered all over the world, generally hated or despised, they had no possibility of recovering their lost homeland. Some clung despairingly to any faint hope, some renounced their religion with the aim of starting a new life, others immersed themselves ever deeper in a strict observance of the rites, in an excessive and blind orthodoxy. For them, the only hope was in God. The history of the Jews is full of incredible instances of frightened people leaving their homes and possessions in masses to follow some new "Messiah" who, generally, did not even succeed in leading them to the nearest frontier. So many failures, however, did nothing to weaken credulity, and new sects constantly arose—secret sects, mystical sects, most of them dubious—and there was always someone to believe in them, hoping to find salvation, a way of escape.

Everyone believed he knew the road to salvation. In the nineteenth century, Russo-Polish Judaism was divided into several movements all hating and mutually excommunicating one another. The mass of the people was enchanted by the open-mindedness of *Hassidism,* which believed God could be reached through joy, through dancing and singing. Orthodox Judaism, rigidly opposed to any change in the traditional rites, was an implacable enemy of this "profanity." A third movement called itself *Haskala,* "Culture," and was an attempt to embrace the culture and civilization of the modern world, taking for example the outlook of Jews in Western Europe. Between these movements and the many splinter groups around them existed a fierce hatred, which inevitably fostered bitter conflicts, and leaders of rival groups even denounced each other to the Czarist government.

Russia was then a vast ghetto. Yet the Jews had been expelled from the country on several occasions. During the eighteenth century, Catherine, Anne and Elizabeth had each in succession signed a ukase to that effect. But such was the irony of fate that after each exodus large areas of Poland were absorbed into the Russian Empire, and their Jewish populations also. Against her own desires, Russia had become the cradle of Judaism. The region bordered by the Dnieper and the Vistula, the Baltic and the Black Seas, contained the largest concentration of Jews in the world.

They lived apart from the Russian or Polish peasantry, withdrawn into themselves, suspicious and uneasy. The men wore long black gowns and a skullcap or fur hat, spoke Yiddish and lived in the past, obsessed by their persecutions. They were poorly housed, mostly in wooden shacks along filthy unpaved streets which never saw the sun. The majority of them were shopkeepers, traders or agents, innkeepers. And a not inconsiderable number spent their days reading the Scriptures by candlelight in the chilly synagogues. Very few worked productively, and this mode of living affected their outlook—they had the mentality of persecuted, humiliated men. Nevertheless, they had an unshakable hope for a better future and a determined faith in their God.

The wave of pogroms seemed likely to put an end to this state of affairs. Before the century was out, nearly a million Jews had fled from Imperial Russia, most of them to emigrate to the New World. But a much greater number preferred to remain where they were, bending their heads to the storm and hoping that, like others before, it would pass over. Nothing roused them—neither the "May Laws" of 1882 which expelled hundreds of thousands of them, nor the creation of a terrorist group approved by the Czar, called the "Black Hundreds," whose aims included the massacre of Jews.

The pogroms spread into Poland and reached Warsaw. A small town on the river Plonka was spared the terror. Its name was Plonsk, and two-thirds of its popluation of ten thousand were Jews, proud of their synagogue, which was the finest in all Poland. They were for the most part traders and shopkeepers, tailors and artisans, divided among themselves by being Orthodox, *Hassidim* or progressive in their religious beliefs. As a community it was a perfect reflection of the world of Polish Jewry.

In this town of Plonsk, in a wooden house on the muddy Street of the Goats, David Grin—later to be known as David Ben-Gurion—was born on October 16, 1886.

His origins and his childhood background set him apart from the other Jewish children. His father was neither a poor trader nor fanatically Orthodox. His grandfather, although a practicing Jew, was a man of wide culture, a fervent admirer of Plato, Spinoza and Kant; in addition to speaking Polish and Yiddish, he was fluent in Hebrew, Russian and German.

Victor Grin, David's father, was even more of a progressive, a member of the *Haskala* movement, that compromise between the world of Judaism and the world of Western culture. He was the first, and for a long time the only, man in the town to abandon traditional Jewish dress. He usually wore a well-cut frock coat and a stiff collar, and he smoked cigarettes—an unpardonable crime in the eyes of Orthodox Jews. He was a lawyer (admittedly without qualifications) and his practice took him outside the Jewish world and brought him into contact with the Polish population and the Russian authorities. He often pleaded in the court at Plonsk, and at Warsaw, and was on friendly terms with the local civic authorities.

The Grin family was quite well off, though not rich. Sheindal Fridman had brought her husband a dowry of two houses that were partly rented. Although David never knew poverty and hunger in his childhood, he was rather cut off from other Jewish children. His father's freethinking resulted in the other Jews keeping their distance and, at times, displaying open hostility.

Yet Victor Grin was a good Jew by his own standards. From his father, he had inherited a strict observance of religious rites and a love of the Hebrew language, which he spoke without any difficulty. David learned his first words of Hebrew from his grandfather, and when the old man died David was taught by his father.

Victor Grin also inspired in his son, from a very early age, a deep love for the old country, Palestine, which he imbued with a legendary halo. He held the hopes of the Zionists fifteen years before the movement was born. He had no illusions as to the chances of assimilating the Jews into the Christian world by a cultural bond. He was aware of the ideas being spread by Jewish thinkers such as Hess and Smolenskin, who dreamed of reestablishing a Jewish nation in Palestine, but he knew that the mass of Jews was not behind them. The Jews prayed for "the return to Jerusalem next year," but if someone seriously proposed it to them he would have been thought a visionary or even a traitor to Judaism.

However, soon after the pogroms in Russia, Leo Pinsker, a Jewish doctor from Odessa, published a pamphlet entitled *Auto-Emancipation*. He wrote of the hopelessness of the illusions of the Jews and called for the establishment of a Jewish center in Palestine. A handful of students had in fact anticipated him and had already gone to the Middle East as members of a tiny organization called *Bilu*. Other Jewish organizations were being formed here and there, all having the name *Hovévei Zion* (Lovers of Zion), and in 1884 they held their first congress at Katowice. Among the delegates were two from Plonsk—Simcha Ayzik and Victor Grin. When political Zionism made its appearance, causing an upheaval in the Jewish world, Grin was one of the earliest members.

David thus grew up in an atmosphere of freedom. His life was not overclouded by poverty, he did not go hungry or suffer humiliations and persecutions, and he never knew what it was to be the victim of a pogrom or to live in a ghetto. He lived in a sheltered little world which was in communication with, but differed from, the ordinary Jewish world. When he joined the Zionist movement it was not as a reaction from despair, but because of his family background. "I have inherited from my father," he wrote on the day Victor Grin died, "a love for the people of Israel, for the land of Israel and for the Hebrew language."

From his mother, he learned of love. As a child, he worshipped her. "My earliest memory," he said, "goes back to when I was two or three. I can see myself sitting at a corner of our big table and looking at my gentle, smiling mother knitting by my side."

He was her fourth child, and her favorite. As a little boy he was thin and frail. When a cholera epidemic broke out in Plonsk, she took him away. She was a simple, religious woman, and hoped that David would become a great rabbi.

He was a retiring child and had little to do with his brothers and sisters; all his affection was centered on his mother. He hardly ever played games, though sometimes he ran about in the large green meadow belonging to the Polish priest, on the other side of the stream at the bottom of the Grin's garden. He wore a long black gown, like other Jewish children, and this made his face seem even paler.

He was not quite eleven when his mother died in childbirth. She had already had ten children, though only six were to survive. It was a terrible shock to the boy.

David Grin was a great reader from his very early years. The first two books which he read, in Hebrew, are symbolic—*The Love of Zion* by the Jewish writer, Mapu, and *Uncle Tom's Cabin*. Later he read the works of Jewish thinkers, and also books in Russian. Tolstoy enthralled him. For some months he was a fervent believer in vegetarianism.

His primary education, however, was a traditional Jewish one. Dressed in a long black gown, he spent some years learning the Bible, the Talmud and books of prayer in the overcrowded classrooms of rabbinical schools. One day he secretly decided to stop praying and ceased to observe the rites of the Jewish religion. This earned him a beating from his father—the one and only occasion. But it had no effect; he still refused to follow religious practices, and his father did not insist. The boy already showed that he had a strong will.

In any case, young David Grin was animated by a new religion, a new faith which was beginning to spread—Zionism.

TWO

THE REBEL

Zionism was born on December 19, 1894, in a most unlikely place—an army courtroom in Paris. The curtain had risen on "The Affair of the Century," and the focal point of the storm was Alfred Dreyfus.

One of the journalists reporting the trial was particularly moved by it. He was a Viennese, the special correspondent of the *Neue Freie Presse*, and a Jew. His name was Dr. Theodore Herzl. As an ardent francophile and republican, he felt that a whole world was crumbling at the Dreyfus trial, and it dawned on him that Jews would never have peace, security or respect while they were scattered among other nations. Only if they had a homeland of their own could they hope for these things. And a homeland existed, had always existed—Palestine. Herzl decided to write a book about the idea of creating a Jewish state. It was published the following year with that title, *The Jewish State*. Translated into several languages, it caused great excitement in Jewish circles.

News of it reached young David Grin in the dimly-lit prayer house at Plonsk. He was told that the Messiah, the real Messiah, had just made his appearance, that he was young and handsome with a big black beard and was going to lead the people of Israel to the Promised Land. Full of a child's wholehearted enthusiasm, the boy sought to win his friends over to this new idea, which henceforth he considered sacred.

At the age of twelve, when most boys were still playing soldiers, he had already embarked on politics. And at fourteen he felt mature and responsible enough to found, along with his two best friends, a youth organization which they called *Ezra*. Ezra, a great man in Jewish history, had been the spiritual leader of the Jews when they returned from exile in Babylon. The aims of this organization were to prepare Jewish youth, spiritually and morally, for their return to Palestine, to teach them Hebrew, and to instill in them a love of the Promised Land. Although David was younger than his co-founders—Shlomo Zemach and Schmuel Fuchs—he soon became spokesman for the group and astonished the Jews of Plonsk with his oratory. He was a spirited and rousing speaker, and even at that age showed great skill in public debate. Often, his opponents could not forgive the virulence of his attack. With strength and enthusiasm, he was waging a Holy War. When he was fifteen, his father wrote about him to Herzl, in Hebrew, calling his son "the apple of his eye," telling of the boy's outstanding gifts and saying that he would like to send him to Vienna to continue his studies.

David knew nothing of this letter, and his father never mentioned it. But there can be no doubt he was proud of his son. For he himself was in the vanguard of the Zionist movement at Plonsk. The house in the Street of the Goats was the meeting place of the town's Zionists. They printed their leaflets there and deposited the money they collected. There was nothing easy about being a Zionist in Poland in the early 1900s. The greatest opponents of the movement were the Jews themselves. Fanatical Orthodox Jews and *Hassidim* rooted in the past waged unremitting war on Zionism.

The ferment was not confined to the small world of Polish Jewry. More rough winds were sweeping across Russia. This time, it was in the Bessarabian town of Kishinev that anti-Semitism broke out. Forty-five Jews were killed and six hundred injured. At Plonsk, the Grin house became the center of defense. Under the walls of the house, the family hid a stock of weapons. Nevertheless, David and his friends felt humiliated and helpless; they had their first doubts about the Zionist movement as it then existed. The World Zionist congresses met regularly and were the theater for heated discussions and debates on Zionism. But no deeds resulted from the words. What was the use of holding one congress after another? Would it not be better to act, and to act now? Herzl believed in diplomatic means to help the Jews establish themselves in Palestine —and in the meantime Jews were being messacred in Russia! At the last congress, held in Basel, Joseph Chamberlain, the British Colonial Minister, had proposed the establishment of a Jewish Home in East Africa, in Uganda—and Herzl had seemed to approve of the idea.

The news from Basel reached Plonsk one day in August. The three inseparables, David Grin, Zemach and Fuchs, had just been bathing in the cool waters of the Plonka when they read the account of the congress in a newspaper. They felt lost and betrayed. This Uganda plan would only turn people's minds from the primary objective—Palestine. There and then, sitting on the river bank and still dripping wet, the three lads made the most important decision in their lives. The only way to achieve the aims of Zionism was by *Aliyah,* emigrating to Palestine. They had had enough of meetings, speeches and hollow words. There was but one means of making their dream come true, and that was to act, each for himself and all together. The Jewish people must stake their claim to Palestine not by words but by deeds.

It was then, too, that a deep distrust of speeches, protocol and wordy diplomacy was born in the young Ben-Gurion. Henceforth he would be a man of action. "For me," he later wrote to his father, "the founding of a new village in Palestine is more important than a thousand congresses and conferences. The real, the only, Zionism is the colonization of Palestine; everything else is just eyewash, blah and a waste of time."

That day, on the bank of the river, young Grin made up his mind; he would leave for Palestine as soon as possible. He thought out his plan very carefully. The new state would need builders; so he would go to a technical college, and once he was a qualified engineer he would set off for the Promised Land. In any case, he had already decided not to stay in Poland. A friend once expressed surprise at his making so little effort with the Polish language. "It's Russian that interests me," he replied. "Polish is just a dialect, and I've no intention of staying in Poland."

When he was sixteen, David went to Warsaw to study for his matriculation certificate. He earned his living by giving lessons in a modern Jewish school. This only brought him twenty rubles a month, but it was enough for him. He read a great deal, and was very active in the Zionist movement, which was much bigger in the capital than at Plonsk.

He was enthralled by the life around him. He was a handsome young man and could have been popular with girls. But he made only one attachment, and that was with lovely Rachel Nelkin, the adopted daughter of the Zionist, Simcha Ayzik. Their relationship lasted for many years.

On one of his visits to Plonsk, in July 1904, he heard of the death of Herzl, which came as a great blow to him. Herzl had died a disappointed man, worn out by his fruitless campaign. The news spread dismay in Jewish communities throughout the world. Did it mean the end of the Zionist movement? A few days later, when back in Warsaw, David wrote a very pathetic letter to his friend Schmuel Fuchs: "The loss is as great and cruel as the everlasting sufferings of such an unhappy race as ours." But he did not despair: "The sun has vanished, but its light still shines forth."

The Russian Revolution of 1905 ended in a blood bath, with long columns of chained men being marched off to Siberia. But the winds of revolution were felt by many young Zionists, who saw in a socialist society the ideal order which they wished to establish in their future homeland. David Grin joined a Zionist-socialist youth movement called *Poalei Zion* (The Workmen of Zion) at the Warsaw home of one of his friends, Itzhak Tabenkin (later to be an opponent). David started a cell at Plonsk. He and the other members played at being revolutionaries, going armed to the synagogue. He could not help smiling at the warlike accoutrement. It was the rule of the game, but ceased to be a game when the Czarist police began to search the Grin house. By some miracle, the weapons and the tracts of *Poalei Zion* were not discovered, although the police made several visits. After one particularly thorough search, Victor Grin decided to transfer the cache of weapons to a safer place. This was done under the noses of the Czarist police and in an original manner. He and his friends, dressed in black and wearing mournful expressions, carried a heavy coffin—a *very* heavy coffin—out of the house and so deposited the weapons in a less frequented house.

One might think that all this political activity had driven thoughts of Palestine from David's mind. Not so. He and his two friends, Fuchs and Zemach, held a council of war and decided that Zemach would go to Palestine first, and the other two would follow when he had prepared the ground. So one day, Zemach pocketed the 300 rubles which his father had sent him to collect from the bank, and left. He stayed in Warsaw with David Grin for a few days, then left for Palestine. For a whole year he sent David long, detailed letters whose vivid style was a sign of the future writer. They gave David an excellent idea of the distant land that so fascinated him, and when he himself arrived in Palestine he felt he had known the land and its people for a long time.

Fuchs was the next to leave. But the first letter that David received from him bore a London postmark, and the following one came from New York. At the last moment Fuchs had lost courage—the courage that distinguished the tiny band of Zionist pioneers from the mass. Fuchs had joined the hundreds of thousands of Jews who had chosen the easiest solution—emigration to the United States.

David was the last to go. He was nearly twenty, small in build but with a lively mind. He had grown a moustache and looked mature for his years. His usually amiable expression could become quite arrogant at times. His thick, wavy brown hair was rather untidy, in the manner of revolutionaries. In fact, it was sufficient cause for a Czarist policeman to arrest him in Warsaw. He was put in prison on political grounds, but his father hurried to the capital and obtained his release after a few days. He was arrested a second time for being in possession of compromising papers relating to his political activities. This could easily have resulted in his being sent to Siberia. But through the Grins' connections and friends in Warsaw plus a "softener" of one thousand rubles, he was released. David was able to continue his work as political agitator and took part in public debates in Plonsk and its neighborhood.

But he had had enough of words. Zemach returned to Plonsk after a year, as he had promised, and David decided to go back with him to Palestine. Victor Grin would have liked his son to finish his education before leaving, but gave way as usual in face of the young man's determination.

David went first to Odessa, traveling under a false name and with a forged passport. At Odessa he met a farm worker who had come from Palestine on business, a Jewish pioneer who tilled the soil of Israel!

At last, in August 1906, David Grin embarked on an old Russian cargo ship, together with Turks, Russians, Greeks and a few Jews, to sail to the land of his dreams, the country that he had never seen.

THREE

THE HEROIC YEARS

Palestine, the land overflowing with milk and honey, as it had been for centuries.

Since the days of the Kingdom of Israel much water had flown down the winding River Jordan and into the Dead Sea. The Jewish nation had lost its homeland, the Wandering Jew had begun his sad travels, and control of Palestine had passed from power to power.

At the time when Zionism was sending forth the first Jewish pioneers, Palestine was held by the ailing but tenacious Ottoman Empire. The country then had nothing in common with the earthly paradise described in the Old Testament. The ravages of successive wars, erosion and lack of cultivation had turned the fruit groves, vineyards and streams of the Song of Songs into arid and desolate wastes. The fertile coastal plains and the lush valleys inland had become malarial marshes. The implacable sun beat down on the mountains of Judaea, on the barren rock. Palestine had become the most neglected part of the Ottoman Empire.

Such was the "earthly paradise." Yet the prayers and the hopes of millions of Jews were directed towards this ailing, desolate land, as well as a trickle of young emigrants who thought they were the advance guard of the Zionist masses. In fact there were still a few thousand Jews living in Palestine, divided between the five large towns of Jaffa, Safed, Tiberias, Hebron and Jerusalem. A few of them were descended from families which had never left the country, and which had succeeded from generation to generation in staying on despite the many laws and edicts expelling them. Others had ancestors who had arrived centuries ago from other parts of the Turkish Empire and the Muslim world. Together they formed a community that was fatalistic and unfruitful. They were waiting, simple and credulous, and with quite Oriental patience, for the coming of the Messiah. . . .

Instead of the Messiah, there came young Jews dressed in European clothes and speaking Yiddish, Russian or Polish, landing in small groups at the primitive port of Jaffa. The majority of them were not experienced at hard manual work and were not strong physically, but they all possessed the real urge and willingness which is the strength of young nations. Brushing aside the specialists and advisers who said their plans were sheer folly, these youngsters flung themselves into the task of wresting a living from the land, and founded farming villages, centers of Jewish stock. The Palestinian Arabs became used to the sight of these young foreigners stupidly pitching their tents on the verge of marshland or by polluted streams, in the heart of unhealthy areas. Many died as a result of this difficult life. At that period, only about one out of ten Jewish immigrants remained working in Palestine.

The pioneers who accomplished the "marvel" in Jewish history, the return to the homeland, could not be counted in thousands and hardly in hundreds; there were just dozens of enthusiasts, sick and famished, treated as fools. The story of an entire Jewish people returning to their homeland is a fable, a legend which conceals a much more modest, and therefore more heroic, state of affairs.

There were some among those "fools" who were quite wealthy, and although they were not foolish enough to work on the land themselves, they used their money to help the pioneers. The first colonization project was put forward by Sir Moses Montifiore in 1839, and he was responsible for the first orange plantation in 1856. Charles Netter founded an agricultural school at Mikve Israel in 1870. Then Baron Edmond de Rothschild bought some land and founded farming communities, and sent out instructors to help those early pioneers.

The Jewish laborer, however, was at a disadvantage compared to the sturdier and more practiced Arab workman. The former's first struggle was to find work, to be allowed to work, and he often came up against the "seigneurs" of his own race.

Such was the sad state of affairs, the reality of the situation, which was waiting for David Grin when he first set foot in the Promised Land. The day, September 9, 1906, was hot and dusty. His first sight of Palestine was the port of Jaffa, an ancient town with a glorious past but now repulsively dirty and squalid—the Orient in all its starkness. When he landed and mixed with the crowd, he looked with disgust at the horde of hawkers and the dull-eyed shopkeepers sitting by their goods. It disgusted him that a number of these traders were Jews. "I shall leave Jaffa this very day," he told his companions, "and go to a farming colony. I can't stay here, not even for a single night."

He experienced another disappointment before leaving Jaffa. To his astonishment, the reception committee of the *Poalei Zion* Party took him off to one hotel for a short rest, while his friend Zemach was taken to another hotel by members of Zemach's party, *Hapoel Hatzaïr* (The Young Workman). The divergences between the two parties were very slight, but their ridiculous rivalry had created a barrier of jealousy and hostility. The young emigrants to Palestine had gotten rid of many prejudices, but still had a liking for the division and the sectarianism which separated Jews in Russia and Poland into different camps. Grin soon came up against this barren hostility. "I had just arrived in Palestine," he said some years later, "and was marveling at being in my homeland, burning with enthusiasm for building it up—and all that those men did was criticize my views on historical materialism."

That very first evening, David Grin and Shlomo Zemach, having met again, arrived on foot at the Jewish colony of Petah Tikva. David spent his first night in Palestine under the starry sky.

"That first night on the soil of my homeland," he wrote, "has left a memory of triumphal joy in my heart. I was unable to get to sleep. There I was in Israel, in a Hebrew village of the Holy Land, in a Jewish village called Petah Tikva—the Door of Hope. The howling of jackals in the vineyards, the braying of asses in the stables, the croaking of frogs in the ponds, the heavy scent of acacias, the sound of the sea in the distance, the shadows of the orange trees in the half-light, the stars twinkling in a dark blue sky that was glistening and unreal—everything was so wonderfully strange, as in some legendary realm. I thought of all the stages of my journey—the farewells, the sea passage and the approach to the coast of Palestine. And now I was in Israel. Was it really true? I sat up all night, communing with these new skies . . ."

The sky was wonderful. But the land yielded little. David Grin became a farm worker, hiring himself out by the day. The relatively comfortable life at Plonsk was a world away. He had never handled a spade before, but he plunged enthusiastically into this new life. Work was not easy to find, and he wandered from village to village, poorly dressed and often near exhaustion. He worked for a few days at Petah Tikva, for a few weeks on the plateau of Kfar Saba, and in the vineyards of Richon-in-Zion. He planted bushes, attacked virgin ground and dug up stones and boulders, shifted manure, made irrigation channels and ploughed the land. The torrid heat of the summer was followed by the icy showers of winter. David Grin shivered in his thin cloak, and was often up to his ankles in mud. It was a hard life, like that of all the other pioneers. And, like many of them, he caught malaria. But fighting against the terrible fever of the marshes was a mark of the true pioneer. The doctor in Jaffa said he would not survive the attacks, he must leave the country. David Grin shook his head: "Not me!"

Fever was not the worst; work was still difficult to find. Jewish employers preferred Arab workmen, who were much hardier and more compliant. When David was out of work he appeased his hunger by munching a chunk of Arab bread, which he could buy for a few coppers. But there were times when he could not even find a few coppers.

His father, alarmed by the news he received indirectly, sent him ten rubles. David returned it, saying "I've no need of money. Thank you for sending it, but I'm returning it to you. I'm managing all right . . ."

It was his pride in keeping himself in his homeland which caused him to write those words; and that pride and love of the country comes through in the descriptions in his letters to his father: "The days are lovely in our country, days bathed in clear light, full of splendor and rich in views of the sea and the hills . . . Yet how much more splendid are the nights: drops of liquid gold sparkling under the light blue dome of the sky, the delicate purity of the mountains, the crystal-clear air on the heights, all vibrant with desires, pulsing with hopes and secret murmurings. You are aware of urges which are not of this world. . . ."

Young Grin's political beliefs were beginning to take shape. The fighter of Plonsk and Warsaw had not given up. He attacked the Jewish landowners who employed Arabs and who scorned the poor wretches of Zionists trying to settle in Palestine. He was disgusted, seeing in their attitude a similarity to the despised Jews in Europe who sought nothing but gain and to be left in peace, and who cared little for the ideal of a free nation. He attacked the owners of vineyards and the vine-growers too, who treated their workmen as they liked. His first victory as a trade union leader was wrung from the "seigneurs" of the Richon vineyards, after he had organized a determined strike. His own scorn for the Zionists abroad kept increasing. A quarter of a century later, Weizmann could write that the years before the First World War were "unexciting." But not for David Grin and his friends. They were decisive years, a time when the capacity of the Jewish people to take root in their country of origin was being tested. And theirs was the victory—the victory of a few hundred pioneers who differed from tramps and beggars only by the light shining in their eyes and by the driving force which impelled them to gather late at night, although worn out by the day's work, to sing and dance until dawn. The voice of David Grin was never absent from these improvised choirs.

His voice was also heard in the small, dingy rooms where the first meetings of the Jewish workers' movements were held. His party, the *Poalei Zion*, the Workers of Zion, was opposed—for the membership of a few dozen workmen—by the *Hapoel Hatzaïr*, a less socialistic and combatant movement but led by an extraordinary man, A. D. Gordon, a venerable white-bearded patriarch. He called for a return to the land, but otherwise the *Hapoel Hatzaïr* had no strong political belief.

The leaders of the *Poalei Zion*, however, were doctrinaires marked by a rigid socialism, an uncompromising Marxism. They had reached Palestine in the second wave of immigrants after the failure of the Russian revolution in 1905, and they wanted to build the kind of model society which the Russian revolutionaries had dreamed of. Class warfare and historical materialism were fascinating subjects, but how could they be reconciled with the needs of the moment? This was a delicate question to which they turned a deaf ear.

David Grin attracted attention in the *Poalei Zion* Party not so much for his qualities of leadership as for his nonconformism. He was a Socialist, of course, but he wanted the party's doctrine to include the idea of a "Jewish national movement." He had already met with opposition. For instance, he tried in vain to persuade his friends to speak Hebrew. One said to him: "I'm quite prepared to speak Hebrew, but how could that be explained from a Marxist point of view?"

Less than a month after arriving in Palestine, David Grin attended the inaugural congress of the *Poalei Zion* Party in Jaffa. It was decided to create a "Workers' Confederation." He pressed for the word "Jewish" to be added. Everyone was against him at first, but in the end he succeeded. He was elected to a ten-man committee which was to draw up the party's political program.

While in Russia, meetings of that kind were kept highly secret, in Palestine, there was nothing to fear. But tradition was very strong, and the ten committee members met like conspirators in a dingy room at the Arab inn at Ramleh. In great secrecy they spent three days drawing up the "Ramleh Program," which was in fact a slightly modified version of the Communist Manifesto. At the next party meeting Grin succeeded in getting his nationalist point included in the program: "The party aims at the political independence of the Jewish people in this country."

From then on, Grin made every effort to bring his nationalism into line with the socialism he wanted to put into practice. But his socialist ideas became increasingly elastic in order to serve the nationalist movement.

In his early twenties, while still known as David Grin, he was a lonely person with hardly any real friends. But when he had been in Palestine for a year there arrived one of the favored few ever to win his affection and trust. This was a tall, slim young man with a sad face, Itzhak Shimshelevitch. Although a scholar and an intellectual, he had organized Jewish self-defense units in Russia. When his identity was discovered he had fled to Palestine disguised as a priest. He took the name of Itzhak Ben-Zvi, and became the inseparable friend of David Ben-Gurion.*

David Grin first met Ben-Zvi in 1907, while at Petah Tikva. But he left this village in the coastal plain before the end of the year, and made his way northwards to Galilee. He had had enough of the life of a farm worker at the mercy of Jewish overlords, a life that was no more than the Eastern version of that of all Jews in exile. He wanted to find a Jewish settlement where he would truly be working with his fellow Jews. He went on foot through Judaea, crossing the uninhabited valley of Izreel, and sleeping under the starry sky. Eventually he arrived at a small village at the foot of the green hills of Galilee. Its name was Sejera, and there he spent the happiest years of his life.

It was during his time at Sejera that his nationalism went a stage further. Until then, his aim and object had been to find work. This was no problem at Sejera. There were no haughty overlords or humiliated Jewish workers at Sejera, nor any rivalry between immigrants and landowners. Everyone in the village worked side by side, and Jews of all origins lived together.

"After Judaea, Sejera had almost the same effect on me as Petah Tikva after exile," he wrote. "I had at last found the atmosphere of a real homeland. There were neither shopkeepers nor speculators, mercenaries nor parasites. All in the settlement were workers . . . farm workers, peasants, smelling strongly of manure and the fields, with faces tanned by the sun."

He was soon tackling another matter—to have Jewish land

* Many years later, Ben-Zvi became President of the State of Israel.

guarded and defended by the Jews themselves. Everywhere in Palestine at that time the villages were guarded by Arabs, Circassians or Turks. Not that the villages were in any great danger; admittedly, the roads were not safe, but the Jewish villages suffered only from petty thievery, and killings were rare. The Jews had never carried arms, so why should they start now?

David Grin was thoroughly aroused. A nation had to be created in this country, a nation which must govern itself. It could not lean on the guns of mercenaries who might abandon their posts or even turn against it. The Jews must see to their own defense.

He tried to convince the villagers of this, but the farm manager was dubious. The village was guarded by Circassians, hard and cruel men. It would be courting danger to show distrust of them. To arm the Jews would lead sooner or later to bloodshed between them and the Arabs. The aim was to live together in peace, not to kill each other. But David Grin believed that a trial of strength was bound to come some time. He continued to press his point of view, and eventually succeeded—a cart was sent to the coast, near the town of Haifa, and returned loaded with rifles which were carefully hidden away. A short time later, David and his friends staged an attempted robbery. The farm manager was called, and discovered that the Circassian guards had done nothing to protect the village. They were dismissed, and Sejera became the first Jewish village in Palestine to be guarded exclusively by Jews.

A few months later, a bloody incident proved that David Grin had been right.

FOUR

BLOODSHED IN GALILEE

Passover 1909 saw the usual festivities in the inn at Sejera. The walls of the public room were adorned with agricultural implements and firearms, symbolic of the pioneers' two aims—work and defense. But on this day they were thinking only of singing and dancing.

A shout brought a sudden stop to the merriment. Standing in the doorway was a distraught young man. In a hoarse voice he told how he and two friends had almost reached the village on their way from Haifa when they were attacked by three armed Arabs, who tried to rob them. After a desperate struggle they had managed to drive the Arabs off, wounding one of them badly.

There was a deathly silence in the room. They could only guess whether the robbers came from the biblical town of Cana, whose inhabitants hated the Jewish colonists, or from Lubia, an Arab center which could muster 500 rifles, or from the aggressive Zubh tribe. But that was of secondary importance, for the pioneers were well aware of the code of Arab vendettas. If the wounded man died, the members of his tribe would wreak their vengeance for a week. They would steal sheep, burn crops and kill. It was the age-old law of the East that blood must be wiped out with blood. "From that moment," wrote David Grin, "we knew that one of us would be murdered. The question was, who?"

They did not have long to wait for the answer. The wounded Arab died, and sheep belonging to the Jews were stolen. Armed horsemen were roaming menacingly round the village. On the seventh day after the initial attack a new arrival, Israel Korngold, went on guard duty. At two in the afternoon he left the inn, armed with this rifle. A few minutes later, shots rang out. The Jews snatched up their weapons and ran towards the sound of the firing. But it was too late. Korngold had been fatally shot and his rifle stolen. That same day another Jew, a carpenter named Shimon Melamed, was killed by Arabs.

"That day opened my eyes," Ben-Gurion said later. "I realized that sooner or later there would be a trial of strength between us and the Arabs. From that moment at Sejera I felt that conflict was inevitable. What happened that day in my village was child's play compared with the dangers that the future had in store for us. We had to be prepared to meet them."

The Judaeo-Arab struggle did not begin in Sejera, but it was there on that day in April 1909 that several of the future Jewish leaders realized that sooner or later the two races would clash and that might would prevail.

"By fire and blood Judaea fell, by fire and blood she will rise again." This was the slogan of the association that Ben-Zvi and some of his friends had founded, even before the Sejera incident. This militant organization, *Hashomer* (the Guardian), which they had created was along the lines of the secret Jewish self-defense groups in Russia. Its aim was to guard and defend the Jewish villages and colonies. *Hashomer* was intended to be a closed, secret society. A cloak-and-dagger atmosphere prevailed in this private army, which consisted at most of a few dozen pioneers.

David Grin's convictions should have made him a member of this group. But, ironically, the *Hashomer* warriors would have none of him—he was too much of an intellectual. "We already had a socialist rabbi in Ben-Zvi," said one of the members in later years. "We didn't want another intellectual."

Grin, an intellectual? Never. He even took his name, David Ben-Gurion, from one of the last defenders of Jerusalem against the Roman legions. He claims that he adopted it only because it sounded well; but the famous Ben-Gurion of antiquity had fought desperately for his country's independence. It was a symbolic choice, proclaiming the young pioneer's conviction that the history of the Jews in Palestine was a continuation of the ancient history of the people of Israel. The two thousand years of exile did not come into it.

When Ben-Zvi sent for him to go to Jerusalem, Grin exchanged his rifle for a pen. And in 1910 he became one of the editors of *Ahdut* (Unity), the *Poalei Zion* periodical which was published in Hebrew. The heroic period of manual work at Sejera had come to an end. The armed farm worker was transformed into a journalist, who signed his articles "Ben-Gurion."

Ben-Gurion had no great faith in journalism, any more than he had in the Zionism of well-dressed gentlemen who frequented drawing rooms, the corridors of power and conference halls. The game would be played out in Palestine, at Sejera, Kinneret, in the first kibbutzim and the cooperative villages; it would depend on the efforts of a nation to take root in an arid land.

It was his love of the Hebrew language that made him decide to go to Jerusalem to become a journalist. He knew that the revived language would bind the nation together. However, he suffered hard knocks and heartbreaking setbacks in his struggle to promote Hebrew. At the *Poalei Zion* Congress, about two months after the first publication of *Ahdut,* he gave a speech in Hebrew, to the general consternation and anger of the delegates. They left the conference room in protest—they would never give up their native Yiddish. Neither would Ben-Gurion give up, and he went on talking to the almost-empty room. Three delegates only had remained—Ben-Zvi, his brother, and a girl member of the *Ahdut* editing committee. She was Rachel Yanait, and fifty years later she would still be with Ben-Zvi, her husband—in the official residence of the President of the State of Israel.

At that time Jerusalem was a miserable, dirty, ugly town, inhabited by people of every nationality. In winter, an icy wind swept through the narrow streets. Ben-Gurion, wrapped in his black cloak, became a familiar figure, hurrying from one meeting to another, taking part in editorial discussions and presiding at conferences. Most of the time he was quiet and thoughtful, but he sometimes threw himself into a discussion with an ardor and a power of expression which astonished his colleagues. However, it was in his articles for *Ahdut* that he best expressed his ideas. The romanticism and overworked sensibility of his letters to his father had vanished. His style was now sharp, clear, and straightforward. He followed his own path with determination, not worrying about other people's feelings. In his very first article he pointed out the wide gap which existed between new immigrants and those long established in the country, and called for a reform of outdated social structures. The urgent need of union between the different classes of Palestinian Jews was ever foremost in his mind.

He expressed these ideas with even greater vehemence at the World Congress of the *Poalei Zion* Party at Vienna in 1911. For the first time, he was one of the Palestinian delegates to the Congress. The other delegate was Ben-Zvi. Early discussion was on the subject of the Workers' Bank which had been established in

Palestine. "It is not for the World Congress to decide on the Bank's policy, but the Jewish workmen in Palestine," Ben-Gurion asserted. The other delegates were indignant, and he and Ben-Zvi remained very much a minority.

Another storm broke a few days later. "It is not the Zionists living in foreign countries who will achieve the aims of Zionism, but those working in Palestine," decared the two delegates. "Those who want to work for the cause of *Poalei Zion* ought to emigrate to Palestine instead of wasting their time here!" The congress was most indignant, and voted a motion of censure on the "separatist" delegates from Palestine.

Back in Jerusalem, Ben-Gurion continued to fill *Ahdut* with his diatribes. But how many people read this small paper? There were a mere 250 readers in Palestine, 100 abroad. The Jewish nation was still a dream. . . . There were no more than 70,000 Jews in the whole of Palestine, a few of them were prosperous farmers but the majority little better than beggars. Hundreds of thousands of young Jewish immigrants were needed, but only a few thousand a year were arriving, lonely idealists for the most part. They fell ill, some died, others left for countries offering a better future, for America chiefly. There had certainly been an impressive exodus from Russia and Poland, but it had taken the wrong direction.

This was a period when national liberation movements were shaking large areas of the Ottoman Empire. The first uprising, in 1908, brought young Turkish officers to power. They spoke of liberty and progress, and there were enthusiastic demonstrations in the large towns of the Middle East and a forest of flags was waved, among them—making its first appearance—the blue-and-white flag with the Star of David. The Jews were at the celebrations too, and they thought that *Huria,* Liberty, was almost in sight. They felt sure that the Young Turks would sweep away the obstacles to Jewish immigration and thus give it fresh impulse. Great was their disappointment. The *coup d'état* by the Young Turks was but the first of several upheavals, which ended in the collapse of the Ottoman Empire. The third *coup d'état,* on January 23, 1913, made Enver Pasha the new leader of Turkey.

The demise of the Ottoman Empire had long been expected in European diplomatic circles, but most of the Jews in Palestine, confined within their little provincial world, falsely put their hopes in the new Turkish Government. Ben-Gurion and Ben-Zvi made their first error of judgment when they campaigned for the integration of the Palestinian Jews into the Turkish Empire. Ben-Gurion even sported an upturned moustache in the best Turkish style. His ideas, mistaken though they were, had some foundation. He maintained that the Jewish minority in Palestine needed competent leaders to guide it, to represent it and protect its rights by acquiring a deep knowledge of Turkish laws. Ben-Gurion thought it possible for him to become a member of the Turkish Parliament in Constantinople, even to become a minister. He would thus be well placed to work for Jewish immigration.

His way seemed clear, and he left for Turkey to study law and to launch into politics. He landed at Salonika in the late summer of 1911, and after a few months, having acquired a rudimentary knowledge of the language, he went on to Constantinople.

Ben-Zvi soon joined him, along with one of the leaders of *Hashomer,* Israel Shochat, a young man with a fierce moustache and an ardent look. Another young Jew was already studying law at Constantinople University. His name was then Moshe Shertok, and many years later when known as Sharett he was to become the second Prime Minister of Israel.

Ben-Gurion was in relatively easy circumstances while at Constantinople. His father was happy to learn that the young rebel had at last decided to continue his education, and sent him thirty rubles a month. He dressed like a middle-class Turk, complete with fez, frock coat, stiff collar and pocket watch with gold chain. He and Ben-Zvi prepared a thesis on Turkish law, and he became acquainted with Montesquieu's *L'Esprit des Lois.* At the university he met young men of many different nationalities, the sons of wealthy Turks and of Arab sheiks, and became friendly with a well-known Zionist journalist with a biting style—Jabotinsky. He also met a good-natured giant of a man who had lost his left arm in the Russo-Japanese War. This was Joseph Trumpeldor, a living symbol of Jewish heroism.

Ben-Gurion spent his nights engrossed in his law books, with excellent results. But he failed to notice that all around him history was being transformed. The Balkan Wars ended disastrously for Turkey, who lost nearly all that remained of her European territories. Ben-Gurion and Ben-Zvi took no interest in this. They thought only of Palestine and the roles they would play in the country's revival.

Even the opening cannon roar of August 1914 did not shatter their illusions. They were on their way back to Palestine when they learned of the outbreak of war; the Russian tramp they sailed on was attacked by a German warship. When they finally reached Palestine it was to find despair and famine. The Jews and others were cramming into ships and trains, fleeing to Europe and Egypt. The efforts to establish Jewish colonies were failing. Weizmann in London, Trumpeldor and Jabotinsky in Cairo, called on the Jews to support the Allies. But the Allies included Russia, the Russia of the Czar, of despotism and pogroms. Ben-Gurion and Ben-Zvi were against this policy, fearing that the remaining Palestinian Jews might be the object of reprisals by the Turks, who were experts in the matter. So the two continued to campaign for Jewish integration—a barren and outmoded idea, but one which they were unable to discard. They felt it to be the only means of remaining in Palestine and safeguarding the fragile bridgehead which had been set up there. They became active in trying to form a volunteer Jewish militia for the defense of Palestine.

In the end, it was the Turks who tore the veil from their eyes. Their Zionist activities were becoming suspect, and the Turks heard of the secret stores of weapons and the *Hashomer* organization. It was feared that the Palestinian Jews might be a fifth column of the British. In the summer of 1915 a wave of arrests descended on the Jews. Ben-Gurion and Ben-Zvi were the first to feel it. However much they protested their loyalty to Turkey, their links with Zionist international organizations were only too evident. They both received expulsion orders.

Just before his enforced departure, Ben-Gurion met one of his Arab friends, Ihie Effendi, who had been a student with him at Constantinople.

"What are you doing here?" said the Arab in surprise, on seeing Ben-Gurion in the courtyard of the prison in Jerusalem.

"I'm being expelled from the country," replied Ben-Gurion.

Ihie Effendi's comment on this gave Ben-Gurion his first indication of nascent Arab nationalism. "As a friend of yours, I'm very sorry to hear it. As an Arab, I'm pleased about it."

On Ben-Gurion's expulsion order had been stamped in bright red letters: "Expelled for ever from the limits of the Turkish Empire."

"I'll be back one day!" he exclaimed.

Late in the summer of 1915 he and Ben-Zvi stepped ashore at New York.

FIVE

PRINCE AND PEASANT

Three years later the two were back, proud and triumphant and wearing British Army uniforms. They had been thrown out of Palestine and put on a ship for Alexandria, and then had begun a long odyssey which was now ending. They were back with troops who were given orders in Hebrew and who marched under the blue-and-white flag with the Star of David—the first Jewish troops in modern times to go to free the country of their ancestors. Bearded patriarchs in Jaffa and Jerusalem, who seemed to have stepped straight from the pages of the Bible, watched these Jewish soldiers marching in the land of Israel and thought a miracle had occurred. It was no miracle, but the World War had hastened a number of things.

Several Jewish leaders had dreamed of this Jewish Legion soon after the outbreak of war, in particular Jabotinsky, the brilliant writer and orator, and Joseph Trumpeldor, the veteran of the Russo-Japanese War. In Egypt, they had been very active in trying to interest the British authorities in the idea of a Jewish force to fight alongside the Allies to liberate Palestine. The British refused to form a Jewish combatant force but agreed to a transport unit of muleteers, composed of voluntary recruits. Jabotinsky was deeply disappointed. Having dreamed of an army of warriors, he refused to join a muleteer unit which would not even see Palestine, since the British proposed to use it on another front. But to Trumpeldor, the principle of a Jewish unit mattered more than battle honors. "The trenches or transport, it's practically the same thing," he said. "And all fronts lead to Zion."

The "Zionist Muleteer Corps" had embarked at Alexandria for Gallipoli in March 1915. Ben-Gurion and Ben-Zvi were among the public who watched the Jewish volunteers leave, and the former made no attempt to hide his objections: most of the volunteers were refugees from Palestine, and the Palestinian Jews ought to do all in their power to remain in the homeland. He feared that the Turks might carry out reprisals against the Jews who had stayed in Palestine. Moreover, the outcome of the war was still very uncertain, and Trumpeldor might well be backing the wrong horse. Years later, Ben-Gurion admitted that he was probably mistaken. "But if history were to repeat itself," he said, "I should still take the same attitude—the Palestinian Jews ought to remain at all costs in the land of Israel."

New immigrants were needed to replace those who had left, and Ben-Gurion went to seek them in the United States, where there was a vast reserve of Jews.

After a long and difficult voyage which lasted several weeks, Ben-Gurion and Ben-Zvi landed in rags on Ellis Island one hot summer morning in 1915. They were on American soil, and turned over the Turkish page in their lives for good. Ben-Gurion at once threw himself into his self-imposed task. He had meetings with hundreds of Jews who belonged to the many Zionist organizations which made up Jewish society in New York. But he discovered they were Zionists in word only.

His immediate aim was to mobilize an army of pioneers to go out to reclaim the homeland and defend it. Aided by Ben-Zvi, and despite the scepticism of the American Jewish leaders, he founded the *Hehalutz* (The Pioneer) organization and went crusading across the country. He addressed meetings of young Jews in town after town, but all his efforts ended in bitter disappointment. The New York skeptics had been right; hardly a hundred Jews in the whole of the United States joined *Hehalutz*.

Ben-Gurion tried to rouse the Zionist conscience of the Jews through the power of the printed page. He and Ben-Zvi and two other friends wrote and published a book entitled *Yizkor (In Memoriam)* and wrote another work lovingly describing in great detail the land of their fathers. Both books had a great success.

But time was passing, and the United States had not yet entered the war. Ben-Gurion continued hastening from one meeting to another, writing articles and raising funds. At the same time, he was preparing himself for the part he intended to play. He wrote in his diary that he was deeply impressed by American propaganda and political systems, but he called these politics and democracy "illusory."

However, he remained a stranger to America. He traveled a great deal, observed and noted, but all that really interested him, everything he wrote in his diary, was concerned with Zionism. He discovered a deep and bitter truth—in order to create a "national home," a Jewish center, he had to battle against several nations, against Arabs and British, but above all against the Jewish people themselves, their indifference, their quarrels, their rival interests, their doubts and fears. Ever since his arrival in the States he had been battling against those people who were demanding the immediate creation of a Jewish state, to be given to the Jewish people by the victors and guaranteed by them. He never ceased protesting against this policy of seeking support in foreign capitals by diplomatic advances and by approaches to those in power, in accordance with the purest Jewish tradition.

In September 1915 Ben-Gurion wrote: "There are several ways of conquering a country; it can be seized by force of arms, it can be obtained through political moves and diplomatic treaties, it can even be bought with money. All these methods have but one aim— to seize power and enslave and exploit the native population. We, however, are seeking something very different in Palestine—a homeland. And a homeland cannot be taken just like that, like a gift, it cannot be acquired by concessions or political agreements, it cannot be bought, neither can it be seized by force. A homeland has to be built by the sweat of your brow. . . ."

There was a profound truth in those forceful phrases. Yet proof to the contrary seemed to be contained in the bombshell which soon brought joy to the Jewish world. This was the Balfour Declaration. On November 2, 1917, Balfour, then Foreign Minister of Great Britain, wrote to Lord Rothschild: "His Majesty's Government view with favour the establishment in Palestine of a national home for the Jewish people, and will use their best endeavours to facilitate the establishment of this object, it being clearly understood that nothing shall be done which may prejudice the civil and religious rights of existing non-Jewish communities in Palestine, or the rights and political status enjoyed by Jews in any other country."

This surprising declaration delighted the Jews, and exceeded the hopes of the most fervent optimists. For the Zionists, it meant that their wildest dreams had come true. And it brought into prominence a man who was to dominate the Zionist world for the next thirty years—Dr. Haïm Weizmann, unquestionably the architect of the Balfour Declaration.

Weizmann would seem to be the direct successor to Herzl, but how had he reached a position which enabled him to influence the British Government? Through shrewd diplomacy he had already gained strong support, but he first came into the limelight in 1916, when he presented the British Government with a solution to the munitions problem—synthetic acetone, which made possible continuous production of munitions. Lloyd George, then chairman of the War Munitions Committee, was particularly grateful to Weizmann, and when he became Prime Minister a few months later he asked Weizmann how he could best reward him. The reply was "by doing something for my people." Weizmann's influence with Jewish circles in the United States was no secret, and those circles could bring pressure to bear on the American Government to enter the war against Germany. There was also the fact that the creation of a Jewish home in Palestine, under British protection, would give the British control there. These advantages were apparent to the Government, ant it approved the Declaration, which took into consideration the feelings of the Arabs.

The Jewish world celebrated. Palestine had been given to the Jews. However much Ben-Gurion and his handful of fanatical pioneers proclaimed that they were the ones who held Palestine, Weizmann had proved that the diplomatic efforts of Zionists abroad could be much more important and effective than all the efforts to drain and cultivate the marshes of Izreel and Sharon.

Weizmann's triumph was unanimously acclaimed, with only one discordant note, that came from Ben-Gurion, who wrote in an article he published on November 14, 1917: "Britain has not given Palestine back to us. Even if the whole country were conquered by the British, it would not become ours through Great Britain giving her consent and other countries agreeing . . . Britain has made a magnificent gesture; she has recognized our existence as a nation and has acknowledged our right to the country. But only the Hebrew people can transform this right into tangible fact; only they, with body and soul, with their strength and capital, must build their National Home and bring about their national redemption."

In those phrases can be seen all the difference between Ben-Gurion and Weizmann, between the little ploughman of Sejera and the prince of the Manchester laboratories. Ben-Gurion admired Weizmann, but did not see in him the man who could bring about a solution. And for the next thirty years, these two men, so different and so removed from each other, were to dominate Zionism in Palestine and elsewhere.

The Zionists in America celebrated for many months, but Ben-Gurion was not present at the ceremonies. He and his inseparable companion, Ben-Zvi, were on their way to Palestine in the uniform of British soldiers. His attitude had greatly changed since leaving Alexandria for the States. Now that America had entered the war he believed that his duty was to help in liberating Palestine. He was not the first. Some months previously, in London, the persistent Jabotinsky had succeeded in getting his Jewish Legion, and in June 1918, it was fighting with the British Army in Palestine. Ben-Gurion's battalion, composed of volunteers recruited in the United States and Canada, did not arrive until much later. A third battalion was later formed from volunteers among the Palestinian Jews.

Ben-Gurion landed at Port Said with his battalion on August 28, 1918. "The Jewish flag is flying under the Egyptian sky," he wrote. He had been given the rank of corporal almost without his knowledge. He felt proud, believing that he could serve his cause better on the battlefields of Palestine than on the platforms at Zionist meetings, even though he was just a single soldier among many.

He was in fact no longer single, having married Pauline Munweis, his Paula, as she became known to the whole Zionist world too. They had been married almost in secret at the City Hall in New York on December 5, 1917. The event was noted in his diary in the briefest manner: "December 3, 1917—meeting of the Work Committee in the evening. December 4—meeting of the committees of our Associations. December 5—got married at 11:30 this morning. December 6—meeting of the Central Committee."

Pauline Munweis came originally from Russia. She was a wan girl with a serious face, but she had a pleasant smile. After having been forced to break off her medical studies, she worked as a nurse at a hospital. Palestine and Zionism meant nothing to her; if anything, she was a bit of an anarchist. But the ardor and grandeur that she sensed in the young pioneer greatly attracted her. Ben-Gurion had asked her to copy some passages from books for him, at the Municipal Library, and their romance began. She was open and sincere, and always spoke her mind. She was prepared to sacrifice everything for "Ben-Gurion," as she always called her husband, and devoted her whole life to him. Several of his friends named her "Ben-Gurion's life insurance." She has a character of her own, though, and has never allowed herself to be eclipsed by the great man.

She slipped away from the hospital for a few hours in order to get married, but after the ceremony had to go back to assist at an operation. Ben-Gurion hurried off to a meeting. It was not until a few days later that they began to look for a place to live.

Ben-Gurion sailed for Palestine with his battalion about four months later, leaving Paula in New York. She was expecting a baby, which proved to be a girl. The father received the news while suffering from dysentery in a hospital in Cairo. He never saw active service; neither did any of his battalion. The war was over when they arrived in Palestine, and the country was under British control.

An important delegation soon arrived in Palestine from London, headed by Dr. Weizmann. They had come to revisit the country he had presented to his people. Before leaving London he had long meetings with members of the Government, and George V granted him an audience. The Balfour Declaration had been approved by France, the United States and all the great Powers. The British, however, still had doubts about the reaction of the Arabs. Weizmann helped to reassure the British by meeting Prince Faisal and signing with him a treaty of friendship which was drawn up by Lawrence of Arabia.

In the face of such spectacular successes, the small band of pioneers led by Ben-Gurion, Ben-Zvi, Katzenelson and a few others were neglected, and naturally felt frustrated. They appreciated the worth of Weizmann's work, but had little illusion about the treaty of friendship with Faisal. Ominous rumblings were coming from Arab quarters. British protection would be of little use unless the "national home" was firmly established in Palestine, thought Ben-Gurion, and he began to devote himself to this end as soon as he was back in the country.

He no longer held the rank of corporal. He was so occupied with his political activities that he sometimes forgot a soldier must not be absent from camp without permission. His officers showed great tolerance and allowed him all the leave he asked for. But, nevertheless, he eventually was court-martialed and reduced to the ranks. This did not trouble him much; being a soldier in the Jewish Legion was important during the war, but only political action mattered now. The future builder of the Israeli Army was, in short, a bad soldier.

He launched his campaign for workers' unity even before reaching Palestine. In February 1919 a new party was born—*Ahdut Haavoda,* Labor Union. It came to an agreement with the *Hapoel Hatzaïr* movement the following year, and thus *Histadrut,* the Confederation of Labor, came into being. *Histadrut* was a means to an end, an instrument and not an objective. Its aims were political—to prepare the way, to build the framework for the future State of Israel. In a sense, it was Ben-Gurion's reply to the Balfour Declaration.

His very first workers' slogan clearly expressed his thoughts: "We must make a nation of the class we represent."

A number of writers and journalists have described Ben-Gurion in the 1920s as a workers' leader and militant trade-unionist. "Who can say," one of them wrote, "at which moment Ben-Gurion the trade-union leader suddenly changed to a political leader?" But there never was such a change. From his first days at the head of the labor movement he was the leader of a political party.

Ben-Gurion was one of the founding members of *Histadrut* in 1920; his membership card was number three. He became General Secretary of the only organized political body in Palestine.

SIX

THE BITTER YEARS

In 1920, the Secretary of *Histadrut* was 34 years old, and his army was only 4,433 strong. Around them were some tens of thousands of Palestinian Jews, 800,000 Arabs, millions of Zionists organized in a powerful world federation, and the British Empire. Only a madman would have said that these few Socialists would influence the Jewish population, stand up to the Arabs, defy the British and dictate the policy of world Zionism. To think that at the time, one had to be mad—or have infinite patience.

Ben-Gurion waited ten years before attempting it. They were the hardest and the most bitter years of his life. And yet they were the most important too, the decisive years which shaped the national Jewish movement in Palestine as well as the character of its leader.

The decade began in bloodshed and tragedy. For the first time, Arab crowds attacked the Jews, having been roused by one of their religious leaders, Hadj Amin El Husseini. In 1921 there was another outbreak of violence, bloodier than the first. That most heroic of pioneers, the one-armed giant, Joseph Trumpeldor, was shot and killed by Arabs in 1920, at the isolated post of Tel Haï, on the borders of Galilee. His martyrdom became a symbol of courage. The following year the writer and poet, Joseph Haïm Brenner, and his family were savagely murdered by Arabs in Jaffa. Was Palestine to become another land of pogroms? The answer of the Jews was the organization of a secret armed force, *Haganah* (Defense), the successor to *Hashomer*. It became part of the *Histadrut* organization, so the rudimentary political force in Palestine soon had its spearhead.

The British Mandate over Palestine and the creation of a Jewish national home were approved at the League of Nations Conference in San Remo in 1920. A White Paper, penned by Churchill and aimed at appeasing the Arabs, tore the areas east of the Jordan from the mandated territories and established the capital of Transjordan in the village of Amman. Palestine was invaded by British officials and by Scottish and Welsh battalions sent to maintain order, and more particularly by representatives of the Zionist organization, who arrived in business suits to take charge of the country's revival.

Weizmann had his headquarters in London. Ben-Gurion had his in a shabby little office in Jerusalem. He had scarcely any contact with the British administration; the few officials whom he knew were subordinates. In London, he was completely unknown. The ministers with whom Weizmann was on good terms had never heard of Ben-Gurion.

What could anyone have said about him? His record was of no interest, his life had been hard and monotonous. From morning to night, Ben-Gurion was busy looking after the interests of building workers and railway employees, organizing strikes . . . trying to find jobs for another ten or fifteen workmen, protesting over the dismissal of a woman at Jaffa, of three pioneers at Richon . . . negotiating interminably for an increase in wages of just a few coppers. He traveled incessantly, visiting towns and villages, and when he got back in the evening it was to attend a meeting or to write an article for the workers' paper.

His passionate belief in socialism was strengthened over the years, and he fought for better working conditions and against the employment of Arabs, who accepted very low wages, by Jews. The Jews had need of all the work available. The way into Palestine was half-open, and ships crammed with immigrants were beginning to arrive. The numbers increased still further after 1924, when the United States denied them entry. Work had to be found for these immigrants. But unemployment increased alarmingly, and trouble broke out here and there. By 1927 the crisis was at its height, and the numbers of bitter, disillusioned men leaving Palestine exceeded new arrivals.

Ben-Gurion was far from living in comfort himself. He and his family had a tiny apartment in Jerusalem—and they now numbered four, Paula having given birth to a boy, Amos, while on a visit to Europe with her husband. The small salary he received as Secretary of *Histadrut* was barely sufficient to keep his family. Ben-Gurion's diary for the years 1920–23 is full of figures, of daily reckonings of household expenditure. Each page contains the mute question—shall we have anything to eat tomorrow? *Histadrut*'s General Secretary was often reduced to borrowing a little to get over the ever-recurring hurdle known as the end of the month.

But that was how Zionism was built up in Palestine—without funds, living from day to day, traveling all over the country and addressing small groups in the hope that one day they would be large crowds. Ben-Gurion had regular bouts of malaria which kept him in bed. Although still young, he had little hair left, and that little was turning gray. In the winter he wore a lumber jacket and thick khaki trousers, somewhat reminiscent of the Bolshevik uniform. In the summer, he wore white linen. He had no leisure time at all.

He tried very hard to get his wife to change her name from Paula to the Hebrew equivalent, Pnina. But he had to admit defeat. If there was one person who could stand up to the authoritarian Ben-Gurion it was his wife.

He was successful in imposing his authority over *Histadrut*, however, and concentrated power in his own hands. One of his colleagues said of him: "That's the man who'll be dictator of Palestine when the social revolution takes place!"

Ben-Gurion did not believe in a revolution. He was a convinced Socialist, but against Marxism. He launched vehement attacks on the Zionist-Marxist movement which was spreading in Palestine— and that was not the only movement to call down his wrath. His tongue could be gentle at times, but was sharp and biting when attacking opponents of the party. When one of his best colleagues, the pioneer woman Mania Shochat, mistakenly proposed a form of agreement between Jews and Arabs, he silenced her with: "You know nothing about politics, so keep out of them!" On the other hand, he could be deeply moved, by a speech in memory of Herzl for instance. His friends were fascinated by him. He aroused their admiration and their affection.

The man who emerges from these contrasts is one living only for his ideas, concentrating all his energies in the struggle to attain his aims, and neglecting minor matters.

Ben-Gurion lacked the education and culture of Weizmann, Jabotinsky, Brandeis. He had never completed his studies at Constantinople University. But he was steadily acquiring an encyclopaedic knowledge during his years in the political arena, and he became very learned in philosophy, history, natural science, comparative religion and, of course, the Bible. He devoured books. In Jerusalem, he bought at least one every day, and he ordered books from Germany, France and England. Often he had not enough to eat, but he always had enough money to buy books. He learned Greek in order to read Plato in the original, as years later he learned Spanish to read *Don Quixote*. With similar insistence, he filled his diaries with everything he learned, not only in Palestine (there are several volumes of information about the Jewish population) but during his travels. Whether at Moscow, Rome or Stockholm, at an international congress or a world exhibition, he noted down facts and figures, conversations overheard, copied out whole brochures and put down detailed descriptions of the monuments and buildings he visited. He has always had a photographic memory.

Berlin, London, Moscow . . . He did an enormous amount of traveling during these years. At least once a year he went abroad to attend meetings of the Zionist Executive or to represent his party at Jewish international congresses. They were not pleasure trips. His expense allowances were modest, too modest. He noted methodically the smallest items of expenditure. The poverty, the wretched conditions he knew in Palestine followed him abroad—dirty trains, overcrowded dormitories, dingy hotel rooms. Paula stoically put up with long separations which sometimes extended to several months.

In 1922 he was at the Zionist Congress held in Carlsbad, Czechoslovakia. The following year he was the representative of the Palestinian Jewish farmers at the Moscow Exhibition. He wrote in his diary of his admiration for Lenin, but his feelings towards the Soviet Union were very mixed. The Revolution meant a lot to him, yet he could not help being critical. On his return home he drew up a memorandum setting out the improvements needed in the attitude of the U.S.S.R. towards his own country. He knew there was little hope for the moment. When he was in London the following year, an official of the Colonial Office asked him why he thought the Communists were opposed to Zionism. "It's because they regard Zionism as an agent of British Imperialism," replied Ben-Gurion.

He allowed himself a small luxury—he flew from Dantzig to Marienburg. He thought it a wonderful experience, and made a careful note of the plane, an Elberfeld D-24. A few days later, with the same pilot at the controls, it crashed.

His third child, a girl, was born in 1925 at Jerusalem, and was given the name Renana. She became his favorite. In July of that year his aged father, Victor Grin, came to live in Palestine.

A few days after his father's arrival, Ben-Gurion was on his way to France. He was enchanted by the country when he reached Marseilles, but did not like Paris very much. He preferred London and Rome to the French capital.

In London, he made his first speech in English, to an English audience. He was nervous beforehand, but once he began to speak his self-confidence returned. While in London he spent one free evening at a movie. He greatly enjoyed the film. It was neither a thriller nor a romance—such things did not interest him—but a German film on the wonders of nature in the Tyrol. Even these few hours of absence from his mission were not wasted. He made notes of his impressions—all part of his continual effort to prepare himself for the tasks ahead.

Every one of the little notebooks in which he was always jotting something down has a detailed list of contents at the end. But the most striking thing about them is the detached, impersonal nature of the entries. He describes events with great care but rarely expresses his intimate feelings, his thoughts and reactions. When something extraordinary occurs, or he is greatly upset by something, he does give way to impassioned remarks—but this is rare. In general, he contents himself with brief, laconic comments and a quotation or two, and he always adds his beliefs and opinions, which show him to be constantly thinking of the next stage in his program, in his long-term plan.

"My forecasts are coming true," he wrote in Berlin in 1923. *"Histadrut* is forcing all the parties which hate each other to work together for the good of Palestine. They don't yet realize that, whether they wish it or not, they are but tools in the hands of History, which follows its course relentlessly."

In 1924 he added:"To succeed in our task abroad we must first unite in Palestine, within the Party and *Histadrut."*

In 1925 he quoted Marx: "Each step of a real movement is worth more than a dozen platforms."

The platforms that Ben-Gurion despised were those at the innumerable Zionist congresses. After the publication of a White Paper which was particularly disastrous for the Palestinian Jews, Ben-Gurion learned that the Zionist leaders abroad had decided to call a congress. "The congress is the one plague omitted from the White Paper," he wrote to his friend Berl Katzenelson.

The struggling pioneers in Palestine had little love for these "first-class," top-level Zionists. But they could not deny that some of them, notably Weizmann, made an immense contribution to the Zionist cause.

But despite everything, Ben-Gurion did not like Weizmann. However, he supported him. He was critical of his hesitations, his moderation and too-docile attitude towards the British; but in general Ben-Gurion agreed with his policy. After the bloodshed in Palestine in 1921, Ben-Gurion said to Itzhak Grinbaum, one of

Weizmann's opponents: "What has recently occurred is nothing compared with what we can expect in the future. Cooperation with the mandatory government is a basic condition for the growth of our population and for the increase of our strength in the country."

The policy and ideas of the hard core of the pioneers did not meet with Weizmann's approval either. He thought they were in too much of a hurry, and accused them of taking themselves too seriously.

Ben-Gurion led the attack on the entire Zionist "Directory," whose members had been elected by the congress and which represented the Zionist movement, above even the Jewish Agency, with the British authorities. As the years passed, the tone mounted and in 1925 Ben-Gurion spoke out against Weizmann at the Zionist Congress: "Weizmann has meekly accepted all the restrictions that the British impose on us." In 1927, in Paris, the leader of world Zionism returned the attack with a few meaningful phrases.

That same year, at Basel, the home of political Zionism, Weizmann made a speech that carried little conviction. Ben-Gurion jotted down his impressions: "In my opinion it was the most important Congress since the war. The period of fine phrases and hollow sentimentality is over. A healthy realism has established itself in the movement. I believe that Weizmann's personal fetishism has reached its end. He has flung down his favorite saying for the last time—'Take it or leave it'. I hope that next time it will be the majority saying that to Weizmann. And if he doesn't submit to the majority, he will have to quit."

At the next meeting of the Zionist Executive, in 1928, the Palestinian delegation waged open war on Weizmann. Ben-Gurion was at the head of this opposition to "Herzl's heir" and campaigned for his replacement. When Weizmann threatened to resign, Ben-Gurion described it as a political maneuver. He saw the Zionist leader as a crafty politician.

A last-minute compromise enabled the Executive to save face, and the Zionist Directory remained unchanged. But Weizmann's authority had been seriously undermined. Ben-Gurion noted in his diary: "Weizmann has left us. He looked pale and tired, depressed and wretched. So ends the tragi-comedy of the latest 'Weizmann crisis' . . ."

Ben-Gurion's mounting attacks on him were not only due to the divergences between them. The former was becoming more and more impatient. Important events had been taking place in Palestine and abroad. The long period of preparation within the party seemed to be approaching its end. After the successes in 1919 and 1920, the *Histadrut* leader was ready for the next move.

His plan was daring and ambitious—to make an onslaught against the bastion of world Zionism, the Executive itself. The purpose was plain: the small group of pioneers had to conquer that strong position, seize the controls, so that world Zionism could be made to serve the national interests of the Palestinian Jews.

But first, the two big socialist parties in Palestine had to combine forces. In 1920 the *Hapoel Hatzaïr* party had prudently refused to associate itself with the extreme socialism of Ben-Gurion and his friends, and their slogan of class warfare, fearing to be swamped by their more determined and better disciplined mass of members. Ben-Gurion had for years impressed upon his *Histadrut* colleagues the need and, indeed, benefit of union with other parties. His arguments finally succeeded, and in 1927 a conference was held in Tel Aviv. The discussions raged for seventeen days, and still there was no agreement on union. Ben-Gurion, ill and weary, left the conference and went to get some sleep at the small apartment he had recently moved into with his family, in Pinsker Street, Tel Aviv.

Suddenly, at about five in the morning, the silence outside was shattered by joyful cries. A crowd of workers and trade-union leaders, members of the *Ahdut Haavoda* and the *Hapoel Hatzaïr* parties, had gathered in front of the house. Despite Paula's protests, Joseph Shprinzak went and woke Ben-Gurion. He told him that the leaders of the two parties had argued all night long and had finally come to the decision which met with Ben-Gurion's dearest desire— to unite. The General Secretary of *Histadrut,* who a few hours earlier had thought he was in a minority, was deeply moved by the news. He went out on the balcony with Shprinzak and waved to the friendly crowd.

However, the effective union was some time in coming. After many long and wearing negotiations, the new party was formed in 1930. It was called the *Mifleget Poalei Eretz Israel* (MAPAI)—the Palestinian Labor Party.

The ink was scarcely dry on the agreement when Ben-Gurion advanced another pawn in his attacking game. He had said that after combining forces in Palestine, a united front needed to be established abroad. So in September 1930, in Berlin, he officially opened the World Congress of Jewish Workers. He presided over a packed hall holding delegates from Jewish workers' movements all over the world and representatives of labor parties of many countries. Among them were Edouard Bernstein, the doyen of the

World Socialist Movement, and Léon Blum, the leader of the French Socialist Party.

The purpose of congress was to demonstrate to the whole world, and in particular to the Zionist movement, that behind the 150,000 Jews in Palestine stood a strong and determined international mass of supporters. It was a success, and founded the World League for Palestinian Workers. Although this soon fell into oblivion, the desired effect had been obtained. In a statement to the press, Ben-Gurion said: "The Congress has proclaimed the idea of the national hegemony of the working class in the Jewish renaissance movement. The League has to convert this idea into acts."

It was time for the next step in Ben-Gurion's plan. The Zionist movement was going through a grave crisis; the Palestinian Jews had felt for the first time the full force of the British Mandate, and their whole future was at stake. A White Paper had just been published which imposed harsh measures on the Jewish population. The decade was ending as it had begun—in destruction, hatred and bloodshed.

SEVEN

THE CONQUEST

Hadj Amin El Husseini was a lanky man with a swarthy face and a crafty smile. He wore the fez of the Grand Mufti, the head of the Muslim religion in Palestine. His great ambition was to seize power in Palestine and restore the Caliphate, symbol of the great days of the past when Islam was all-powerful over a huge area extending from the Atlantic coast of Morocco to the Indian Ocean. There were several obstacles—not the least being the influx of thousands of European Jews who were taking root in Palestine and fostering an aggressive nationalism.

A second Jerusalem was growing beneath his eyes—the New City, that of the Jews, for whom he had nothing but hatred. He was prepared to use all possible means to destroy them. The day would come when he would not flinch from an alliance with Mussolini and Hitler. For the moment, the best means was to have a blood bath.

For months past, his agents had been spreading rumors that the Jews were preparing to rebuild their Temple, and the site they chose was where the Mosque of Omar stood, which those dogs of infidels would entirely destroy. It was sacrilege. Death to the Jews!

The order went forth on August 23, 1929, a Friday, the Muslims' day of rest. At midday hundreds of young Arabs invaded the Jewish district and started attacking with clubs and daggers, in the age-old tradition of pogroms. The killing, the raping and looting continued for two hours. British forces did not intervene until later. The terror spread to Hebron, Jaffa, and to Safed, where Jewish houses were set on fire. Altogether 140 Jews were killed and thousands injured. Some Arabs were hurt while the British were restoring order.

The Muslim masses, although they had not taken an active part, gave moral support to the Arab gangs carrying out the Mufti's orders. Arab nationalism was being revived.

The British reaction was exactly as the Mufti had hoped. The Labor Government hurriedly sent out a commission of inquiry and then published the White Paper, which forbade Jews to purchase land in Palestine and imposed restrictions on Jewish immigration that almost completely put a stop to it. For the first time, the Jews were faced with the possibility of remaining permanently in the minority in Palestine—which meant that eventually Palestine would be just one more ghetto added to those already existing in the world. The Mufti had won the first round.

The *Yishuv*, the name given to the Jewish community in Palestine, was badly shaken. Voices were raised, especially in extreme Left-wing circles, clamoring for a peaceful settlement with the Arabs, even if it meant renouncing all hopes of creating a Jewish state. For the promoters of this movement, a dual-nation state was the formula which would calm the Arabs. For the leaders of all other political tendencies, it was the death sentence for Zionism.

This crisis also involved world Zionism and, on a personal level, Weizmann himself. He had succeeded in winning the confidence of the British to such an extent that they had presented him with the land of his fathers, but he had thereby become a prisoner of his gratitude to the British. In bringing about the aims of Zionism, the brilliant scientist had almost come to behave like an English lord—and, like any real lord, he found it impossible to attack the Crown. The 1930 White Paper was the first British betrayal of him. From then on, the crises between Britain and Zionism were to undermine and break him, torn as he was between love for his homeland and loyalty to the British Government. As for the Zionists, they looked upon him as being too meek, as the man who made concessions to the British and never had the courage to revolt against their betrayal.

It was he who paid the price of that betrayal. At the 1931 Zionist Congress in Basel a strong coalition demanded his resignation.

The British Prime Minister told Ben-Gurion, who had gone to see him in Weizmann's name: "I have complete trust in Weizmann and wholly support his policy. If he is not reelected I shall continue the same policy with his successor, but I shall always consult Weizmann because I've confidence in him." And Winston Churchill declared: "I don't believe the Jewish people are so stupid as to let him leave."

At Basel, the discussions soon turned into open warfare between "maximalists" and "minimalists." The former, led by Jabotinsky, wanted to proclaim that the definite objective of the Zionist move-

43

ment was the establishment of a Jewish state in Palestine. The latter, who were followers of Weizmann, merely expressed a vague hope for a Jewish majority in Palestine, and were opposed to any debate on a Jewish state.

Just before the congress opened, Ben-Gurion put on paper his personal thoughts on the subject, with an eye to Weizmann being replaced. But, in the end, he stood behind Weizmann. Ben-Gurion's ideas in favor of a Jewish state were no secret. But why proclaim to the world that the aim and object of Zionism was the establishment of a Jewish state? In his opinion, considering the prevailing circumstances, it would be mere arrogance, serve no useful purpose and would only harm the movement. So the workers' delegates and their supporters stood behind Weizmann. However, his opponents proved to be the stronger and carried the day. Weizmann was defeated, and resigned. His place as President of the Zionist movement was taken by Sokolov.

Although Ben-Gurion had opposed Weizmann in many matters over the years, he nevertheless, was upset by his humiliating downfall.

Zionism had never been so divided in itself, so disabled. For the next four years it had in Sokolov a second-rate figure at its head. During most of that time its only real strength was provided by the workers' parties in Palestine, the great majority of them being contained in Ben-Gurion's MAPAI. It was a propitious moment for taking control. On April 1, 1933, Ben-Gurion sailed from Alexandria to win over the Jewish nation.

The greater part of it—six million Jews at least—still clung obstinately, blindly, to the soil of Poland, the Baltic States, Hungary and Rumania. Whoever could obtain the support of a majority would be the leader of the Zionist movement.

It was not easy, with the Jewish areas swarming with political parties and movements. Ben-Gurion had the support of the moderate Left-wing elements, and it was in their name that he started on his electoral campaign—for that is what his tour of central Europe became.

The Zionist movement had created an electoral system that was unique and which embraced the whole world. A Jew who wanted to take part in the elections of members to the congress had to buy a "sheckel," a piece of blue-and-white paper which served as a ballot. The money went to the movement's funds. A congress was held every other year, and a certain number of members representing the various political parties was elected from each country by proportional ballot.

To conquer the Zionist movement, Ben-Gurion had to obtain a majority of congress members whose parties supported him. The Central European Governments, although traditionally anti-Semitic, did not object to these "private" elections. After all, the aim of Zionism was to lead the Jews into Palestine—to clear them out of Europe.

The elections were due to be held in July 1933. By mid-April Ben-Gurion had begun his vast electoral campaign, and for many weeks traveled from town to town, from country to country. He addressed two or three meetings nearly every day, set up election committees, started periodicals, sometimes spent all night in discussions or at a meeting. He proved to be an excellent organizer, a talented speaker and a determined leader. He succeeded in putting in the field a whole army of disciplined militants, spread over central and eastern Europe.

Judaism was torn asunder by heated passions, deep gulfs had been driven between the various factions. In Warsaw, on Passover, smoke bombs and tins filled with stones were thrown at Ben-Gurion. The brave attackers were young supporters of Vladimir Jabotinsky and his Revisionist party. The elections, the decisive struggle, had become a fight between Ben-Gurion and Jabotinsky.

Jabotinsky had a gift for holding a crowd, for rousing and convincing it by his wonderful flow of language. Everything about the man was spectacular, and at the same time this was his chief weakness. He had fathered the Jewish Legion in the First World War and, like Weizmann, had become a prisoner of his own idea, even when it had lost its power. He had also helped to start the self-defense organization in Palestine, *Haganah*. But he had far less faith in that than in the idea that a Jewish legion, under British protection, was the only means of defending the Palestinian Jews against Arab attacks. Even in the early 1920s he had opposed Ben-Gurion, who never ceased saying that the solution was not in a Jewish legion nor in British protection but could only be found in the pioneers' own strength and self-defense efforts.

Ben-Gurion and Jabotinsky were both, in their different ways, prophets of a Jewish state. But the means each wished to employ in the struggle were far apart. Ben-Gurion insisted that the country had to be conquered through the work of an army of pioneers. Jabotinsky had never believed this possible, nor did he have any faith in Ben-Gurion's workers' movement. He came from a middle-class background, and had no sympathy for Socialists and their methods. He was something of a dreamer and poet. His idea was to liberate the homeland by means which would shake the world, arouse public opinion and cause a great outcry among Jews and Gentiles alike.

He might be compared with some of the authoritarian figures then emerging in several countries, such as Pilsudski, Kemal Ataturk, even possibly Mussolini. In 1925 Jabotinsky broke away in disgust from the other Zionist leaders and formed his own movement—Revisionism. The pioneer workers in Palestine were revisionists too, but they saw hard work and patience as the only means, in the long run, of winning the struggle against British and Arabs. Jabotinsky's Revisionists were too impatient, unrealistic—they called for the creation of a Jewish state when there were only a few tens of thousands of Jews in Palestine against 800,000 Arabs. They were reckoning, in fact, not on actual accomplishment but on the hope that the effect produced by their spectacular acts would bring about the Jewish state. A movement such as Jabotinsky's was bound, sooner or later, to slide into extremism. And that is what happened.

"For Zionism to succeed," Mussolini said to Rabbi Prato in 1935, "you need to have a Jewish State with a Jewish flag and a Jewish language. The person who really understands that is your fascist, Jabotinsky."

This was enough for Ben-Gurion to stick the label "fascist" on Jabotinsky, and to call him "Vladimir Hitler." To which Jabotinsky replied, somehat clumsily, with the epithet "Ben Bouillon" (Hot Air). They addressed each other in violent terms during the 1933 election campaign in Poland. Their supporters needed no more to come to blows. However, worse happened in early June, when Haïm Arlozoroff, one of the MAPAI leaders, a specialist in international affairs for the Jewish Agency and an opponent of Jabotinsky's Revisionists, was mysteriously murdered in Tel Aviv. The Jewish world was aghast. It was the first political assassination in the Zionist movement. Who was the assassin? The inquiry pointed to some notorious Revisionists, but their party retorted that the MAPAI gangsters were behind the accusation. The killer or killers were never discovered. But during the last month of the election campaign the Right-wing Revisionists and the workers attacked each other with deeper hatred than ever before.

In his letters from the depths of Poland, Ben-Gurion repeatedly gave his opinion that, from the information he had received, the Revisionists were the authors of the crime. A few days before the murder, Arlozoroff had signed an agreement with the Nazi Government which permitted several thousands of German Jews to emigrate to Palestine.

This revelation had a terrible effect on the mass of Jews. The strength of the Revisionists in Palestine was shattered. Having been named as assassins, rightly or wrongly, they were forced to sink into the background and their attempts to win over the working classes came to nothing.

The election results were known at the end of July. The workers' parties supporting Ben-Gurion had won nearly half the seats at the forthcoming congress. Thanks to the coalition, the workers' movement in Palestine gained control of the organization.

Ben-Gurion had been carried to power by his friends and supporters, and he was to command Zionism for the next thirty years. A handful of determined men had seen to it that the policies of Zionism would no longer be issued from London or Basel, but from Jerusalem.

EIGHT

INTERLUDE FOR FRANKNESS

The defeated Jabotinsky rebelled against the authority of the congress, and Ben-Gurion's riposte was not long in coming—a motion was adopted which deprived the Revisionists of their quota of immigration certificates. As long as they refused to accept the directives of the Zionist Executive they would be unable to obtain entry into Palestine for any more of their militants. These certificates constituted a new weapon in Ben-Gurion's armory.

At the same time as Ben-Gurion in Palestine, Hitler had come to power in Germany. The dark clouds were gathering over Europe, and action to save the Jews was becoming urgent. In 1935, *Aliyah*, immigration to Palestine, reached its highest figure—61,000 Jews.

The dangers looming over European Jewry indicated that it was time for the parties in Palestine to unite. Ben-Gurion and Jabotinsky met in London in October 1934. There was a distinct coolness between them at first. Jabotinsky held out his hand to Ben-Gurion, who pretended not to notice it. After several hours of discussions, they left together. "Why did you refuse to shake hands with me?" asked Jabotinsky. "I didn't want to put you to the test," Ben-Gurion replied with a smile.

These two men who heartily detested one another nevertheless found they had something in common, and they remembered the old sympathy which had existed in the glorious days of the Jewish Legion. In short, an agreement on practically every point seemed possible, including the fusion of their two political parties in Palestine. Jabotinsky made only one condition, that the combined party should not be called MAPAI (Palestinian Labor Party) but MABAI (Palestinian Builders' Party). Ben-Gurion agreed. He wrote in his diary, however: "It's too good to be true!"

In the world of politics there is no place for frankness, as the two leaders were reminded when they returned to Palestine. Their supporters rejected the agreement, and the two parties were soon as bitter enemies as ever.

In 1935 Jabotinsky walked out of the Zionist Congress. He started one of his own, but it was a fiasco, and in 1940 he died without seeing his dreams come true.

At that 1935 congress Ben-Gurion was elected chairman of the Zionist Executive and head of the Jewish Agency, which was the embryo of the future government in Palestine. He went to see Weizmann in his semiretirement and offered him the position of President of the Zionist movement again. The reason for this gesture was that Weizmann still remained the most respected leader of the Jewish world and that he still held the confidence of the British. His presence with Ben-Gurion was therefore necessary. But while voting for Weizmann, the Nineteenth Zionist Congress had no doubts that the real head of the movement was Ben-Gurion.

"When did you first feel that you had become the leader?" a young colleague asked him one day. "When I realized there was no one I could put questions to," he replied.

When Ben-Gurion became chairman of the Executive, Berl Katzenelson explained to his friends that he had managed to escape that thankless task. Ben-Zvi, Jerusalem's leading Jewish citizen, withdrew for some years from the political scene—which had never been his strong point. Tabenkin moved further to the Left and concentrated on developing the kibbutzim. Arlozoroff was dead. Other leading figures in the MAPAI—Remez, Shprinzak, Kaplan —lacked initiative. Shertok, who as head of the political and diplomatic section of the Jewish Agency became Ben-Gurion's right-hand man, was not the stuff of which leaders are made. Jabotinsky had been expelled from Palestine by the British. Weizmann was too much a middle-of-the-road man, and too much of an aristocrat, who knew nothing of the daily problems of the Palestinian Jews. He had never been one of them, and never would be. He lived in London, not in Israel; and when he did go to that country, it was to build himself a splendid residence.

Ben-Gurion adapted himself to his new life with surprising ease. He often went by air to Europe. In evening dress, he and Paula attended the balls and sumptuous receptions given by the Zionist movement. But such gatherings bored him, and he sought to draw the most interesting person present into a corner for a long conversation. He often met high British officials and members of the Government. He had his own bodyguard, and the British added another to his entourage. But, Ben-Gurion remained the same—

modest, straightforward, frank, at times blunt. His one aim was still that which he had fixed for himself since the early years—the establishment of a Jewish majority in Palestine, with a view to the creation of a Jewish state.

This ambition was dependent upon the attitude of the British Government to Jewish immigration and aspirations, and at that period there was every indication that the British would help the Jews—as, indeed, they had done since the Balfour Declaration. Not until many years later did they become the enemy. So far, the British had done all in their power to protect the small Jewish minority, to assist settlement and create the best possible conditions for the growth of the *Yishuv*.

From the British point of view, fewer than 200,000 Palestinian Jews, aided by the members of their race throughout the world, were worth more consideration than the millions of Arabs scattered over the whole of the Middle East.

But what would be the attitude of the Arabs? Ben-Gurion had little doubt that a clash between Jews and Arabs was inevitable. The latter would never willingly accept the idea of a Jewish majority in Palestine, let alone a Jewish state. They were already protesting strongly against the principle of parity.

And yet perhaps a chance existed, however slender, of reaching an agreement. Perhaps the opposing leaders could prevent disaster, despite every sign to the contrary. Ben-Gurion made the effort, although he had little belief in a successful outcome, and in the greatest secrecy sought to make contact with the Arab leaders. The year 1934, the year of the truce with Jabotinsky, also saw the hope of another peace—with Moussa Alami.

Ben-Gurion had never liked the Arabs, but never said so, and in his work as a trade unionist he often assisted them. However, whenever he mentioned them in his personal notebooks he usually treated them as adversaries.

He was not impressed by the Arab way of life, nor by their culture. His attitude can be easily understood when one remembers the young David Grin making his first contacts with Arabs—the filth of Jaffa, the thefts and killings at Sejera, the massacre of Jews in 1920, 1921, 1929. . . . The Arab world was completely different from his own.

Nevertheless, he made this effort to reach an understanding with some of the Arab leaders. As with everything he undertook, he went about it conscientiously and earnestly. But obviously his heart was not really in it, and as soon as he met with rebuffs, he gave up.

The man with whom he made contact was worthy of his admiration. Moussa Alami had been chief public prosecutor before becoming one of the leaders of the Palestinian Arabs. He was rich and influential, very knowledgeable, and although he had little liking for politics was closely connected with the Mufti of Jerusalem and the leaders of *Istiklal,* the Arab Independence Party. On several occasions in September 1934, Ben-Gurion had meetings with him in his house in Jerusalem. The two took an immediate liking to each other, and talked sincerely and freely. Alami was alarmed by the influx of Jews and their purchasing of land, worried by the economic and cultural differences between the two populations, and anxious over the refusal of Jews to employ Arab workers, whose poverty was becoming more acute. Ben-Gurion had a ready reply—he promised large-scale financial aid from the Jews to improve the Arab economy, on one condition: that the Arabs accept the establishment of a Jewish state in Palestine. This state, he added, with its large Arab minority, would join a Middle East Federation of purely Arab countries.

Alami was interested. He raised objections, however, to Ben-Gurion's proposal that the Jewish state extend westwards to include Transjordan, which he considered a purely Arab territory. Ben-Gurion was prepared to concede the point. "If you would agree to the establishment of an unlimited number of Jews in Transjordan, then we should be prepared to come to some special arrangement over Transjordan, either a temporary or a permanent one."

Alami was particularly interested in the idea of a federation and the offer of Jewish financial aid to the Arabs. He went at once to report on the conversations to the Mufti, and on his return conveyed the Mufti's reactions to Ben-Gurion. Apparently the Mufti had been astonished—he had never imagined that the Jews would be prepared to come to an agreement with the Arabs and to cooperate with them. If the religious, economic and political interests of the Palestinian Arabs could be safeguarded, the Mufti would raise no objections to the proposals. However, he prudently refrained from making any definite statement himself, and suggested that Ben-Gurion go to Geneva to put his proposals before the Committee of Syrian and Palestinian Arabs.

Switzerland, however, was not Palestine, and the attitude of the Arab nationalist leaders, Gabri and Arslan, towards Ben-Gurion was tinged with hatred: "You want us to agree to you, the Jews, becoming a majority in Palestine? Why, even the British would not allow it!"

Moussa Alami refused to be discouraged and pressed Ben-Gurion to continue his efforts on the lines that the two had agreed upon. But the Arab nationalists in Geneva put a stop to the talks by publishing a report of the secret meetings in their periodical *The Arab Nation*. Moussa Alami did not dare see Ben-Gurion again.

The latter had not confined his contacts to Alami. In equal secrecy he had had meetings with other Arab leaders—Auni Bey, Abdul Hadi and Moussa Husseini. He had refused to support them in their struggles against the British and the French. In all sincerity he said to Auni Bey, the head of *Istiklal*, "We will not fight against the British; they have helped us, and we want to benefit from their help in the future. We are loyal to our friends." Ben-Gurion had even informed the British High Commissioner of his meetings, without naming the other side's representatives, and had been encouraged to continue his efforts.

Whatever hopes there may have been were soon shattered. While in 1935 a record number of 61,000 Jewish immigrants reached Palestine, the same year marked the Italian invasion of Ethiopia, and the infiltration of Italians into Arab ultranationalist circles. Ben-Gurion had a hard awakening from his pacifist dreams. At Passover, 1936, a new series of massacres inflamed the whole of Palestine. Behind the killings, the looting and the burning loomed once again the enigmatic figure whom Ben-Gurion had thought he could win over—the Mufti of Jerusalem.

NINE

WHO WANTS A STATE?

During the night of April 15, 1936, two Jews were murdered on the Nablus–Toulkarem road by an armed band of young Arabs. This was the start of a wave of terror which swept across the country. On April 19 a fanatical crowd attacked the Jews in Jaffa, killing sixteen. The leaders of the *Yishuv* barely managed to hold back the young men of *Haganah* from wreaking vengeance. There was to be no retaliation, no massacre of the innocents as the enemy was doing. The situation remained explosive, nevertheless. On the orders of their leaders, the Arab workers started a general strike. It was total in the port of Jaffa, with the admitted aim of bringing Jewish immigration and trade to a standstill. Supported by the vast movement he had set afoot, the Mufti called on the British Government to stop Jewish immigration, prohibit Jews from buying land, and give the country a government and national assembly to be elected by the Arabs. The British, in their perplexity, sent out some of their best battalions, but the Arabs stood firm in their demands, and the killings and strikes strengthened their position. In addition to clandestine support from Rome and Berlin, the Palestinian Arabs were encouraged in their extremist activities by the coming independence of Egypt and Iraq, and the probable independence of Syria. The winds of nationalism blowing over the East had not spared Palestine. And the Jews were paying the price of being the one obstacle to the Arab plans for an independent state.

Meanwhile, defeatism was demoralizing the Jewish world. The reaction of many Zionists in this time of crisis was to favor any sacrifice which would restore order and peace.

The attitude of Ben-Gurion and his supporters was expressed in a forceful statement made by Moshe Shertok to the London *Times* in May 1936: "If the demands of the Palestinian Arabs are met (by Great Britain), this would mean the end of the Jewish people's hopes of taking root as a nation in their homeland . . ."

The day after this statement appeared, Ben-Gurion received a cable from two American Jewish leaders, Warburg and Strauss: "This statement seems extremely unreasonable to us. It makes the situation in Palestine worse and loses us friends all over the world. We think resignation of Shertok desirable to dissociate us from his words and to prove our desire for peace . . ."

Ben-Gurion was furious. "We cannot pass over in silence the vulgarity, impudence and idiotic fears of these two gentlemen concerning Shertok's statement. It is time they realized that they are not in charge of the national undertaking in the land of Israel. These Jews want to leave the ship which they think is sinking. I fear this arrogance springs not only from the coarseness of these 'money-bags' but also from the moral weakness of the American Zion-ists. . . ."

The "moneybags" were not alone in beating a retreat. Some months later, Ben-Gurion heard that Professor Magnès was said to have had conversations in Beirut with the Mufti and the Iraqi Foreign Minister, Nouri Saïd. According to this source, Nouri had declared that no Judaeo-Arab agreement was possible except on the basis of the Jews remaining permanently in a minority of no more than 33 percent of the population of Palestine, and Magnès had said he would try to get the Jewish Agency to accept this principle.

However, the most shocking act of defeatism (hushed up previ-ously) came from Weizmann. On June 9, 1936, he had a meeting with Nouri Saïd, who was playing an important role in the crisis, and as a means of restoring peace proposed nothing less than to put a temporary halt to Jewish immigration into Palestine!

Ben-Gurion was terrified when he heard of this. He was then in London with Weizmann, and tried to explain to him the disastrous effects of such a proposition. And disaster was not far off. As might have been expected, Nouri Saïd did not keep Weizmann's sensa-tional proposal to himself, but hastened to inform the British ambassador in Baghdad, who in turn cabled the news to the Colonial Secretary, Ormsby-Gore. And Ormsby-Gore did not wait long before raising the matter with Weizmann. Ben-Gurion wrote despairingly in an urgent letter to Shertok: "I don't know if I ought to continue my activities here, especially to collaborate with Weiz-mann. Will he never change? If we were not in deadly danger I should probably have drawn the obvious conclusion; but just now a split between us might well ruin our political position . . ."

Did Weizmann realize his mistake? Ben-Gurion went to see him, and the two had a long and painful talk. Finally they went together to call on Ormsby-Gore. The Colonial Secretary, aware of Nouri Saïd's meeting with Weizmann, put the question: "What do you think of the idea of halting immigration while a commission of enquiry goes out to Palestine and examines the situation?"

Ben-Gurion looked tensely at Weizmann. The latter merely said: "I am unable to give a reply now to your question."

Another page had been turned in the complex relationship between Ben-Gurion and Weizmann. Ben-Gurion would never again place any confidence in Weizmann. He feared he could harm Zionist interests inadvertently through negligence. Henceforth, he kept a close check on every statement or speech that Weizmann wished to make in the name of the movement.

This internal crisis came just at the time when the larger crisis, that between Jews and Arabs, was reaching its height. What action would the British take? Ben-Gurion was still hopeful. He was used to hard knocks, and could draw on reserves of strength and tenacity just when everything around seemed to be collapsing. In 1930, when the previous conflict with the Arabs had led to rigorous measures being taken by the British against the Jews, Ben-Gurion had said to a despondent audience in New York: "I will let you into two secrets. The first is that my whole life in Palestine has been a succession of crises. The second is that all our great accomplishments have sprung from some critical situation. We went to Israel because of the historic crisis among our oppressed people; we built up a powerful workers' organization and a collective economy to overcome the crisis among the Jewish workpeople, who were unable to find employment. *Hashomer* came into being because of the crisis following Arab attacks. The growth of Tel Aviv, too, was given incentive by a crisis, the massacres in 1921. And this present crisis ought to lead to the crystallization of the national effort and the growth of the population in the land of Israel . . ."

He thought that the 1936 crisis, too, would in the end prove to be of benefit to the Zionist movement. In the course of a brief return to Palestine in July he had been overjoyed to find that a harbor had been built at Tel Aviv in record time, thus overcoming the difficulties caused by the Arabs' strike in Jaffa and freeing the Jews of dependence upon them. A port at Tel Aviv was one benefit resulting from the gravest crisis yet to shake Palestine. Something far better was to come—the Jewish state.

The year 1936 was one of anxiety and tension for the Zionist world. Did the hesitations of the British, confronted with the strife in Palestine, presage a change in their policy? There were fears that

Jewish immigration might be restricted or even suspended, that the Jews would be kept in permanent minority in Palestine as in the ghettos of Eastern Europe. A powerful international campaign was organized to prevent such disaster. The Jews not only mobilized their communities throughout the world, especially in the United States, whose attitude affected British foreign policy, but they also put into action a worldwide ramification of propaganda and personal contacts.

In Britain, carefully-prepared questions were asked in the House of Commons by members faithful to the Zionist cause. Lloyd George received Weizmann and Ben-Gurion at his home in the country and said to them: "So the Arabs fear that Palestine might become a Hebrew State? Well, a Hebrew State it will become!" Ormsby-Gore told all the Jewish leaders that he was a Zionist. Attlee was sympathetic and expressed the hope that a peaceful solution would be found. "The Jews have done some splendid things in Palestine," he said.

Whether or not it was the effect of all these efforts, combined with the worthy and courageous attitude of the Palestinian Jews, one way or another the Zionists began to register some success. Thousands of young Palestinian Jews were armed by the British and organized in territorial units to help keep order, thus becoming the nucleus of an official Jewish Army side by side with the clandestine *Haganah* forces. Moreover, the British rejected Arab requests to put a halt to Jewish immigration. The Arab general strike was called off after six months, and an atmosphere of defeatism led to quarrels amongst the Arab leaders themselves. Ben-Gurion triumphantly called the pro-Zionist attitude of the British "the greatest political success since the Balfour Declaration." Then came the sensational recommendation of the Peel Commission— the creation of a Jewish state in Palestine!

Who would have believed it? The Jewish leaders who had given evidence before the Peel Commission in Jerusalem were all flatly pessimistic. Weizmann, at his first appearance before the Commission, had made a moving plea for the rights of the Jewish people to Palestine. In a flash of prophetic vision he had foreseen the disaster looming over the six million Jews in Europe. But his statements at later appearances had been much less inspired. He had been unable to refrain from having a few digs at his colleagues. But much worse was the impression he gave that the Jews would be quite satisfied if the *Yishuv* were allowed to increase by one million immigrants: ". . . by stages, over twenty-five or thirty years; there is no hurry. We must not forget that if we go too quickly we risk a fall . . ."

Ben-Gurion was incensed. To him, the ultimate aim of Zionism had never been the transfer of one or two million Jews to Palestine, but the complete solution to the problem. He believed that the rhythm of building up the national home should in fact be increased. The crisis which had long been brewing between the two men finally came to a head. ". . . I find that our differences are neither temporary nor fortuitous, but go very deep," Ben-Gurion wrote to Weizmann on December 24, 1936, "and I have come to the conclusion that it is no longer possible nor useful for me to continue to exercise my functions in the political section of the Executive . . ."

The rapid intervention of a few mutual friends smothered the blaze between the two leaders before it was too late. But trust between the leader of the Jews and the leader of the Palestinians was wearing very thin.

A few weeks later the Zionist world was shaken by another explosion, and this time the two leaders were on the same side. The conclusions reached by the Peel Commission were that the British Mandate could not be effectively exercised in the prevailing circumstances, and the solution recommended was the partition of Palestine into a Jewish and an Arab state. The Jewish state, as recommended, would consist of only a small part of historic Palestine.

The Jewish world rose in protest. Objections came from all sides, and there were threats of secession from the Zionist movement. Standing firm against all this indignation were two fierce supporters of the recommendations—Weizmann and Ben-Gurion.

The report of the Peel Commission was not published until July 1937. But in February of that year the possibility of partition had already been raised at meetings of Zionist organizations in many countries. And the reply heard everywhere was "No." The territory to be given to the Jews was indeed small—about a quarter of Palestine, chiefly Galilee and the coastal plain to just north of Gaza. All the remainder, including the Negev Desert, would become an Arab state. Britain, however, would continue to exercise her mandate over Haifa, Jerusalem, Bethlehem and Nazareth, as well as a corridor to the sea.

It was little enough for the Jews. Yet Ben-Gurion was overwhelmed—an independent Jewish state! He showered his friends and colleagues with enthusiastic and moving letters, in which he gave free rein to his joy. He wrote to Moshe Shertok, who thought as he did, revealing his innermost thoughts: "We shall smash these frontiers which are being forced upon us, and not necessarily by war. I believe an agreement between us and the Arab State could be reached in a not too distant future. And if we bring hundreds of thousands of Jews into our State, if we can strengthen our economic and military position, then a basis would be established for an agreement on the abolition of the frontiers between ourselves and the Arab State."

He deplored the loss of the Negev, which had seemed to him in 1935 to hold the future of Palestine. But he had hopes for that too: "The Negev will remain an arid desert in Arab hands, but sooner or later the dynamic spirit of Jewish colonization will prevail over the barren Arab patriotism . . ." In other speeches he was equally clear: "This Jewish State now being proposed to us is not the Zionist aim, for it's impossible to solve the Jewish problem in such a territory. But this will be a decisive stage in bringing about the great Zionist aims. In the shortest possible time it will build up the real Jewish strength that will carry us to our historic objective." All of Ben-Gurion's political philosophy was contained in those few phrases.

What would have been the destiny of the Jewish people if this state had been established, even in a small part of Palestine, before the Second World War? The temptation to make such speculation is almost irresistible, if only because six million European Jews might have been saved. Yet could the proposals ever have been given effect? No sooner had the Peel Commission Report been published than the Arab world began seething in revolt. Terrorism reared its head again, more deadly than before. As for the Jews, they seemed not to understand what a great opportunity was being offered. Two thousand years of dependence had sapped their national aspirations, and they stuck grimly to the mentality of the past, as when in exile. They preferred the continuation of the British Mandate.

Ben-Gurion fought futilely against friends and colleagues at the Zionist Congress in Zurich. One after the other, opponents of partition addressed the delegates—Berl Katzenelson, Golda Meyerson, Bentov, American rabbis, Palestinian leaders, members of MAPAI . . . A telegram from South Africa expressed indignation that the subject was being discussed at all.

In the opposite camp were Ben-Gurion, Weizmann, Shertok and Remez, and a handful of their friends. The congress prudently took a neutral line and passed a motion calling on the British for "supplementary details." But this was only throwing dust in people's eyes. It could not hide the fact that Zionism was refusing to accept its responsibilities.

In Britain, too, there were many opponents of partition, and the outbreaks of terrorism in Palestine strengthened their position. In the House, even members sympathetic to the Jews voted against the Peel recommendations, thinking they were serving the Zionist cause, but in fact were ill-informed on the matter. Conservative leaders, including Churchill—whose sympathies with the Zionist cause were well known—voted against the Report. Ben-Gurion had lost.

The following year, 1938, the idea of a Jewish state was definitely dropped. The British, in view of the split in the Zionist movement and the growing violence of the Arabs, gradually changed their policy. The Anglo-Zionist idyll had ended, and British friendship with the Arabs had begun. It was the year of Munich, the year of appeasement, inaugurated at an imposing conference in St. James's Palace. There the illusions of the Jews were finally shattered and Ben-Gurion began his fight against his recent allies.

TEN

THE POINT OF NO RETURN

Shortly before noon on February 7, 1939, Neville Chamberlain and some of his ministers entered the splendid Picture Gallery at St. James's Palace in London to open the Round Table Conference to seek a final settlement of the Palestine question. The Jewish delegates were not overawed by the splendid surroundings—they all suspected that the scene had been set for the deathblow to the agreement started by the Balfour Declaration. The British, increasingly anxious in face of the gathering storm, and uneasy at the growing Arab unrest, were preparing to impose restrictions which would stifle the growth of the Jewish national home and put an end to Zionist hopes. This was the real reason for arranging the round table talks between Jews and Arabs there in London.

The St. James's Conference was, in principle, an attempt to bring Jews and Arabs together. Actually, there were three distinct conferences. There was not a single Arab delegate in the Picture Gallery—they had all refused to sit at the same table as the Jews; instead they held meetings with the British, who acted as liaison between the two sides. To make matters more difficult, the Arabs were divided among themselves. There were the followers of the Mufti, headed by the Husseini family, and the *Istiklal* party, led by another important family, the Nashashibi. A deadly feud existed between these two families, and they refused to meet and held their talks in different rooms.

The Jews were very pessimistic. The British had already refused immigration permits for ten thousand Jewish children escaping from Nazi persecution. And they had invited Arab kings and potentates to the conference, thus widening Arab representation and confronting the Jews with the whole Arab world. And the numbers of Zionist sympathizers in the British Government and high official circles had considerably decreased. Ormsby-Gore had been replaced at the Colonial Office by Malcolm MacDonald. The High Commissioner in Palestine was no longer Wauchope but Sir Harold McMichael, described later by Ben-Gurion as a "nasty person, arrogant and bureaucratic, a real disaster for the Jews, Palestine and the British."

Ben-Gurion had no illusions about the outcome "I think no good will come of these talks," he wrote to Paula. "There will be no agreement between the Jews and the Arabs, nor between the Jews and the British either."

The Arabs were intractable. World events were strengthening their position, they were backed up by Hitler and Mussolini, and had to deal with a weak Britain. So they insisted on a Palestine under Arab domination and with a small Jewish minority.

After several days of fruitless talks, they agreed to meet the Jews unofficially, with Malcolm MacDonald presiding. Ben-Gurion again put forward his scheme for a Jewish state within an Arab federation. The chief Arab spokesman, Ali Maher, proposed a halt to Jewish immigration and expansion in order to reestablish Judaeo-Arab friendship. Weizmann smiled at Maher's speech and said: "For the first time in twenty years, I have heard friendly words from a Muslim. We can reach an understanding in this spirit. For our part, we are ready to negotiate on a basis of mutual concessions. If we are told that an agreement can be reached by slowing down immigration a little, we will find common ground for negotiations."

MacDonald, who had said nothing up to that point, seized upon Weizmann's words. "This meeting has achieved something," he said. "There is mutual agreement on the slowing down of immigration. The meeting is adjourned until tomorrow."

"I am sorry," Ben-Gurion said, "but there is no common agreement. Dr. Weizmann spoke of concessions on both sides, but there can be no question of slowing down immigration."

And he added, "But we might perhaps discuss a speeding up of immigration."

MacDonald was completely taken aback, then he stormed: "No agreement can be reached on the basis of speeding up immigration!"

"Well then," retorted Ben-Gurion, "neither can an agreement be reached on the basis of slowing it down."

This was a determined, arrogant Ben-Gurion, refusing to give way, attacking to avoid defeat, carrying the fight into the enemy camp. His reply to the demand for concessions was calmly to put forward new demands.

A few evenings later, an official envelope bearing the seal of the Colonial Office was delivered to Weizmann. The old man could hardly believe his eyes when he opened it and read the contents— the details of a forthcoming White Paper which would satisfy all the Arab requirements. The immigration of 75,000 Jews was to be spread over a period of five years, then the Jewish immigration would be brought to an end, except with the agreement of the Arabs. The Jews would not be allowed to buy any more land, and a minority status would be fixed for the Jews, whose numbers would not be allowed to exceed one-third or perhaps one-quarter of the population.

This top secret document had come into Weizmann's hands by mistake, as was revealed by a secret inquiry. It was destined for the leader of the Arab delegation. Perhaps some official at the Colonial Office thought that the Jews ought to know of the disaster in store for them.

Lord Halifax, the Foreign Minister, turned the knife in the wound by informing the Jews that in ten years' time an independent State of Palestine, with an Arab majority, would be established. Ben-Gurion angrily banged the table. "Let me tell you that Jewish immigration will be brought to a halt only with the aid of British bayonets. And Palestine will never become an Arab State without the aid of those bayonets!"

The Jews left the conference on March 16. Two months later, the British Government published the White Paper, "Order 6019," which gave details of all the disastrous measures to be imposed on the Palestinian Jews.

Back in Palestine, Ben-Gurion called together the leaders of *Haganah,* the clandestine defense force. "Until now," he told them, "we have acted according to the spirit of the law. From now on, some of our activities will be directed against the law and with the aim of making that law powerless."

It was a declaration of war. "Zionism is entering a new phase," wrote Ben-Gurion. "The first phase was that of 'the love for Zion' and illegal entry into Palestine. That ended with the Great War. The second phase, political Zionism, began with the Balfour Declaration and ended with the publication of the White Paper in 1939. The third phase, militant Zionism, is now beginning."

While this David was declaring war on Goliath—the weak *Yishuv* against the powerful British Empire—the world was shaken by the outbreak of a bloodier and more tragic war. Hitler had invaded Poland.

In this war against Nazism, the Zionist leaders came out unhesitatingly on the side of the British. They used everything at their command in the fight against the common enemy, while continuing their private war in Palestine against the British Crown. One of Ben-Gurion's most famous sayings sprang from this odd situation, and was to be the slogan of the *Yishuv* for many years: "We will make war as though there were no White Paper, and we will fight the White Paper as though there were no war."

After the bitter blow of the London conference, Ben-Gurion made a Jewish state his main objective. He wrote to his friend Itzhak Grinbaum: "It's either the Mandate or a Jewish State. Britain has definitely come out against a Mandate, so it must be a State."

He did not reserve these opinions for confidential letters to friends. He expressed them openly, challenging the British during the gravest period of the war, "as though there were no war." While Zionism in Europe was being killed in the gas chambers, in Palestine it was being strangled by strict security measures and military censorship of the press. Ben-Gurion decided to shift alliances, and appealed to the New World. A few months after the disaster of Pearl Harbor he was in New York, attending the American Zionist Congress. There, he buried political Zionism and gave a spectacular start to militant Zionism. His new objective was unanimously adopted—the creation of a free Jewish "commonwealth" in Palestine.

There were three forces opposing his political and nationalist aims. First, the mass of Arabs, which carried increasing weight in the balance of power as the war spread. Second was the enemy of recent date, Great Britain, who was trying to destroy with the aid of White Papers and useless conferences what she had built up in Palestine. Third was the enemy of all time and the most dangerous, the enemy within—world Jewry.

There had been a time when Ben-Gurion had almost had victory within his grasp. He had conquered the Zionist movement, the Arabs were split by internal quarrels and Britain was proposing to establish a Jewish state. The opportunity had slipped away. And now, while Britain was facing a German-occupied Europe, Ben-Gurion was preparing his plans for the future, between voyages, between a secret conference and a chilly interview with the British High Commissioner in Palestine.

"Our greatest concern," he wrote, "was the fate of Palestine after the war. I was convinced of the necessity to establish a Jewish State.

It already appeared evident that the British would not keep their Mandate. While there was every reason for believing that Hitler would be defeated, it seemed equally obvious that Britain, even though victorious, would be considerably weakened by the war. However willing, she would not be strong enough to exercise a new Mandate, nor carry out the project of partition in the face of opposition from all the Arab countries. For my part, I had no doubt that the center of gravity of our political efforts had shifted from Great Britain to America, who was making sure of being the world's leading power and where the greatest number of Jews, as well as the most influential, were to be found. All Europe was under Nazi domination. Hitler would be defeated in the end, but Europe would emerge from the war enfeebled and dependent for many years upon economic aid from the United States."

European Judaism was dead, and new allies had to be won for the Zionist cause—America and its Jews.

On May 12, 1942, at New York's Biltmore Hotel, six hundred delegates gathered for the congress extraordinary organized by the American Committee for Zionist Affairs. On the platform, among the best-known names in American Judaism, was the "lion" from Palestine, David Ben-Gurion.

He had had great difficulty in getting this congress organized. The year before, when he had gone to the United States to suggest to the Zionist leaders that demands should be made for a Jewish state in Palestine, he had been regarded as mad. Several of the Zionist leaders remembered the names he had called them in the past, such as "moneybags." Now, in his abrupt way, he was making a complete about-face, and wanted to turn the "moneybags" into allies in order to proclaim a bold and dangerous policy.

There were some convinced pacifists, who would have nothing to do with a policy bound to anger the Arabs. Some feared future repercussions from this defiance of the British, and others obstinately repeated their ideas for a dual-nation state in Palestine. Weizmann was against Ben-Gurion's program; Magnès, the Dean of Jerusalem University, was against it, and so was Henrietta Szold, the founder of the influential women's movement *Hadassa*. Brandeis, the head of American Zionism, was hesitant. The leaders of the pioneers' Left-wing party, *Hashomer Hazaïr,* were in open opposition.

How it came about no one knows, but in spite of the obstacles on that May 12 the six hundred delegates unanimously adopted (with one abstention—the extreme Left-wing delegate) the motion that

Ben-Gurion put to them: war to the bitter end on the White Paper and its repressive measures, unrestricted immigration into Palestine under the authority of the Jewish Agency, and—most important of all—the transformation of Palestine after the war into a Jewish commonwealth, to be part of the setup in the postwar world.

Why a commonwealth and not a state? The ambiguity of the term could but assist a wily tactician like Ben-Gurion. There were three possible meanings: an independent republic, a dominion within the framework of a community of nations, or a country belonging to a federation of states. Any of these was acceptable to Ben-Gurion. The word "commonwealth" had an historic significance too, for Ben-Gurion and his friends had used it in 1917 to describe the manner of the national home they wanted to see established in Palestine.

The Biltmore Program was in any case an insolent smack in the face for Britain. Weizmann was in complete disagreement with Ben-Gurion, as he told his close associates (he was too honorable a man to say so publicly). The break between the two, who until then had been at variance on the tactics to adopt but united on the aims, now became complete.

While in New York, Ben-Gurion received a distressing cable— his father had died in Tel Aviv. He wrote home to say how grieved he was at the loss of the man who had sown in him the seeds of Zionism and inspired him to restore the Kingdom of David.

On his return to Palestine, Ben-Gurion was bitterly attacked by the Left-wing parties. He realized that restoring the Kingdom of David would be paid for in blood, and that when the crucial moment came there would be no one but themselves to rely upon. The destiny of the Palestinian Jews depended on their own military strength. If the Biltmore Program were not to remain just a scrap of paper, the whole of the *Yishuv* must be turned into a loyal and bold army.

A new period in Ben-Gurion's life began on that May 12. He had always been a prophet; now he was an armed one.

ELEVEN

WAR ON THE BRITISH

The Palestinian Jews had been preparing in secret for this trial of strength. In the spring of 1939 *Haganah*'s secret stores of weapons dispersed about the country totaled 6,000 rifles and a million rounds of ammunition, 600 machine guns and submachine guns, 80,000 grenades and 12,000 mortar shells. In addition there were the few thousand "legal" rifles of the Jewish auxiliary security force, and the weapons of the illicit organizations *Etzel* (from the initials of the "National Military Organization") and *Lehi* (initials of "Fighters for Free Israel").

Grenades and bombs were being made in the cellars of an inoffensive-looking tannery at Tel Aviv owned by the brothers Levkovitz. Another secret arms factory was in the peaceful surroundings of Kibbutz Naan. Some technicians were secretly assembling the first mortars "made in Palestine," which were successfully tested under the very noses of the British. The outbreak of war brought an increase in gun-running, and weapons were smuggled into the Holy Land in many different ways. Some dozens of roller drums began to be unloaded at Haifa, each of them filled with rifles and explosives. The other end of this illicit organization was in Poland, where some senior army officers—having been approached by one of the *Haganah* leaders, Yehuda Arazi—had sold large quantities of arms to the Jewish "resistance."

Behind this growing traffic was the illicit military force *Haganah*, which had developed since its creation at the end of the First World War to become a powerful, national organization. "*Haganah?* Never heard of it!" was the invariable reply of Jewish leaders to the British authorities, who returned a tolerant smile. They tolerated this military force, which had training camps in several kibbutzim and organized instructional courses under the guise of sports meets, because *Haganah* had teeth but did not bite. It was not a fighting force in a military sense. Its role was to protect Jewish villages and districts against attacks by Arab bands, but it never attacked the Arab population or carried out reprisal raids. It was the only nonpolitical Jewish organization in a country that was intensely politicized. From a military point of view, *Haganah* was a kind of Home Guard and presented little real danger. Its units could guard a village and beat off an attack, give first aid to the wounded, but could not pursue attackers, and carry the fight into enemy territory. *Haganah* was not even a guerrilla force.

However, this began to change with the arrival of a British Army captain, Orde Wingate, an austere Scot with a fascinating personality. When he first met the *Haganah* leaders, David Hacohen asked him if he had read anything about Zionism. To which Wingate dryly replied: "There is only one important book on the subject, and I know it thoroughly—the Bible." He soon won the confidence of the Jews. He learned Hebrew and set about creating a Jewish fighting force. With the aid of other British officers he succeeded in the improbable feat of making soldiers out of Jews, capable of carrying out daring raids into enemy territory, of pursuing Arab bands back to their base and then wiping them out.

Unfortunately, he appeared to his superiors to have too much sympathy for "the natives." He was replaced, and given a post in another part of the world. He later achieved fame in the Burma campaign, as General Wingate, and was killed in an air crash in 1945. "If he had lived," Ben-Gurion said later, "he would have been the man to command the Israeli Forces during the War of Independence."

Wingate's teachings had lasting effect. The Jews had learned that it was not enough to hold the shield; they must also wield the spear. Nevertheless, *Haganah* still refrained from acts of terrorism and remembered its directive of "hold back."

"A tooth for a tooth, an eye for an eye." The Bible is cruel, and life no less so. Jabotinsky's disciples, the young Revisionists, did not agree with the idea of "holding back" and could not understand *Haganah*'s passive attitude in face of Arab terrorism. They wanted to reply to it with terrorism of their own. Jabotinsky was against this, right until his death in 1940, but for the first time a number of his disciples disobeyed him. *Etzel* became an extremist organization which believed in taking a life for a life. Sooner or later, *Etzel* and *Haganah* were bound to come into conflict.

Ben-Gurion sent an ultimatum to *Etzel* in 1937—either accept the supreme authority of the *Yishuv*'s institutions or be banished.

Some of the terrorists submitted, but the others rejected Ben-Gurion's conditions and became even more extremist. This he could not accept. "The only condition," he repeated, "on which *Etzel* can be brought into our ranks is for it willingly to accept the political discipline of the Zionist Executive." While in London in September 1938 he learned that *Haganah* and *Etzel* had come to an agreement, and he threatened to resign. On several occasions, the two had been close to making a truce, even an alliance. But Ben-Gurion has never liked compromise, and he would not make a compact with anarchy by letting into the movement people who spurned legal authority.

The outbreak of the Second World War added a new dimension to the problem. While the hatreds decreased, others were driven to fanaticism. The gap between opposing political tendencies in Palestine grew even wider, and the most reckless of the terrorist groups, *Lehi,* came into existence.

The *Yishuv* was still despairing over the publication of the rigorous measures contained in the White Paper; and the bitterness resulting from the St. James's London Conference had driven many Palestinian Jews to extremist views. *Etzel* was seriously considering rebelling against the British. Ben-Gurion had a succession of anguished and embittered men visit him at his office. He noted in his diary on May 27, 1939: "It has been a week of delegations. They all say the same thing—that what we need now is a dictatorship, otherwise there'll be great confusion . . . I replied that our chief quarrel is with the British Government, but that we have no wish to make war on the British people; and it's not easy to draw a line between the people and the government . . . For the moment, the greatest danger here is a split among ourselves."

The danger soon became a reality. Many were unable to distinguish between the British Government and the British people, and when war broke out, the extremists adopted radical methods. Supporters of Abraham Stern, who dreamed of a Kingdom of Israel extending from the Nile to the Euphrates, fired the first shots against the British. They even committed the unpardonable crime of recommending an alliance with Nazi Germany, against Britain. When the British shot Stern, his gang avenged him by bomb attacks. These men were few in number and represented a very small part of the *Yishuv,* but their terrorist activities began a new, violent phase in the struggle against the British, a phase which was to lead to open warfare between various factions and groups in Palestine, when Jew fought against Jew and disaster almost came to the Zionist cause.

In the midst of all the strife and confusion, Ben-Gurion continued methodically to follow the path he had laid down for himself—to fight the White Paper and its measures, but above all to fight the common enemy, Nazism. The modest but zealous contribution of half a million Jews to the Allied cause would give them a share in final victory. "The First World War brought us the Balfour Declaration," said Ben-Gurion. "The Second ought to bring us the Jewish State."

When victory came, the Jewish state was still a dream, a vague and distant hope, although the Jews had done all in their power to help the Allies. Swallowing their bitterness against the British, they had made war as though there were no White Paper.

More than 30,000 men and women took part in the fighting in Greece, North Africa and Sicily. These Jewish units, prudently given the name of Palestinian, honored their flag with the Star of David. At Bir Hakeim, General Koenig's Free French saluted the Jewish flag of a company of the King's West African Rifles which had lost 450 men, nine tenths of its strength, during the battle. At Fort Gouraud, on the borders of Syria, the start of the campaign was marked by a sharp and bloody battle between French Somali and Jewish units. It was there that Moshe Dayan, the future Chief of Staff of the Israeli Army, lost his left eye. Jewish men and women were parachuted into German-occupied Europe on dangerous missions. The Jewish Brigade, the formation of which was due to the protracted efforts of Weizmann and Shertok to convince the British Government, took part in the final fighting in Europe with the British Army.

Ben-Gurion had not forgotten the White Paper. The Jews were forbidden to buy land, so new villages would be created in spite of the British. Ben-Gurion gave details of his plans to his colleagues on the Zionist Executive and of the Jewish Agency's Directory, the general principles being to support Britain in the war but to fight against the new laws, organize passive resistance and demonstrations, and appeal to world opinion. But, once again, he found himself in the minority. There was agreement on supporting the British war effort, but fears were expressed about opposing British policy in Palestine. To overcome this opposition, Ben-Gurion relied on a weapon which he often used with skill—the threat to resign, the ultimatum. He got his way, and started his fight against the measures contained in the White Paper, particularly against the restrictions on immigration. The British had closed legal entry to Palestine, so the Jews would force their way in by the back door.

Mass illegal immigration began at the height of the Second

World War. Ships that were hardly seaworthy, veritable "floating coffins," were packed with men, women and children forming the *Aliyah Beth,* Immigration B. Immigration A was the legal one, for the favored few who had been able to obtain an official entry certificate. All the others, tens of thousands of them, tried to reach Palestine by one of the long escape routes which curled across Europe to some southern port; then one or two thousand were crammed into a ship which usually carried one or two hundred passengers.

Sometimes a ship was intercepted and her passengers were taken to internment in a faraway place, such as Mauritius. Other ships were refused entry to the port of Haifa and had to cruise around for weeks; a few were even obliged to return to their port of departure and then cast back into the Nazi hell from which they had tried to escape.

The first tragedy was on November 26, 1940, when the *Patria* sank in Haifa harbor with 1,800 illegal passengers on board. Two hundred and fifty of them were drowned. The survivors had at least the consolation of being allowed into Palestine by the British, who had been holding them aboard ship and were embarrassed by the disaster. The decision to allow them in was made in London, at the highest level. Churchill noted in his diary: "Everything went without a hitch, not even a dog barked . . ."

Things did not go well for the *Salvador,* a miserable cargo boat flying the Uruguayan flag, which went down in the Sea of Marmara with the loss of 200 of her 326 passengers, 70 of them children. Tragedy also came to the *Struma,* a Panamanian ship, which struck a mine in the Black Sea, in February 1942. She went down with all her 770 illegal immigrants.

Ben-Gurion gritted his teeth when he read in pamphlets distributed in the United States by the British Information services that the Gestapo was behind the Jewish illegal immigration, and that many of those from Germany were Nazi agents with the mission of organizing a spy network in Palestine. . . .

Yet Ben-Gurion did not hold a grudge against Churchill. He never accused him of having forgotten, when he was out of power, the promises made to the Zionists, nor failing to take steps to rectify the White Paper, nor even of refusing to bomb the concentration camps of Auschwitz and Treblinka in order to destroy the gas chambers and so put a stop to the terrible slaughter. Ben-Gurion, grieved to death, told his intimates that Churchill doubtlessly had other, more urgent and vital, preoccupations.

Ben-Gurion had a great admiration for Britain and her war effort. His respect for the adversary and his endeavors to keep the fighting clean have to be borne in mind in order to understand his attitude toward Britain throughout his long struggle to establish a Jewish state.

On a personal level, however, his attitude was quite different, particularly in his relations with certain British ministers and high officials. For instance, in August 1941 he met Lord Moyne, the new Colonial Secretary, in London and spoke to him of the need to open Palestine, after the war, to three million Jews spread over ten years.

"That's 300,000 a year," said Lord Moyne with hostility. "Where are you going to house them all?"

"Lord Passfield told Weizmann in 1930 that there was no room left in Palestine to swing a cat in," retorted Ben-Gurion. "But since then, hundreds of thousands of Jews have entered the country."

"I can see only one solution—to create a Jewish State in Europe," replied Lord Moyne. "We shall crush the Hitler regime, then throw the Germans out of East Prussia and establish a Jewish State there."

Ben-Gurion breathed fire. "I believe in an Allied victory, and you can do whatever you like with the Germans. You can chase them out of Prussia at the point of machine guns. But even with machine guns, you won't be able to drive the Jewish people into Prussia. Our only country is Palestine."

That was Ben-Gurion's last attempt to overcome the hostility of British ministers. On his return to Palestine at the end of a long journey which had taken him to the United States and Africa, he had his reply to Lord Moyne's theories—the Biltmore Program, approved by American Zionism. This was his declaration of war on the British. It was also a declaration of war on some of his closest colleagues in Palestine.

TWELVE

JEW AGAINST JEW

The Palestinian Jews were uneasy and undecided. They were half a million in the midst of a sea of Arabs, they were a dot in the vast British Empire, destined for sacrifice by the Nazis, hated by their neighbors, and an embarrassing problem for the British. And they did not even know themselves exactly what they wanted. This was understandable to some extent. These Jews had just been wrenched out of an age-long exile and were still affected by the complexes of the past and by the habit of dependence on others. Most astonishing was that the ghetto world produced a man like Ben-Gurion.

The hesitations and weaknesses of the Jewish community did not greatly hinder him. As soon as he saw what road to follow he pressed on to the end with only a few lieutenants. Everyone else lined up behind him, willy-nilly—even if not in complete agreement. Whenever he found himself in a minority, whether among his party or on the Zionist Executive, he had only to offer his resignation to be implored to pick up the reins again. His responsibilities were heavy and onerous, and few people would have dared to assume them. But he knew what he wanted, and on his return from New York, he lost no time in casting the Biltmore Program onto the political stage.

To say that no Zionist was against the idea of a Jewish state would be to oversimplify the problem. The majority were not "against" it, but on the other hand very few were sincerely "for" it. Ben-Gurion repeatedly used the phrase: "My ideas and propositions met with no objections from my colleagues." He could have added: "nor with their enthusiasm."

But the way was not easy. The Biltmore Program met with fierce opposition in some quarters. The terrorist groups favored a more radical solution—they wanted a state with the historical boundaries of the Kingdom of Israel. On the opposite side of the political arena, the Extreme Left was up in arms too; the *Hashomer Hazaïr* was the only party with the courage to oppose the idea of a Jewish state to the very end. In the party's kibbutzim there was general refusal to fly the blue-and-white flag and to sing the national anthem, *Hatikva* (Hope). They sang the *Internationale* instead. This fanaticism was responsible for a keen animosity between Ben-Gurion and the Extreme Left which never entirely disappeared. The later attempts to form a workers' front were doomed from the start by sharp political divergences.

Further opposition to the Biltmore Program—but harmless and even understandable—came from recent German immigrants. They were intelligent, polite, earnest people, but had little knowledge of political realities in the Middle East. At their head was Martin Buber and other thinkers and philosophers of world renown. For humanistic and moral reasons they were inclined to support the idea of coexistence with the Arabs. The slogan of their party was "Hitler is the greatest enemy of the Jews and of the Arabs," which proved that they had never noticed the enthusiasm with which the Arab masses greeted each Axis victory, nor heard the Mufti of Jerusalem broadcasting regularly from Berlin and inciting the Arabs against the Jews.

The other parties stood behind Ben-Gurion, although the strongest of them, the MAPAI, was shaken by a domestic crisis before finally accepting the Biltmore Program—a crisis which ended with Tabenkin and his "Kibbutzim Union" leaving the party.

The MAPAI Congress was held at Kfar Vitkin in November 1942, and Ben-Gurion presented his Biltmore Program. The groups forming a fractious element in the party had the elderly Tolstoy-like figure Tabenkin as spokesman. They were too engrossed in their dreams of pure socialism, too immersed in an ideology which placed the kibbutz at the summit of human society and which went beyond nationalist aspirations to statehood, and they listened to Ben-Gurion with only half an ear. They preferred to attack him on his ground, on trade union matters. Ben-Gurion replied by having a motion adopted which eliminated the fractious groups from the party. At the next meeting of the *Histadrut* Executive, these elements joined the extremists in voting against the Biltmore Program.

Ben-Gurion succeeded in pushing through his policy, in having the Biltmore Program approved and the fractious elements expelled; but Tabenkin took with him the best of the young leaders of the kibbutz development program and the best officers of *Palmach,* the shock brigade of *Haganah* which had been created with British support. This scission in the ranks of the MAPAI could have been avoided had Ben-Gurion not been so intransigent; but Ben-Gurion would not have been the man he was if he had given way to a wing of his party.

Leaders such as Tabenkin, some of the best in the party, failed to grasp the real problem confronting them, which was to establish a scale of priorities in which the national interest came first. Ben-Gurion was astounded when he spoke to these men of realizing something which had been dreamed about for two thousand years, and in reply had to listen to diatribes on trade union matters. The two sides did not speak the same language. If the Jewish state were to become a reality it would not be due to the masses but to the bold efforts and superhuman striving of a few who prevailed over the others and drew everyone with them.

The Biltmore Program was only the first of several conflicts. The following year, 1943, there was yet another clash between Ben-Gurion and Weizmann.

After opening the congress at the Biltmore, Weizmann had said nothing against the resolution which was finally adopted. But he had given his opinion in veiled terms at another meeting, held at the Commodore Hotel. "The art of politics is to aim at what is possible," he said, "to foresee what can be obtained, to select the best means of attaining it and have the talent not to waste those means." Ben-Gurion did not have to be very perceptive to see that these diplomatic phrases were directed at him. Wiezmann was in agreement over fighting the White Paper, but was not prepared to engage in what he considered fanciful undertakings. He returned to London and opened talks with the British Government. Back in Palestine, Ben-Gurion blew up and once again threatened to resign.

Jewish leaders asked Weizmann to go to Palestine and explain his point of view to Ben-Gurion, but he refused. His prestige was declining, whereas Ben-Gurion's was rising. A delegation hurriedly left Palestine to see Weizmann in London, and obtained from him a promise that in the future he would take no action without the agreement of the Zionist Executive and its leader. Once again, Ben-Gurion had used the power of the ultimatum to effect.

The differences between the two were now public, but Ben-Gurion was in a strong position. However, although the clash had ended with Ben-Gurion triumphant, it had revealed another split in his camp. Among those who had sided with Weizmann in this latest quarrel was a new name, Moshe Shertok—the faithful lieutenant of Ben-Gurion for many years, who had supported him in his hardest battles with Weizmann. But this time Shertok had changed sides. Almost imperceptibly, a gap had opened between him and Ben-Gurion, had gradually grown wider until they eventually found themselves too far apart. It was inevitable because once Shertok became Weizmann's spiritual heir he ceased to have common ground with Ben-Gurion.

So the 1943 victory was a bitter one. Ben-Gurion's authority within the Zionist movement was so secure, however, that Shertok never became a serious rival—in fact, he continued to back Ben-Gurion until the definite break between them some years later. More correctly, he had become a troublesome ally.

The real enemy that Ben-Gurion had to face, a deadly enemy whom he fought ceaselessly and intensely, came to the surface during the third conflict which shook the *Yishuv* at this period. This conflict was the most terrible that the Palestinian Jews were to experience, a shameful, unequal struggle in which violence, denunciation, terrorism and hatred all had a part. It was a conflict that none who were involved like to remember, and is referred to simply as "the season"—"the hunting season," explain those who have not forgotten . . . the manhunt.

Hunters and hunted were Jews and patriots, all faithful in their different ways to the common aim of independence. The hunters were the members of *Haganah;* the hunted were the dissident bands, especially the terrorists of the clandestine *Lehi* and *Etzel.*

One night in January 1944 posters calling on the population to revolt appeared on the walls. They had been put up by members of *Etzel,* which had nevertheless agreed to keep the truce with the British. But the tragedy of the Jews in Europe and the uncertainty as to the fate of Palestine after the war had driven these men who believed in violence as a political weapon to take action. Jabotinsky, the leader who could have prevented bloodshed, was dead. *Etzel* had thrown up a new leader, Menahem Begin. The British were never to succeed in laying their hands on him. He would change his disguise and identity as easily as changing a shirt, and changed his hideout just as often. This commander of a phantom force became a legendary hero to his followers.

This terrorist revolt against a Britain fully engaged in a world war was hardly the right remedy—it seemed more like stabbing Hitler's enemies in the back. *Etzel* plunged the country into violence, demanded independence for Palestine and committed acts of sabotage against the British. Attacks were made on Arabs too, and banks were robbed to obtain funds for the terrorists. Threats of all kinds were directed at members of *Haganah*. Then the *Lehi* group went into action too. Lord Moyne, whose anti-Zionist attitude was well known, was assassinated by them in Cairo on November 6, 1944.

Ben-Gurion was firmly against this wave of terrorism; it had to be stamped out by all possible means, he declared. Yet he himself had considered using terrorism in 1939, after the disastrous conference at London. He had been tempted, but neither he nor anyone else had dared to employ terrorism as a political weapon. And he had abandoned the idea when the war broke out.

He knew that after the war, the question of an independent Jewish state would be put before Britain. If she refused, it would be time to turn to warlike methods; but not now. Ben-Gurion knew only one way to deal with opposition to his line of action—to crush it. However, he first attempted, through his lieutenant, Moshe Sneh, to get the dissident groups to accept the orders of the central authority. When that failed he declared merciless war on them.

The order went forth on November 20, 1944. It was not given in a confidential document with restricted circulation, but publicly, in a speech which would reach the whole of the *Yishuv*, given before the annual *Histadrut* Conference. In short, sharp phrases, banging the table for emphasis, Ben-Gurion pronounced his four-point plan against the terrorist bands:

(1) Dismiss from their work all people who gave any help to the terrorists. (2) Refuse them shelter. (3) No giving way before the threats of the terrorists. (4) (the hardest of all) Collaborate with the British police and authorities in this matter of stamping out terrorism.

That word "collaborate" left a bitter taste. But, bitter or not, total warfare was waged on the terrorists for many long months. All over the country, *Haganah* commandos arrested members of the dissident bands. In some cases, brutal reprisals were carried out by the terrorists. Several members of *Etzel* and of *Lehi* were kept in prison for long periods. *Haganah* gave the British police lists of hundreds of terrorists, with their addresses and their false names.

It was a nightmare for the Jews, a tragic period which has left wounds that are still unhealed. Ben-Gurion became the *bête noire* of the terrorists. He took full responsibility for the activities of *Haganah* against the terrorists, even though he was far from knowing all the details and horrors of these activities.

While there can be little doubt that Ben-Gurion took the right course, that terrorism would never have led to a Jewish State, and indeed could but hinder the effort to attain it, no one who took part in "the season," whether as hunter or hunted, pursuer or victim, likes to be reminded of it.

Ben-Gurion had brought off his third victory in this succession of conflicts which shook the *Yishuv,* but it was a mournful victory. The *Yishuv* had survived the war, had helped in the struggle against Hitler and earned its part in final victory. It had adopted the Biltmore Program, and had stamped out the terrorism which could have plunged it into anarchy. It emerged strong and capable of continuing, of intensifying the struggle. But the domestic conflicts and crises had heavily scarred men's minds, created new rivalries and hatreds, which were to saddle the State of Israel as soon as it was proclaimed.

THIRTEEN

THE GREAT POWERS STEP IN

Spring was in the air on May 8, 1945; with the war over in Europe, a new era was beginning.

Ben-Gurion stood watching the joyful London crowds from the window of a small furnished apartment. He wrote only a few words in his diary that day: "VE Day. Sad, very sad."

It was not a victory for the Jews, who had lost six million of their people during the war—over a third of their numbers had perished in the Nazi concentration camps. Other peoples would demobilize and return home, but the Jews still had no home. Palestine was closed to them. For the Zionists, for those who still dreamed of a Jewish state, the war had only begun.

Ben-Gurion was thinking of the struggles and fights to come, as he stood at the window. While others were thinking of present victory, he was fearing the fight ahead.

He was more than ever on his own. Weizmann, bent under the weight of years, was a sick man undergoing one operation after another. "Old age is a shipwreck," someone once said. Ben-Gurion's closest friend, Berl Katzenelson, had died from a stroke a few months previously; when Ben-Gurion heard the news he had fainted. Dov Hoz, a brilliant trade-union leader, had been killed in a car crash, and Eliahu Golomb, one of the chief architects of *Haganah,* was dead too. American Jewry was split by stupid personal rivalries and by opposing influences. The Jews in Europe had been nearly all exterminated, and most of the survivors would soon be confined behind the Iron Curtain. The *Yishuv* was in a state of confusion. There had been a definite split in the MAPAI in 1944, and although Ben-Gurion, by a clever maneuver, had succeeded in gathering about him a "league of non-party Socialists," which had neutralized the effect of Tabenkin's departure, the workers' movement was greatly weakened. Meanwhile, the Arab world was gathering strength. In Cairo, Arab leaders from all over the Middle East had laid the foundations of the Arab League, under the paternal eyes of Anthony Eden. The victory parades in Damascus and Beirut had ended in anti-Jewish riots. The King of Saudi Arabia had been confidentially telling visitors that the United States would soon be helping the Arabs against the Jews.

However, the general picture was not altogether hopeless. A top man in British Intelligence had confided to Ben-Gurion that at Yalta the three Powers had decided that a Jewish state ought to be established in Palestine. Churchill was said to be studying a plan of partition. Roosevelt, on his return from Yalta, had said to Stephen Wise, one of the leaders of American Jewry: "There is no foundation for suspicions that Stalin is against you; he is with us. Winston is in agreement on a Jewish State too . . ." As for the fourth Power, Ben-Gurion was confident of De Gaulle's support. During the war, representatives of De Gaulle had contacted the leaders of the Maronites, a sect of Syrian Christians dwelling in Lebanon. They too were agitating for a state of their own, and would be greatly pleased to have a Jewish state for a neighbor. The two states, Jewish and Christian, would thus join forces against the vast Muslim population. The Maronites also had confidence in French support—not from the Vichy Government, but from De Gaulle's Free French. When De Gaulle later visited Palestine he was greatly impressed. Some months afterwards, when Ben-Gurion was in Paris to see Georges Bidault, the latter confided to him: "When I went to London to see Bevin, De Gaulle said to me, 'Tell Bevin that I've been to Palestine and saw that the Jews are the only people who are developing the country.' "

However, how much reliance could be placed in these inspired rumors and whispered promises? At the Kfar Vitkine Congress in 1942 Ben-Gurion had made an assertion which raised a storm of criticism: "No one will give us this country. In order to take it, we must rely on our own strength."

Weapons alone, he felt, would in the end decide the fate of Palestine. And these weapons had to be obtained, or better, had to be made on the spot "by our own strength."

On June 18, 1945, Ben-Gurion arrived in New York.

On July 1, about a score of Jewish millionaires gathered in an apartment at 455 East Fifty-seventh Street. A daring and unusual conspirary was being hatched. Ben-Gurion outlined it in blunt, direct terms. In the near future, probably very soon, the Palestinian Jews would have to fight for their existence against several Arab forces, and the Jewish state-to-be would need an armaments industry. The United States was about to cut back its armaments production and was selling whole factories for ridiculously low sums. It was now or never. But much money was needed, some millions of dollars.

Ben-Gurion spoke for three hours. Then two of his aides, Kaplan and Shiloach, gave surveys of the financial problems and the political situation in the Middle East. The meeting lasted until five in the evening. Before leaving, the participants gave their full support to Ben-Gurion's plan and created a secret organization with the innocent name of the Sonneborn Institute.

During the following months, the eighteen Jews behind the organization made millions of dollars available to the Institute. The first million went to buy machinery and heavy equipment. In the euphoria of the immediate postwar years, the United States Government disposed of armaments and war machinery without worrying too much about the identity of the purchaser. The Sonneborn network saw to the rest—the machinery was dismantled, put in crates and shipped to Palestine as industrial equipment. The British allowed it into the country without knowing its real nature. And when independence was proclaimed, this machinery began hectically producing light armaments for the Israeli Army.

Ben-Gurion made no reference in his diary to the nature of the secret meeting on July 1, 1945. He merely entered the names of those who attended it, and added: "This was the best Zionist conference during my stay in the U.S.A. . . ."

While returning to England on the *Queen Elizabeth*, he heard that the Labour Party had won the general election. Attlee was Prime Minister, and Ernest Bevin had been given the Foreign Office. In Palestine there was dancing in the streets—the Labour Party was known as a great friend to Zionism, and the Jewish state could not be far off. In 1944 the Labour Party had voted in favor of a "Palestinian Programme" which even the most extremist of Jews would not have dared hope for—the creation of a Jewish state in Palestine which would be brought about by evacuating the Arabs and transferring them elsewhere. And one of the Labour leaders most in favor of this program was the man who had just become Foreign Minister, Ernest Bevin. The whole of world Jewry was firmly convinced that the Labour Party would carry out its promise.

There were some Jews, nevertheless, who retained a few doubts. One group of prominent Zionists, arriving in London at the same time as Ben-Gurion, saw in the *Times* a photograph of Attlee and Bevin with Nouri Saïd, who was in Arab Army uniform.

Ben-Gurion, who had often put his trust in the Labourites only to find himself mistaken, thought he ought to moderate the enthusiasm of his colleagues. "Don't rely too much on this change of power," he warned, speaking at the Zionist conference being held in London. "It is only right to wonder whether a party in power will maintain the same attitude as when in opposition. I want to say this to the British Labour Party—if, for one reason or another, the policy in the White Paper is maintained, a policy which ignores our historic rights and deprives us of the right of becoming a State, then we in Palestine will not submit; we will not shrink before the might of Britain; we will go to war against her!"

Before long he discovered how right he had been. An adversary of his own weight appeared in the "brotherly government"—stubborn, strongminded Ernest Bevin, who opposed Zionism with all his strength and did all he could to prevent the establishment of the Jewish state. However, the "Bevin period" proved to be only an interlude, a desperate effort by one man to oppose a movement which outstripped him.

For this postwar world was a very different place. Deep feelings of guilt towards the Jews were aroused as the full horrors of the concentration camps and gas chambers were revealed. The survivors, hundreds of thousands of living skeletons, were seeking a haven, and world sympathy was with them. This moral debt towards the Jews was by no means the only factor in their favor. The Russians had ceased attacking Zionism for the first time since the October Revolution. They now saw that the movement provided a means of breaking the British monopoly in the Middle East and penetrating their preserves. Thus Stalin completely reversed his country's Middle East policy, and in so doing found himself allied —for once—with the President of the United States.

Harry Truman was undoubtedly one of the chief architects of the State of Israel. He pursued a Middle East policy diametrically opposed to that of Roosevelt, who, a week before his death, had sent a warmhearted letter to Ibn Seoud assuring him of support in the Arab demands on Palestine. In his *Memoirs,* Truman explains his actions in favor of Zionism by his sympathy for the Jewish people in the great sufferings they had endured, and by his conviction that they had a right to a country of their own in the land of their forefathers. That was very likely true. However, he was also influenced by the forthcoming presidential elections, in which the state of New York would play a determining role, and the Jewish vote in that state could well swing the result in his favor.

The almost simultaneous coming to power of two new men in the

Anglo-American world did not prove harmful, in the end, to the Zionist cause. While an enemy, Bevin, took over the Foreign Office, a resolute friend was moving into the White House.

Events moved fast. Curiously enough, the first demands of the Jews after the war were quite modest. Their leaders seemed afraid to ask for too much, as though they still had little belief in their dream of a state ever coming true. The first postwar Zionist conference opened in London in August 1945. While Ben-Gurion was still on his way from America, Moshe Shertok held a press conference. Shertok told the press that the Jewish Agency was asking for immigration certificates for 100,000 Jews to go to Palestine. Dr. Boger, sitting by him, pulled his sleeve. "What are you saying? Haven't we come to demand a Jewish State in Palestine, in accordance with the Biltmore Program?"

"It can't be helped," Shertok replied. "Those are Weizmann's orders."

When the conference opened two days later Weizmann, a tired and sick man, repeated the demand for 100,000 certificates. Ben-Gurion, who had reached London the previous day, bounded onto the platform and banged the table. "This man speaks for himself alone!" he thundered. "No one has authorized him to propose something which is fundamentally opposed to the decisions of the Zionist Directory in Palestine."

The conflict between the two was revived. On the following day, Ben-Gurion made an impassioned speech on the theme "The Jewish State is our only hope."

However, the demand for 100,000 certificates was maintained. The reaction of the British Government would prove whether the Labour leaders were prepared to keep their promises to the Zionists. Truman and Dewey both appealed to Attlee to grant the certificates. "I would willingly have supported a demand for 200,000 certificates," Truman said to some Zionist leaders. "But you only asked for 100,000."

Rumors began to reach the ears of the Jewish secret service that the 100,000 certificates would be refused. And then it became evident that the Labour Government was not going to keep its promises. Ben-Gurion changed his tactics without hesitation—as he always has done whenever he believed it necessary. The World War was over, and there were no longer any moral obligations towards a Britian at grips with Nazi Germany. The *Yishuv* would make war on the British.

A top-secret document reached the *Haganah* leaders on October

1. It was signed by Ben-Gurion and gave details of the action to be taken against the British. This was the start of a war which, in spite of everything, still aimed at moderation. The action included the founding of new collective settlements in the forbidden zones by stepping up Immigration Beth, the illegal immigration, and by organizing a second illicit line called *Aliyah Gimel* which had its headquarters in France, and not only packed Jewish refugees into ships but also taught them how to resist the British. Other action included civil disobedience, demonstrations, refusal to pay taxes, etc.

Military means were not excluded. Terrorism against the British and the Arabs was still ruled out, but sabotage and attacks on military installations were envisaged.

Haganah acknowledged receipt of Ben-Gurion's instructions by coded cable on October 4. At midnight on October 9, a unit of the *Palmach* shock brigade breached the walls of the fortified camp at Atlit and freed 200 illegal immigrants detained there. This was the first military operation of any size against the British.

The question of whether this resort to force was necessary was answered on November 13, 1945, when Bevin announced in the House of Commons that the Government rejected all the Zionist demands and intended to maintain the restrictions laid down in the 1939 White Paper. Permitted immigration would remain at 1,500 a month. However, to mollify the United States, a commission of inquiry would be set up to study the problem of displaced persons in Europe.

There were demonstrations all over Palestine. In London, Ben-Gurion went to see Harold Laski, the Jewish writer and historian who was chairman of the Labour Party, and told him of the decision to step up illegal immigration and to take up arms against the British. "May God be with you!" said Laski, chairman of the party that was governing Britain. Fortunately, the Zionist movement had friends in high places.

The Jewish resistance soon increased. In November, some British vessels that were to keep watch for illegal entry were sunk, and sabotage was carried out on the railway lines at 186 different places. Later, the radar station at Haifa (which detected the approach of ships carrying illegal immigrants) was blown up. In February 1946 *Haganah* units attacked installations of the mobile police force which patrolled the frontiers. Other illicit bands attacked airfields being used by the British. Ben-Gurion's agents were busy buying German weapons from the American Occupation Forces and were negotiating with the French Resistance for large quantities of arms and ammunition. The members of the commission of inquiry set up by the Labour Government had the impression that Ben-Gurion was playing a double role—as head of the legal Zionist institutions and head of the Resistance organizations.

The commission's report was published in April. It did not favor the creation of a Jewish state but did recommend the immediate issue of 100,000 immigration certificates to German Jewish refugees. Ben-Gurion was disappointed, for it was the Jewish state that mattered to him. Truman sent a message of satisfaction. But would the British Government accept the recommendations of the commission? If so, it could well cut short Ben-Gurion's attempts to hoist the flag of independence; at the cost of 100,000 certificates it could probably satisfy Truman and Weizmann, the pacifists and moderates, alienate the terrorists and isolate Ben-Gurion and his "activists." But in May, Prime Minister Attlee declared: "Britian will do nothing to implement the recommendations until the Jewish Resistance lays down its arms."

The Resistance refused to do so. In Palestine there were massive demonstrations in the large towns, and prominent Zionists began a hunger strike as a protest against the harsh treatment of illegal immigrants. On June 18, 1946 some *Palmach* units attacked eleven bridges over the Jordan and completely destroyed ten of them. The British struck in reply by rounding up the Zionist leaders. Soon after midnight on June 29, a Saturday, troops took up positions round the towns and certain kibbutzim, and at first light moved in. The heads of the Jewish Agency and the National Council—Shertok, Grinbaum, Remez and others—were arrested and taken to a detention camp. A curfew was imposed in the large towns. Some thousands of men were arrested, roughly handled and questioned. There were five deaths. British troops discovered a fabulous quantity of hidden arms and ammunition at Yagour. The offices of the Jewish Agency were thoroughly searched. Altogether, 3,000 people went sent to internment camps.

Ben-Gurion was traveling in Europe at the time. Sneh, the head of *Haganah,* succeeded in slipping through the net and taking a ship to France. Neither Weizmann nor any or the moderates were arrested. Bevin was making every effort to isolate the "activists" and to have new leaders elected from among the moderates, in the hope that they would collaborate with the British.

Ben-Gurion established his headquarters in Paris, at the Royal Monceau Hotel. "The British Government is making a big mistake," he said at a press conference. "It won't find anyone, either of the Left or the Right, who will agree to play the part of a Quisling or a Pétain."

The mounting tension had its effect on the Jewish Resistance itself. *Etzel,* the Right-wing terrorist group, mounted Operation Tchik. On July 22, 1946, some of their saboteurs, disguised as Arabs, managed to enter the King David Hotel in Jerusalem, which was the headquarters of the British forces. A little later, a terrific explosion shook the town, and when the smoke and dust had cleared it was seen that one wing of the hotel had completely disappeared. Two hundred bodies—most of them British, but a few Jews and Arabs too—were found beneath the rubble. There were no casualties in the other wing of the hotel.

The *Yishuv* and their leaders were aghast. The *Haganah* chiefs had known of *Etzel's* plans but hoped that the sabotage would not cause any casualties. When the number of victims became known, *Haganah* dissociated itself from the operation. The explosion at the King David Hotel had also shattered the united front of the Jewish Resistance. *"Etzel* is an enemy of the Jewish people," Ben-Gurion declared in Paris to a *France Soir* reporter.

The ever-fragile union of the Resistance organizations came to an end. Henceforth it was to be a case of "each for himself." *Etzel* engaged in violent terrorism, and the sinister heading "War against the dissidents" reappeared in *Haganah's* budget.

The crisis broke in September. The tragedy at the King David Hotel led to several heated debates in Parliament. Churchill employed all his eloquence to support the Zionist point of view, and Lord Samuel did the same in the Upper House. The Government was hard pressed and tried desperately to find a formula to satisfy everyone, and eventually produced the "Morrison Plan," which was a vague and confused program for dividing Palestine into Jewish and Arab sectors.

The Zionist Directory met in Paris, deprived of many members who were interned in Palestine. The conference lasted three weeks, and in the end the Biltmore Program was approved, and at Ben-Gurion's urgent request, a budget of three million dollars for the purchase of armaments was placed at his disposal. The Morrison Plan was rejected and any negotiations on the subject with the British Government were condemned.

Ben-Gurion and Sneh remained in Paris. A warrant for their arrest had been issued, should they set foot in British territory. But other members of the Directory were able to go to London without risk of being arrested. It was then that the crisis broke. Despite the decisions taken in Paris, the moderates entered into negotiations with the British Government. Bevin had not given up his idea of causing a split between moderates and activists, and of opening talks on the Morrison Plan with Weizmann and his group.

Ben-Gurion promptly used his powerful weapon—he threatened to resign. On September 13 he sent a letter to the group in London: "I no longer consider myself to be your partner in the Directory. From now on, you neither speak in my name nor do I accept responsibility for your actions." At the same time, he made further attempts to revive "Institute X," *Haganah*'s secret committee for terrorist activities. He even considered—as he wrote to Abba Hiller Silver, the American Zionist leader—setting up a "Zionist Directory in exile" to run the campaign in Palestine. This idea came into the long talks he had with a fellow guest at his hotel, an Asian with a long beard and ascetic features whose name was Ho Chi Minh. The two became great friends, and Uncle Ho even suggested that an exile Jewish Government might work from North Vietnam.

However, matters did not go that far. Ben-Gurion's ultimatum to his colleagues and Bevin's uncompromising attitude finally caused the moderates to retreat. They broke off their talks and sent a delegation to Paris to tell Ben-Gurion that they would take no action without him. Bevin had again missed his chance. Had he been more versatile he might have succeeded in breaking the fragile links between moderates and activists.

The first postwar Zionist congress was due to be held in Basel, the cradle of Zionism, in December 1946. The last act in the thirty years of strife between Ben-Gurion and Weizmann was about to begin.

FOURTEEN

BEN-GURION AS MILITARY LEADER

The clash came right at the start of the congress. The delegates had to choose between Ben-Gurion's policy of a Jewish state, of fighting for national independence, and Weizmann's policy of seeking a compromise solution with Britain. There were signs of hesitation among the MAPAI delegates themselves. An important group of moderates headed by Kaplan, the Jewish Agency's treasurer, refused to abandon the aged Weizmann. Disgusted by this, Ben-Gurion seemed on the verge of leaving.

One of the delegates put forward a suggestion: "Let us call an urgent meeting of the MAPAI group delegates at the Congress. If you obtain a majority vote, we all stay. If not, we'll leave with you."

After a long argument, Ben-Gurion agreed. It was to be a night sitting, with Mrs. Golda Meyerson in the chair. Among those present were old hands such as Shertok, Eshkol and Lavon, and two young delegates attending their first Zionist Congress—Moshe Dayan, aged 31, and Shimon Peres, who was only 23. The debate raged all night. At dawn, a vote was taken. Ben-Gurion had won. From that moment, the issue of the congress was never in doubt.

Ben-Gurion had of course done everything possible to secure victory. As he had thought, American Jewry was beginning to play a major role in world Zionism. A new figure had appeared among the American Jewish leaders—the strong personality of Abba Hiller Silver, who had opposed Ben-Gurion's project for a Jewish state in the western half of Palestine by proposing a larger state to include Transjordan, and who wanted world Zionism to be directed from the United States, where there were many millions of Jews. Ben-Gurion had resisted him on both points, but had at least obtained his support for the division of Palestine into a Jewish and an Arab state. With the backing of the American Zionists, Ben-

Gurion had gone to the Basel Congress with every chance of having his policy accepted.

Weizmann was not prepared to admit defeat, but very few delegates retained any confidence in Great Britain. And, after the dramatic all-night sitting of the MAPAI delegates, Ben-Gurion was certain of a majority vote. Weizmann left the congress before its close. Not only was he defeated, he was not even reelected President of the Zionist movement. To smooth his downfall, the congress decided not to elect a new President. They gave full power to the Zionist Executive and its head—Ben-Gurion.

The departure of Weizmann from the scene was the end of an epoch. But he was not the man to guide the movement when it was about to make war on the British. Ben-Gurion had brought him out of semiretirement in 1935 to act as spokesman for world Jewry, but the situation with Britain now seemed to have gone beyond words. Weizmann was an old, sick man, unable to grasp the great changes which had taken place. He had fallen victim to his moderation and his attachment to Britain. In April 1947, little more than a year before the proclamation of the independent State of Israel, he was still opposing the Biltmore Program.

Ben-Gurion saw things as they were—which was why he accepted the new responsibilities conferred on him by the Zionist movement at that Twenty-second Congress. He was given charge of the defense of the *Yishuv*. The future State of Israel already had its Prime Minister and Minister of Defense.

However, his most urgent mission was of a very different character. At the beginning of January 1947, he arrived in London for talks with the British Government and to confront the man he had been fighting for nearly two years. Bevin, however, was now a sick man and sagging under his heavy responsibilities at the Foreign Office. He easily became irritated, and the problems of the Palestine question were driving him to anti-Semitism. He spoke out against President Truman at the Labour Party Conference. "The Americans are supporting the demands of the Jews for the entry of 100,000 of them into Palestine because they, the Americans, have more than they want in New York!" He accused Truman of acting in favor of the Jews for electoral reasons.

The first meeting between Bevin and Ben-Gurion took place in somewhat depressing surroundings, in a room lit only by a few candles (the hard winter and consequent fuel shortages and electricity cuts did not spare government offices). It was an "informal" meeting between the Government and the Jewish representatives.

The "formal" meetings were for the Arab delegates, who were having talks with the British at the same time. These arrangements were reminiscent of the St. James's Palace Conference in 1939. But much had changed since then—the Jews had gained world sympathy and a powerful ally in the United States. One thing had not changed, as became obvious—the intransigence on both sides.

Bevin and Ben-Gurion had a final meeting to try and break the deadlock. "I should like to know the real reasons for your attitude towards us," said Ben-Gurion. "But my impression is that you will never reveal them." Bevin's reply was quite frank. "We seek only to keep the peace in the Middle East!"

"And the Negev—doesn't that interest you?"

Bevin admitted that there was oil in the Negev, and that there was a plan to build a canal. ". . . but every time we start to prospect or to drill, you come and poke your nose in and you establish farming villages there."

Ben-Gurion was ready to swear that a Jewish state in Palestine would safeguard British interests. But there obviously was no hope of reconciling the two points of view.

Three days later, after a plenary meeting of Jewish and British representatives, Bevin capitulated. On February 14 the British Government announced its decision to take the matter to the United Nations. A page had been turned.

Henceforth, the political battle for the establishment of a Jewish state would have the attention of the world's press and world opinion. The American Zionists, wealthy and influential, would continue to press the White House and the State Department to support their case and also to influence other Western countries. The task was not easy, for the Arab states presented a solid front at the United Nations, where the Jews had no delegation of their own.

Ben-Gurion took almost no part in this battle. He concentrated on the task given him by the Zionist Congress. At the age of sixty, with only the most elementary ideas of what constituted an army, he devoted himself to problems of armament, military intelligence and defense.

His study in his modest, gray house on the Boulevard Karen Kayemeth in Tel Aviv soon looked like a military reference room. He read army manuals in all languages, and all the books and treatises on military tactics which he could obtain—Foch, Klausewitz, Liddel Hart and the rest. He made careful notes, copied out figures and details, scribbled down ideas which seemed important. At the same time he set about mastering military matters concerning Palestine. Young men in khaki became daily visitors to the house. Notebook in hand, spectacles on the end of his nose, he listened for hours to the reports of these *Haganah* officers. He asked innumerable questions about equipment, weapons, training, the strength of the units and their morale. The young officers called these long sessions "Ben-Gurion's Seminar."

He called them by their given names. One was Israel—Israel Galili. There were two Igals—Igal Yadin and Igal Alon. The Chief of Staff was Jacob Dostrovski, soon to become Commander-in-Chief of the Israeli Army. Others included Laskov, Dayan, Sadeh. Ben-Gurion was at ease among them. It was here that he began to forge the Jewish Army, and prepare for the creation of a united and solid force out of *Palmach* and *Haganah, Etzel* and the auxiliary defense units. He was to love this army, to make a cult of it and believe in it with all his might.

However, at that time there were important events taking place in Palestine and in the world, and urgent decisions had to be taken concerning *Haganah*. Ben-Gurion was consulted. "No, don't ask me just now," he replied. "I haven't learned all there is to learn. Let me find out everything before taking any action."

He found out everything. He visited all the villages and farming communities where *Haganah* units existed under a thousand different disguises, inspected the defenses, checked the stocks of weapons and attended training sessions. He asked the special services of the *Haganah* for details and figures on the armies of the Arab states. Some surprise was expressed, but his orders were carried out.

The black notebooks filled with facts and figures piled up on Ben-Gurion's desk. *Haganah* kept no secrets from him. In 1947 he knew the exact weapon strength: 10,073 rifles, 1,900 submachine guns, 464 light machine guns, 186 machine guns, 672 2-inch mortars and 96 3-inch mortars. There was one heavy machine gun, but not a single field gun or tank, and no warship of any kind.

As for the combatants, there were 2,200 in the *Palmach* brigade, 7,000 in the mobile units, 27,000 in the local defense units and 9,000 in the youth movement. The total amounted to 45,340 men and women. And all were volunteers, who knew what they were fighting for. But this fact was also a considerable disadvantage— they were not very disciplined, and the great majority had never served in a regular army. They were splendid at defending villages, but how would they be at attacking, at opposing regulars? Could they fight a modern war?

It was not marauders, bandits or the irregular Arab bands in

Palestine that Ben-Gurion feared. While all those around him argued whether the British would quit Palestine, whether the United Nations would grant the Jews their independence and, if so, whether the Arabs would remain inactive, he, the "old man," the lonely one, was looking farther ahead. What he foresaw made him anxious. While the others talked of marauders, he feared the regular armies of Arab countries. No one took him seriously. Among his associates there was some murmuring—as there had been in the past—that he was crazy.

In 1947 the armies of Egypt, Syria, Lebanon, Iraq, Transjordan and Saudi Arabia totaled 135,000 men. The Egyptians alone had 177 planes. Transjordan possessed the best armed force in the Middle East—the Arab Legion, trained and commanded by British officers. If these forces attacked the *Yishuv* what was to stop them from sweeping all before them?

Ben-Gurion had been saying since 1946 that the chief danger to an independent Jewish state would be invasion by the regular forces of the Arab countries. No one had listened.

In May 1947, at his request, the *Haganah* leaders drew up a plan of defense to meet a possible attack by the Arab countries. They envisaged mobilization of up to 60,000 men. Pitched battles were to be avoided, as the Jewish troops were trained only in guerrilla warfare. Instead, they were to organize defense in depth while commandos raided the enemy lines of communication, destroying gas and supply dumps to prevent him using his heavy armament in the battle. The *Haganah* leaders couldn't have been more naive.

A meeting of *Haganah* leaders and MAPAI officials was held at the party's headquarters towards the end of the summer. All the senior officers of the future Israeli Army were present. Ben-Gurion spoke again of the danger of an Arab invasion. "War is inevitable," he maintained. "We shall have to fight on all fronts. We need planes, tanks and guns!"

Everyone was astounded. Some people hardly bothered to conceal their smiles. "He's crazy!" others were saying. "Wanting planes and tanks—sheer folly!"

Who indeed would have believed that a real war was coming?

In those impassioned days of 1947 another kind of war was setting all Palestine ablaze—the terrorism against the British. The audacious acts of members of *Etzel* and *Lehi* were assuming unbelievable proportions. The officers club in Jerusalem was wrecked, gas dumps in Haifa were set alight, a commando attacked the prison in

Acre and freed more than 200 political internees, senior British officers were kidnapped in broad daylight, British Army camps and forts were attacked, weapons and ammunition stolen. The British executed a few terrorists who had been caught red-handed, and *Etzel* retaliated by hanging two British Army sergeants. Palestine became a fortress in a continual state of siege. The 100,000 British troops were in a state of tension. The daylight curfew in Tel Aviv and Jerusalem turned them into ghostlike towns, with armored cars patrolling the deserted streets. The various British headquarters and administrative centers looked like bastions, with their barbed wire, sandbags and machine-gun posts. The Jews' ironic word for them was "Bevingrad." There was grave anxiety in London, reflected in the press and among the public. A strong body of opinion favored withdrawing from Palestine at once.

Resistance movements are usually the expression of the population of a country against the enemy occupying it. This was not the case in Palestine, where 600,000 Jews lived surrounded by twice as many Arabs. The real danger did not come from the British occupants but from the Arabs. If a Resistance movement succeeds in turning the enemy out of the country, it usually takes over. But in Palestine it was only after the British left that the struggle for power would begin. And what hope had small Resistance groups like *Lehi* and *Etzel* against the Arab armies?

There was also the fact that the British never took strong repressive measures. A few terrorists were executed, but the struggle to stamp out terrorism was never intense. The international climate made such measures impossible, and in any case the British were more embarrassed than anything by this encumbrance of a mandate.

Terrorism had certainly added a new dimension to the Palestine problem, but it had not brought a solution any nearer, because it was not capable of doing so. The real enemy of the Jews was not the British but the Arabs—frightened and alarmed, understandably so, by the implantation in their land of a people who were more advanced, more wealthy and energetic than themselves, and who seemed determined to gain ascendancy over them someday.

Meanwhile a special meeting of the United Nations General Assembly had been called at Lake Success to settle the Palestine question.

The outcome was promising. The tireless Shertok, special representative of the Jewish Agency, had some success. United States support for the Zionist cause seemed assured, and a number of

South American countries were favorable to it. Trygve Lie, the Secretary-General, had agreed that Jewish representatives should be allowed to state their case to the delegates, and Abba Hiller Silver, speaking for the American Zionist movement, made a deep impression on them.

The most dramatic move came from the Russian delegate, vigorous Andrei Gromyko. For the first time, the U.S.S.R. gave its views on the Palestine question—in the form of a fervent plea on behalf of the Zionist cause which went even further than President Truman's warm statements. Russia saw an opportunity to supplant the British in the Middle East.

Once the two World Powers expressed similar opinions on the future of Palestine, it seemed evident that the Jewish state would soon become a reality. In June 1947 the United Nations sent a commission of inquiry to the Middle East. The eleven members (representing Australia, Canada, Czechoslovakia, Guatemala, Holland, India, Iran, Peru, Sweden, Uruguay and Yugoslavia) carried out their task conscientiously in an atmosphere made tense by terrorism and the feverish preparations for a military clash. Ben-Gurion, Shertok, Weizmann and other representatives of the *Yishuv* met the members of the commission. The Arab representatives began by boycotting the commission, but then met the members in Beirut. The greatest effect, however, was produced by the fate of 4,500 illegal immigrants packed aboard an old ship, the *Exodus.*

Previously known as the *President Warfield* and bought in America by the "Sonneborn Institute," the *Exodus* sailed from Sète, in southern France, on July 11. Out at sea, she was stopped by three British warships. It was obvious that this largest number of illegal immigrants ever to be put on one ship would never get through the blockade. The organizers of the *Aliyah Beth* might have had other intentions; the fact that the *Exodus* episode was featured in the world press and that the United Nations' commission was then in Palestine makes one wonder.

In any case, the drama aboard the *Exodus* had a profound effect upon the members of the commission. The immigrants resisted the British, and three of them lost their lives in the hopeless fight. Finally, they landed at Haifa and were transferred by force by British military police to three "prison ships" which took them back to France. But despite pressure by their guards, the immigrants refused to go ashore and started a hunger strike. The British Government then bungled the matter further by announcing it would take them to Germany, to the ex-concentration camps from which they had come.

The *Exodus* affair not only roused the whole world, it revived the quarrel between tough Ben-Gurion and the more humane Weizmann. The latter, anxious to bring the sufferings of the would-be immigrants to an end, even if it meant ruining the political campaign being worked up by the Zionist movement, appealed to Léon Blum to contact Bevin and propose that the illegal immigrants be sent to France; in which case, Weizmann promised, the Jewish Agency would instruct them to go ashore.

This was capitulation. Ben-Gurion, who was in Geneva at the time, was enraged. He telephoned London, bestirred his contacts in Paris, and succeeded just in time in countermanding Weizmann's overtures. As Moshe Shertok admitted: "The British use Weizmann to bring pressure to bear on us which would be favorable to them." Ben-Gurion kept saying: "What right has Weizmann to act in this way, now that he no longer has an official post in the Zionist movement?" In a letter to the members of the Zionist Directory in London he added: "I am absolutely opposed to Weizmann interfering in the Directory's activities, serving as emissary or acting as mediator between the Government and the Jewish Agency. I am opposed to his being given any kind of political mission either in England or the United States. The reasons are obvious!"

There was no place for sentiment in the strenuous struggle then troubling the Zionist world.

Nothing could stop Ben-Gurion in his resolute efforts to establish the Jewish state. In July he rejected the advice of the *Haganah* veterans who disagreed with his ideas on the strategy to adopt in the event of war. "The organization of *Haganah,* as I see it," he wrote in his diary, "no longer corresponds to its role. This is not a criticism of the past, but thought for the future."

Through thought for the future he demanded strenuous preparations and general mobilization of the *Yishuv,* despite contrary advice. Although called "crazy," he gave instructions for heavy armaments, and particularly aircraft, to be purchased in Europe and America. He asked for pilots to be ready to come to Palestine, and he tried to get the services of a military expert. He wanted a quarter of the war material acquired to be transferred immediately to Europe, so that if needed it could quickly reach Palestine.

These were by no means unnecessary precautions. In September the United Nations' commission published its report. By a vote of 8–3, it recommended the partition of Palestine into a Jewish and an

Arab state. The General Assembly of the United Nations was to vote on the matter. Loud protests came from the Arab countries, and the armed forces of Syria and Transjordan were alerted.

In the weeks before the vote there was feverish behind-the-scenes political activity. The Zionists of Palestine and the United States, under the leadership of Shertok and Silver, used all their powers to ensure the support of the countries favorable to partition. The Communist bloc and most of the Western countries seemed certain to cast their votes in favor of the project.

Ben-Gurion remained immersed in the problems of defense. He was astounded that no one in Palestine seriously believed in the danger of an Arab attack. The anarchy and the archaic methods which existed in the military and paramilitary organizations made him furious, and he drew up reforms to be applied to the *Haganah* forces.

The decisive vote at the United Nations began at ten in the evening, Palestine Time, on November 29, 1947. Tens of thousands of Jews gathered in the streets and squares of Tel Aviv and Jerusalem, or sat round their radios at home, to await the result of the voting. But Ben-Gurion had gone to bed early. For a man who lives so intensely and is so easily moved he has excellent command over himself. He was traveling in the region of the Dead Sea, and spent the night in the Kalia Hotel. He was awakened in the early hours. Outside, on the shores of the Dead Sea, workers were dancing joyfully in the moonlight. And it was there in the heart of that strange landscape, unique in the world, facing Sodom and Gomorrah, that Ben-Gurion heard the great news—the creation of a Jewish state had been approved by the United Nations by a vote of 33–12, with ten abstentions.

Ben-Gurion returned to his office in Jerusalem next day. The streets were full of joyful crowds. He wrote, "While joyfulness was filling the heart of the House of Israel, I was wracked by deep anxiety." He was thinking of the trials ahead, which were to be the hardest and most bloody yet.

That day, November 30, Arab bands attacked some Jewish travelers and killed seven of them. Despite the presence of 100,000 British troops, and although the Jewish state would not come into existence for another five months or so, armed Arab bands were soon active all over Palestine in a widespread attack on the *Yishuv*. The war had begun.

FIFTEEN

DISASTER

It was a war on a phantom state, one which would not come into being for a few more months; a state which had no existence except on maps of the Holy Land across which United Nations officials had drawn their curving lines. With several strokes of the pen, experts tried to separate zones with a majority population of Jews from those dominated by Arabs. It was an almost impossible task. The Jews were being given three long, narrow strips of territory which touched each other here and there. Similar points of contact were given to the Arab zones. The two states were thus entangled together, overlapping in places, with frontiers which were proportionately the longest in the world for the size of territory they enclosed. Jerusalem was to be an international city. One of the Jewish strips extended from the source of the Jordan to the foothills of the Syrian and Lebanon mountains, and curved around the lush hillsides of Galilee, which were in the Arab zone, to join the second strip which bordered the Mediterranean. This extended from the proud ramparts of St. Jean d'Acre, in the north, to the beginning of the coastal plain which had been the home of the Philistines. Most of the Jews lived in this zone, which contained Haifa and its fine port and Tel Aviv, the Jewish capital. The United Nations was more generous with the southern strip, which was practically the whole of the stony Negev Desert, and was bordered to the east by the salt waters of the Dead Sea and to the south by the waves of the Red Sea. The Jewish territory stopped short of Beersheba, the village of Abraham, and ended just before Gaza, the chief town of a coastal strip given to the Arabs. The only link with Jerusalem was along a corridor between the Arab hills—access to the Holy City would depend entirely upon the goodwill of the Arabs, which meant it would be denied. The Arabs did not want partition and intended to fight it. They were going to make every effort to insure that the Jewish state never became more than a few lines drawn on a map—they intended to drown it in blood, wipe it out before birth.

Blood was what the Mufti demanded in his speeches broadcast from Cairo, where he had prudently taken refuge. And no sooner had the United Nations announced their decision than the *Jihad* started. The 100,000 soldiers of His Majesty did nothing to stop this "holy war" against the Jews. Sir Alexander Cadogan, Britain's delegate to the United Nations, informed the General Assembly that his Government would respect the decisions taken and its troops would leave Palestine on the date arranged, May 15, 1948, thus bringing the British Mandate to an end. In the meantime, the British troops would observe strict neutrality—in other words, leave the Jews and Arabs to kill each other. The outcome was not difficult to see, with 40 million Arabs against 650,000 Jews.

The war spread throughout Palestine while the British were still there, and it was one of the strangest wars in history. There were no defined fronts; the fighting was fluid, skirmishes occurred everywhere—around isolated colonies in the Negev, along pipelines, in the suburbs of Tel Aviv and Jerusalem, at Haifa, along the roads and in the green valleys and the orange groves of Sharon and Jezreel. It was a war of irregulars, of Arab raiders against the still illegal units of *Haganah* and the *Palmach* brigade; of rifle and machine gun against grenade and Sten. The choice before the Jews was to win or be exterminated. And their chances of winning, in the early stages, were very slim indeed.

The war started slowly, with ambushes, attacks on transport and raids on Jewish villages and kibbutzim. But the Arab bands were numerous, and Cairo Radio was promising them Jewish land, possessions and women.

Minarets near Jewish districts in the large towns were no longer being used to call the faithful to prayer. The muezzins had been replaced by machine guns which fired into the Jewish districts. The Arabs were safe enough up there, for they knew that the British would not interfere, and that the Jews would not attack religious buildings.

Before long, however, the scattered attacks of the Arabs became organized and developed into an overall strategy which concentrated on roads and communications. They were still not using regular troops, for the armies of the Arab countries could not take part in the war while the British flag was flying over Palestine. But the Arabs realized that the best way of attacking the Jews in the meantime was to cut their communications, isolate the centers of resistance and deal with them one by one.

The Jews tried to keep the roads open by organizing convoys with armed escorts. Inexperienced at offensive warfare, they relied on defending isolated places and making reprisal raids. Occasionally, in order to strike terror into the Arab population, Jewish commandos raided some Arab village, blew up houses and strategic points and destroyed the wells. But this did not always produce the desired effect—instead, a wave of hatred swept through the country.

The situation grew worse every day. Some of the Jewish leaders came to the conclusion that, in face of the increasing Arab attacks, the wisest move was to withdraw from the isolated and outlying villages and concentrate on organized lines of defense.

The *Haganah* forces had their headquarters at the "Red House," by the sea at Tel Aviv, and it was from there that Ben-Gurion issued his instructions. He refused to abandon a single village, a single outlying post, wherever it might be. He was prepared to make a Tobruk or a Stalingrad of each of them.

His colleagues in the civil institutions which controlled the defense forces were more than skeptical. It seemed sheer folly to send five thousand men to the Negev, as Ben-Gurion wished to do. The Negev was a deathtrap. Withdrawal was imperative, to protect the *Yishuv* and all that had been built up over the years. However, after a stormy meeting, they accepted Ben-Gurion's tactics. Some thousands of soldiers were sent to the Negev, and the Arab bands were not able to seize a single kibbutz, a single house!

A defense force like *Haganah,* recruited from volunteers, could not easily adapt itself to the rigid requirements of military discipline. It performed wonders of improvisation, but lacked the experience of a regular army. Moreover, the standard of training was poor, and administration hardly existed—no lists of recruits were kept, and cases of insubordination were not unknown. The leaders still stuck to defensive methods, and did not seem to realize that tactics which were effective for beating off marauding bands had little to commend them for dealing with regular army units. They all regarded the *Palmach* brigade as a symbol of military perfection, but despite its qualities it had never gone into battle against professional troops. And the only men who knew what modern warfare was really like, the veterans of the Jewish Brigade who had fought in the Second World War, were treated with suspicion by the *Haganah* leaders. Besides, *Palmach* units were used to taking orders only from their staff officers, and refused to recognize any other authority.

Most serious of all, however, was the anarchy which existed at the higher level. Who had the responsibility for the defense forces? There was a kind of "Committee for Security," but it had no say in making military decisions. There was a "National Command," with Israel Galili at its head, which had been set up by the Jewish Agency. But when the State came into existence, this was to be replaced by an Army staff which would come directly under the Minister for Armed Forces. It would be a problem to effect these necessary changes without offending the men who had spent their lives building up *Palmach* and the *Haganah* forces. How to convince them that the romantic period was over and must give way to the routine of a State organization?

Ben-Gurion had other matters on his mind. The numbers of fighting men were proving to be insufficient. The only really effective military force was *Palmach,* which had a strength of no more than 2,500. A good percentage of the tens of thousands of *Haganah* recruits existed only on paper or had never received any military training. But even more serious was the problem of the clandestine *Etzel* and *Lehi* groups—there would be no place for these independent organizations in the State structure, and they would have to be assimilated into the Army.

As for equipment, it was practically nonexistent. There were no uniforms, and not enough weapons to go around. Many of the 10,000 rifles held by the military were good only for the scrap heap, and many of the remainder were needed for defending the villages. In most units, only one man in every two or three had a rifle, revolver or submachine gun. And the submachine guns, which had been secretly assembled from worn-out parts, misfired more often than not. A standing joke was to ask "What's the difference between a broom and a Sten?", and the reply was "There's more chance of the broom firing."

And what were they to fire? For each rifle, there was an average of fifty bullets—to last the five and a half months until the State became a reality. There were machine guns which could fire 600 rounds a minute, but only 500 rounds were available for each.

These were the problems Ben-Gurion had to cope with.

He was looking for a general, too. The most likely place to find one was in the United States, where several Jews had risen to high rank in the American Army during the war. However, no one was eager for the position. The only officer who showed an interest wanted the British Government to approve his appointment first! On the other hand, specialists and experts arrived in Palestine from all parts of the world, as well as army and naval officers and air pilots. "Without their aid," Ben-Gurion said later, "I don't know if we could have won the war."

He set about buying arms with the same energy he was using to seek an officer corps. Dozens of his "special agents" traveled the world buying anything they could—old aircraft, damaged tanks, guns that were almost museum pieces, machine guns, rifles and ammunition. These young agents invented all kinds of stratagems to get their purchases out of the country of origin and to hide them in various places in Europe, ready to be dispatched to Palestine. An airline called *Lineas Aereas de Panama* was a cover for purchasing planes in the United States and flying them to Latin America, from there they were sent out to the Middle East. In England, a film company pretended to be making a war film in order to obtain permission for some planes to take off—which did not land again in England. In Paris, General de Larminat promised that France would help the Palestinian Jews and offered them the use of the airfield at Ajaccio. In Czechoslovakia, an agent signed a contract for the purchase of large quantities of armaments to be delivered to the future Jewish state.

Ben-Gurion needed tens of millions of dollars for all these purchases. At one of the most dramatic moments in the fighting he was thinking of flying to the United States himself to obtain funds from American Jews, but his colleagues opposed his leaving. Instead, Rabbi Hiller Silver raised the money. But it was not enough, and Golda Meyerson was sent on an urgent mission to America. She did wonders. "When these glorious days are talked about," Ben-Gurion said to her, "full mention will be made of a Jewish woman who obtained the funds enabling the State to survive at birth."

However, the armaments were not reaching Palestine. The British prevented entry right until the end of the Mandate. "As long as we're here, we govern the country," they said in effect. "Afterwards, you can do what you like." Shertok's indignant comment on this was: "Britain is trying to be like Louis XIV and XV rolled into one, and saying 'The State is me' and 'After me, the deluge.' "

The Palestinian Jews could only look on from afar as their armaments piled up in Europe, and hope that they would be able to hold out with the inadequate means at their disposal until the time when the blockade was lifted.

The Arab bands became increasingly active. The torrential winter rains did not hinder their attacks on road communications, and they had cut the road to Jerusalem. Ben-Gurion was obsessed by this, and identified the fate of the road with the outcome of the war.

Although Jerusalem had not been included in the Jewish state, Ben-Gurion knew that if the 100,000 Jews living in the city were cut off from the rest of the *Yishuv,* and were forced to capitulate, the morale of the Jews as a whole would suffer a deadly blow. Communications with the Holy City had to be kept open at all cost.

The military leaders were, with all due allowance, the most stalwart supporters of Ben-Gurion in his fight to bring the State into being. A number of the political and civil leaders seemed unable to understand the nature of the war or to grasp the fact that the fate of the *Yishuv,* and perhaps world Jewry itself, depended on the efforts of a few thousand amateur soldiers who were ill-clad, poorly fed and poorly armed. While the fighting spread, the politicians were engaged in shabby negotiations for seats in the provisional assembly and ministerial office in the future government.

In the south of the country were bands of Bedouins, poorly organized and almost inactive. But with them was a large group of fanatics from Egypt led by the notorious Muslim Brotherhood. In the center were two Palestinian bands, about two thousand strong, who took their orders from the Mufti. In the Jerusalem area was the most dangerous band of all, led by the formidable Abd El-Kader El Husseini. In the north was the "Liberation Army" of several thousand Arabs from Syria and Iraq, commanded by Fawzi El-Kaukji, who had taken a prominent part in the anti-Jewish riots in 1929 and 1936. One of his best lieutenants was Adib Shishakli, the future dictator of Syria and a great friend of France. This force was accompanied by several small bands. There were Druzes from the Haifa region and foreign mercenaries of various nationalities— survivors of Rommel's Afrika Korps, deserters from General Anders's Polish army, British members of the "Fascist League," and Yugoslav and Italian refugees. The Germans had their headquarters in Hebron; mercenaries were enrolled at an office in Rome with the name of "Muslim Relief Service" and were then sent by ship to Alexandria.

Early in February all these Arab forces launched attacks, but the Jews managed to hold them. Kaukji was floundering about in the valley of the Jordan, having lost hundreds of men in vain attacks on Jewish settlements. In the Negev, the Bedouins and the "Muslim Brotherhood" were beaten. El Husseini refrained from pressing home his attacks around Jerusalem, while Salame failed to break up the Jews' preparations at Tel Aviv.

The courage and heroism of the Jews had great effect, but a decisive factor in the Arab failure was the lack of coordination, chiefly due to rivalry between Kaukji's forces and those of the Mufti. The Arab villagers, for the most part, preferred to stay out of the fighting, and those who did take part were untrained in military combat. They were adept at raiding villages, looting and setting fire to them, and were tempted by promises of easy victories and spoils, but when up against stiff resistance they tended to withdraw and attack more vulnerable objectives, such as convoys, or to cut communications around Tel Aviv and Haifa, isolate the Negev or encircle Jerusalem.

The Jews in Jerusalem were being demoralized by grave events there. In February, British fascists in Army uniform blew up the offices of the *Palestine Post,* a Jewish daily printed in English, and more than a hundred people were killed. On several occasions, British troops arrested members of *Haganah,* disarmed them and handed them over to the Arab crowd, which promptly lynched them.

The British did nothing to stop the bloodshed. They were preparing to leave the country and were interested only in protecting their communications for the withdrawal. High British officials had said to Ben-Gurion: "If we were asked by the Jews, we would stay to maintain order." While Field Marshal Montgomery had been quite emphatic. "The Jews won't be able to hold out by themselves," he said. "They'll have to ask for our help."

The United Nations expressed some doubts and hesitations. The organization had been proud at first, surprised at its own boldness, but was now wondering if it had really done right in creating a state and whether it had not acted in too much haste. Alarming reports were reaching Tel Aviv from New York that the State Department, the Secretary of War and the big oil companies were lining up against the President. "If only we had the weapons," Ben-Gurion fumed at the "Red House," "we could pull it off by ourselves and we shouldn't need the United Nations!"

In order to dispel the fears and hesitations arising in the minds of people friendly to the creation of the State, the Jews needed a swift, decisive victory. But the opposite occurred.

A crisis arose in the diplomatic and military fields, in the political sphere and in the morale of the Jews. They had never been so near disaster. Many thought the tragic events meant an end to the dreams of a Jewish state.

Ben-Gurion had been demanding a major offensive against the Arabs ever since the beginning of the war. He felt that the proper response to the attacks of the Arab bands was to counterattack the centers of Arab population. At a policy meeting with the senior officers of *Haganah* on December 19, 1947, he had criticized the methods based on reprisal raids and demanded an "aggressive defense." He had repeated his ideas to the *Haganah* leaders a week later. One of his most ardent supporters for offensive action against the Arabs was young Moshe Dayan.

Ben-Gurion remained skeptical about any possibility of coexistence with the Arabs. The fewer there were living within the frontiers of the new Jewish state, the better he would like it. He did not actually say this, but his position was clear—a major offensive against the Arabs would not only break up their attacks but would also greatly reduce the percentage of Arabs in the population of the new state. (While this might be called racialism, the whole Zionist movement actually was based on the principle of a purely Jewish community in Palestine. When various Zionist institutions appealed to the Arabs not to leave the Jewish state but to become an integral part of it, they were being hypocritical to some extent.)

The Palestinian Jews seemed unable to discard their policy of reprisals and adopt bolder tactics. They had struck no great blow at the enemy so far. Although they had not lost a single village or kibbutz, the initiative was with the Arabs, who dictated the course and character of the war. At the beginning of March, the Arab bands concentrated on cutting road communications. The Jews persisted in their reprisal raids and in trying to keep open their communications by forming ever larger convoys, and this brought them very near disaster.

On March 11, the Arab driver of the United States Consulate parked his van in front of the Jewish Agency building in Jerusalem. A few minutes later the vehicle blew up and shattered the building. Although the Jewish Agency had no great part in the conduct of the war, the incident had an enormous effect. The Arabs had shown that the very centers of the *Yishuv*'s institutions were not safe from their attacks. But this was only the first of a series of catastrophes. On March 26 a Jewish convoy succeeded in breaking through the Arab lines encircling the four villages forming the Etzion settlement. But the joy was short-lived, for when the convoy began the return journey it ran into roadblocks, was forced to a halt, and lost dozens of men in the fighting that followed. The survivors were obliged to call for help from the British, who disarmed them and gave their weapons to the Arabs. On the same day the Arabs stopped another convoy in the south. They had cut the road to the Negev, and the Jewish settlements there were isolated from the rest of the *Yishuv*. On March 29 a convoy trying to reach the Yehiam kibbutz in western Galilee was ambushed, and the Jews lost 42 men before managing to withdraw.

On the following day the most tragic of these defeats took place along the winding road to Jerusalem, below the steep wooded slopes near Bab-el-Oued, "the Gates to the Valley." Here, one of the largest Jewish convoys ever formed was attacked by El Husseini's men. Dozens of vehicles were burned and Jewish casualties were heavy. And the road to Jerusalem was cut.

"Your situation is worse than that of Norway in 1940," was the opinion of Colonel Lund, the Norwegian member of the United Nations mission in Palestine. The situation was indeed disastrous. Prominent Jews began sending their children out of the country. The consensus, in leading circles of the *Yishuv,* was that the bloodshed must stop before all the Jews were massacred, that agreement must be reached with the Arabs, that it would be better to forget the ambitious dreams of a Jewish state and rely on the United Nations and the great Powers. This was what the United States proposed too, for the White House had given way to the pressure groups and was preparing to renounce the plan of partition.

On February 13, United States diplomats in the Middle East had sent President Truman a secret report stating that the Arabs were preparing a major offensive against the Jews for the end of March. The American President appealed to the Arabs to hold back, while at the same time he refused to see Zionist leaders. The State Department was considerably alarmed just then by the Communist take-over in Czechoslovakia. In Washington, London and Paris there was talk of the possibility of another world war. And Palestine was one more danger spot which would spark off the conflict. An armistice had to be arranged there at all cost, even if it meant sacrificing the plan of partition. The Jewish state was about to become the first victim of the Cold War. In the greatest secrecy, State Department specialists began to prepare an urgent plan to halt the mechanism which the United Nations had set in motion the previous November. The chief American delegate at the United Nations, Senator Warren Austin, lodged a resolution by which the United States renounced the plan of partition and proposed that Palestine be placed under the aegis of the United Nations.

The defeats inflicted on the Jews during the last week of March caused something of a panic among friends of Zionism. When General Marshall heard of the convoy which had been almost wiped out on the way to Jerusalem he foresaw the Jews being killed like flies. He lost all faith in *Haganah*. A scheme was hurriedly drawn up in Washington to send a delegation of experts to Palestine to convince the Jews of the folly of proclaiming an independent state at this time. The Americans were prepared to send the delegation in President Truman's personal airplane. Several of the American Zionist leaders came in on the project.

They had no conception of the character of the men fighting in Palestine, especially of Ben-Gurion. When, on March 20, he heard of the American resolution to place Palestine under the protection of the United Nations, he could not restrain himself. "The American proposal is more injurious to the United Nations than to us," he declared angrily. "It does not change the situation in Palestine nor can it prevent the establishment of the Jewish State, which does not in fact depend upon the decision taken by the United Nations on November 29, although that decision has immense moral and political value. It depends upon us winning the trial of strength in this country. The State will be created by our own strength. It is we who will decide the destiny of this country. We form the basis of the Jewish State and we are going to create it . . . We will not accept any 'protection,' either temporary or permanent. We will not agree to any form of foreign government in the future, whatever happens. We insist upon the rapid removal of the British domination and the withdrawal of their troops . . . Our political program is the same as a month ago, as six months ago. It can be summarized in three points—security, the Jewish State, Judaeo-Arab peace."

An even more forceful reaction came ten days later, on March 25 when he asked for the setting up of a supreme authority to deal with military matters. The same day a mobilization order was issued. Then, on March 30, when the Americans were placing their armistice proposal before the United Nations, Ben-Gurion defiantly announced the formation of a "Council of Thirteen," the provisional government of the state due to come into being 45 days later.

But he directed his most effective reply at the Arab bands which had almost paralyzed the Jewish communications, cutting the roads to the Negev and to Galilee, to the Etzion group of villages and to Jerusalem. It was a reply aimed, too, at the numerous defeatists in Palestine as well as in New York. On the evening of March 31, Ben-Gurion held a meeting of the Army command and demanded that all available forces be mobilzed to open the road into Jerusalem. Yigal Sukenik, the Chief of Operations, proposed sending four hundred men. To the amazement of the others Ben-Gurion replied,

"Fifteen hundred." That night, units were withdrawn from several fronts to carry out the largest military operation ever mounted by the Jews. That night too, a Skymaster plane landed at a secret airfield after a direct flight from Czechoslovakia. It was carrying the first consignment of weapons and ammunition under an agreement recently signed in Prague. The two hundred rifles and forty machine guns, together with thousands of rounds of ammunition, were issued to the soldiers.

Operation Nakhshon began the following morning, April 1, 1948. Ten days later, El Husseini's forces had been crushed, the strategic points around Jerusalem had been captured and the road to the Holy City was open. In the Arab town, a lamenting crowd followed the funeral of El Husseini, who had been killed in the fighting on Mount Kastel.

This was the turning point. From then on, until the proclamation of their state, the Jews went from victory to victory. Ben-Gurion had struck his great blow and initiative passed to the Jewish forces.

SIXTEEN

THE REVOLT THAT FAILED

In Ben-Gurion's operational room at the "Red House," speeches and political maneuvers and voting at the United Nations lost all significance compared to the daily happenings on the battlefronts. He was more than ever convinced that the struggle would be settled on the battlegrounds and not in conference rooms. When anyone came to ask for his advice on other problems he would impatiently dismiss his visitor. He covered the pages of his notebooks with figures, details, comments on the various military operations, mobilization projects and outlines of offensives. Leaders of *Haganah* and *Palmach* called to see him throughout the day.

Since the fateful night of March 31 the God of Victory had at last begun to smile upon the Jews. That night, in addition to the Skymaster, the good ship *Nora* had succeeded in slipping through the blockade and reaching the coast of Palestine. And Operation Nakhshon had been the turning point of the war.

In the neighborhood of Tel Aviv the Arab bands under Hassan Salame were wiped out, and Salame himself was killed in the later stages of the fighting. El Husseini's forces, deprived of their leader, suffered heavy losses in the fighting around Jerusalem. Kaukji could make no progress in Galilee. In the Negev, the assault waves of the "Muslim Brotherhood" broke against the modest ramparts of a small kibbutz called Kfar Darom. The anarchy in the top echelons of the Arabs made their situation worse. While Kaukji was trying to capture Haifa, the Mufti was broadcasting from Cairo and calling on the Arab population of the town to flee.

The Jews captured Tiberias and some villages near Jaffa, and occupied areas of Galilee and the Negev. Then a brutal act terrified the Arabs. Units of the terrorist organizations, *Etzel* and *Lehi*, attacked a small village called Dir Yassine, west of Jerusalem, on April 9. They captured the village after a fierce fight, and afterwards massacred 254 men, women and children. The whole of the *Yishuv* bowed its head in shame. Ben-Gurion was aghast. The exodus of the Arab population, which had started to get under way because of the Mufti's orders, turned into a panic-stricken flight. The subtle differences between *Etzel* and *Haganah,* between an isolated incident and general policy, escaped the Arab masses. However, this abandonment of large areas by the Arab population eased the task of the Jewish forces.

The Arabs took their revenge with equal cruelty. On April 13 they attacked a convoy taking doctors, nurses and scholars to the Hebrew University on Mount Scopus. Among the 77 killed was the medical student engaged to Ben-Gurion's younger daughter.

But, unlike the Arabs, the Jews did not flee from their homes. Ben-Gurion arrived in Jerusalem with the first convoy to reach the city after communications had been restored. "Jerusalem is Jerusalem, from both the Jewish and international point of view," he declared, "and it might become the capital of the State." It was a secret obsession of his to restore to the Holy City its functions in the time of the Kingdom of David.

Another obsession of his was the need of heavy armaments. But even the *Haganah* staff officers had failed to grasp the importance of possessing tanks and field guns. One day during the winter, Ben-Gurion had summoned the senior officers to a meeting at his house. He at once broached the question of armaments. Joseph Avidar had produced a list of the weapons needed by *Haganah*—so many rifles and machine guns, so many rounds of ammunition. Ben-Gurion noted it all down, then asked: "And how about tanks and artillery and aircraft?" This met with an amazed silence. "Before long," Ben-Gurion continued, "we shall have to defend ourselves against seven Arab countries, against regular armies possessing tanks and aircraft. Without heavy armament, we shan't be able to resist. We must obtain it at all costs—and obtain it we shall."

Many weeks had passed since that meeting. The Jews had won several victories. And it was because of them that Ben-Gurion was convinced that the Jews would soon be facing regular forces. "The defeats inflicted on the Arabs by *Haganah,"* he wrote on April 20, 1948, "have decided the Mufti and the Palestinian Arabs that they cannot beat the Jews with their own means. So the Mufti has appealed to the Arab League. And the League realizes that to succeed it will have to throw regular forces into the battle, supported by tanks and aircraft."

Heavy armament could soon reach the country and be stored in

Haganah's supply depots. But the most dangerous army that Ben-Gurion had to face and fight was *Haganah,* his own men and allies. He was more than ever on his own. It turned out to be a struggle between him and Galili, between him and the leaders of *Haganah* and the civil institutions for the supreme command of the future Israeli Army.

The trouble had been simmering for some time and a trial of strength was inevitable. Ben-Gurion had openly criticized *Haganah,* attacked its defensive strategy, its outdated organization and inability to adapt to the new requirements, the new form of warfare. He was also exasperated by the confusion in the chain of command of the *Yishuv's* defense forces. In fact there was no proper chain of command. There was a "National Command" which had a commander-in-chief; there was a General Staff with its commander-in-chief; and there was a "Committee for Security" whose exact role no one could define. *Palmach,* the crack force, had its own General Staff which took orders from nobody. And the "dissidents," *Etzel* and *Lehi,* were excluded from all these military bodies and had their own aims and means. Ben-Gurion felt all this ought to be swept away and rebuilt as a single command of a national army which would take its orders from the future government.

In addition to this problem of transforming a many-sided Resistance movement into a regular army, Ben-Gurion was greatly worried by an even more important political change. The *Palmach* brigade had been formed and organized by lieutenants of Tabenkin, the leader of the "Kibbutz Union" which had broken away from MAPAI in 1944 and had eventually joined with the Extreme Left to found MAPAM (United Workers), a party with Communist tendencies. The result was that a minority party which represented at most a fifth of the *Yishuv* had sole command of the strongest military force. And the chief of the National Command, Israel Galili, who controlled the whole of *Haganah,* was one of the MAPAM leaders. Moreover, the only military organizations capable of bringing the Jewish state into being by force of arms, *Palmach* and *Haganah,* were under the influence of a political party which had not favored the establishment of a Jewish state—the Extreme Left had wanted a dual-nation state, while Tabenkin and his group had also opposed the Biltmore Program and then lamely appealed for an international mandate over Palestine. The fact that MAPAM and nearly all the senior officers of *Palmach* were pro-Russian was bound to embarrass the new state when it began to form a foreign policy. How would they react, having so much military strength at their command, if the government's foreign policy did not meet with their approval?

These dangers, real or imaginary, haunted Ben-Gurion. Sooner or later he would have to dismiss *Palmach*'s General Staff, modify the political character of the High Command, weaken the position of the pro-Russian elements, and combine the various armed forces all jealous of their independence into a State military organization. He would also have to abolish the controls over *Haganah* and dissolve the National Command, after depriving it of its chief. Ben-Gurion waited a long time before embarking on this very difficult and dangerous undertaking. Then in April 1948, when the military and political crisis was at its height, he struck. This was the first round, and it proved to be a near-disaster for Ben-Gurion.

The spectacular turning point in the Judaeo-Arab war, in early April 1948, coincided with Ben-Gurion's offensive against the National Command. Until then, he had limited his criticism to speeches and to his black notebooks. Ben-Gurion's political development was not in the least inclined towards the Communist bloc. The policy of the Jewish state would be to steer a middle course between the two major Powers, but Ben-Gurion was definitely in favor of the Western Alliance. He did not forget that Russian support at the United Nations and approval of the sale of war material by Czechoslovakia were based upon the hope of supplanting Britain in the Middle East. Ben-Gurion intended to maintain good relations with the Western Powers. In spite of past grievances, he hoped to forge strong links with Britain, even to join the Commonwealth. The United States was an ally to be retained through the great influence wielded by American Jewry.

Ben-Gurion had made no promises to Gromyko in exchange for his support. The exorbitant price for the war material supplied by Czechoslovakia, and the fact that a secret agreement to supply arms to the Arabs had been made at the same time, relieved him of any political obligation. He intended to cooperate with the West, and so the Communist sympathies of the MAPAM leaders were more than a hindrance.

The thorny problem of the *Palmach* leaders had come up again in March 1948. They had demanded that the Negev front be placed under the command of their own General Staff, and Ben-Gurion was categorically opposed to the idea. It was a particularly stormy meeting, but in the end Ben-Gurion's point of view was accepted. However, *Palmach* continued taking independent action in every sector. The time was not then ripe for Ben-Gurion to meddle in

Palmach's affairs. Any attempt to modify its structure just then could have had disastrous consequences militarily and nationally. The dissolution of *Palmach* could only take place when a regular army existed.

Ben-Gurion therefore began a struggle to obtain the legal and complete command over the armed forces. His first objective was the abolition of the National Command and the dismissal of its chief, Israel Galili.*

Ben-Gurion did not have a high opinion of him. Galili was a highly intelligent man, devoted body and soul to Haganah; as its commander-in-chief he enjoyed the complete confidence of all ranks. However, although probably indispensable to the proper functioning of *Haganah* during the British Mandate, there was no logical place for a chief of the National Command in the future Israeli Army. In all fairness, Ben-Gurion offered Galili a number of different posts in the military organization he proposed to create. But he was resolved to abolish outmoded chains of command between the military chiefs and the Ministry of Defense.

On April 30, 1948, the Council of Thirteen assumed the task of governing during the interim period. In an administrative sense, this nucleus of government succeeded the Jewish Agency at the head of the *Yishuv,* and so had provisional charge of defense and military matters. Ben-Gurion took advantage of this transfer of power to abolish the National Command.

Previously, on April 21, despite opposition from everywhere, he had announced at a meeting of the Jewish Agency Executive that the functions of chief of the National Command were suppressed and the supreme command was transferred to the Council of Thirteen.

On April 26 he summoned Israel Galili and informed him that although he had so far refrained from making changes of a political character, he was not satisfied with the state of things within *Haganah*. Matters were at a critical stage and certain changes were necessary, beginning with *Palmach*. This was a private army of a political and sectarian nature; some of its officers were not up to their assignments, others had not been employed in the best way. He told Galili that the position of chief of the National Command had been abolished, but out of consideration for him the decision would not be made public for the moment.

Galili, who was regarded as a high authority, returned in the

* Galili was head of the National Command from early 1947 until the establishment of the State of Israel.

evening with a number of suggestions to meet Ben-Gurion's criticisms of *Palmach* and its staff, but he was violently opposed to the loss of his own post. In his opinion, it was not desirable for the Chiefs of Staff to receive instructions directly from Ben-Gurion. An intermediary was required, and he was the most suitable person. The two had a long talk, but at the end neither had budged from his position.

The following day, the two explained their opposing points of view to the leaders of their parties, MAPAI and MAPAM. The latter were definitely against Galili being evicted.

On May 2 Ben-Gurion offered Galili a position with him in the new organization he intended to set up, but Galili would not give an immediate reply. That evening Ben-Gurion informed the Chiefs of Staff and the National Command of his decision by letter: "In view of the new administrative measures concerning the Zionist community and matters of security, there is no longer any necessity for a representative of the Jewish Agency Executive to be at the head of the High Command. Consequently, the post of Commander-in-Chief is abolished, and this letter brings the functions of Israel Galili to an end. In future, the Chiefs of Staff will receive their orders directly and solely from the head of the Security Forces or his delegate. . . ."

The following morning, Ben-Gurion renewed his offer of a fresh post to Galili. The Thirteen were to meet late that afternoon, and Ben-Gurion wanted a reply by then. Galili sent it early in the afternoon—through the Chiefs of Staff or "Chiefs of Department," as they were called. Four of them arrived at Ben-Gurion's office— General Eliahu Cohen (Ben-Hur), General Zvi Ayalon, General Igal Sukenik (Yadin) and General Moshe Lerer (Zadok). All four expressed their strong opposition to the dismissal of Galili. The absence of the senior officer, General Jacob Dori, because of illness, complicated matters further.

"Who is going to give the orders?" the generals wanted to know. "How will the Defense organization work if Galili is dismissed?"

Ben-Gurion tried to calm them, and explained what he planned to do to reorganize the High Command. The four generals were not convinced, and their attitude on leaving boded little good. A few minutes later, Ben-Gurion received a note from Galili: "I've thought over your proposals again. I cannot and do not wish to act and participate in the kind of setup you propose." The break had come.

The meeting of the Thirteen was stormy. For the first time, Ben-

Gurion felt completely isolated. The members of the Council who belonged to MAPAM furiously attacked the decision he had taken without consulting the Council. They demanded that it be canceled, and that Galili and the Chiefs of Staff be consulted. The members who belonged to other parties did nothing but ask questions. The only member to make any positive effort was Remez, who proposed that the matter be put back for a few days. Ben-Gurion repeated that he would accept the Ministry of Defense only if his plans for a unified army were accepted. The meeting ended without any decision having been taken. It was said behind the scenes that Ben-Gurion was plotting a "palace revolution."

The *Haganah* leaders returned to the attack on May 5 with barely-veiled threats. Galili was again summoned to Ben-Gurion's office. The atmosphere became heated, and Galili would not budge. "I'm prepared to resume my functions on condition that I am given a grade between you and the Chiefs of Staff," he said. "No," replied Ben-Gurion. And so the worst happened.

The following morning, May 6, a letter was delivered to Ben-Gurion's office:

"The situation at the front just now calls for a commanding authority at the head of *Haganah*. The abolition of the post of chief of the National Command and the illness of the head of the Chiefs of Staff have left *Haganah* without a leader having authority to command the brigades and direct the Chiefs of Staff. This state of affairs has already proved disastrous for the conduct of the war during the past three days. The Chiefs of Department of the Staff consider that the days to come will be decisive for the conduct of the war and the preparations for May 15. They cannot continue to assume their heavy responsibilities while this matter remains unsettled. They demand the reinstatement of Israel Galili until definite arrangements are made. If the matter is not settled within twelve hours from now, the Chiefs of Department will no longer consider themselves responsible for the conduct of the war." The letter was signed by Zvi Ayalon, Igal Yadin, Eliahu Ben-Hur, Moshe Zadok and Joseph Avidar.

It was an ultimatum, almost a revolt. In the face of this threat by the Chiefs of Staff, Ben-Gurion had either to give way and reinstate Galili or resign. The war was at its height, the country was being torn apart, and the United States, the Zionist organizations, and leaders of the *Yishuv* were all pressing him to give up the idea of proclaiming the Jewish state. Abandoned by his friends, violently attacked by the Extreme Left and most of the political parties, defied by the Army command, he had to sacrifice his prestige or resign.

He did neither. He refused to give an inch. At one o'clock that afternoon he summoned the five signatories to his office. He maintained an icy attitude to their threats, and all he proposed to them was that when General Dori returned to duty they could raise their grievances and state their problems at a meeting at which others would be present, including Levi Shkolnik. As an additional concession, Ben-Gurion asked for Galili to work as one of his assistants —without defining the nature of the work.

Confronted by his iron will, the Chiefs of Staff gave in and agreed to continue with their duties. Three days later, Galili took up his position in the military organization. His duties were still left vague, but this was just a small concession. In fact he later became, like Shkolnik, one of Ben-Gurion's assistants at the head of the country's defense organization. He was in charge of mobilization and manpower and military specialists.

The MAPAM leaders continued to attack Ben-Gurion at committee meetings, to accuse him of seeking to establish dictatorial control over military operations, and they fulminated against his "totalitarian intentions" in their paper *Al Hamishmar*. But nothing could now shake Ben-Gurion: "In accepting the Ministry of Defense I had but one aim—to ensure our country's security," he said at a MAPAI meeting. "As head of the armed forces, I acknowledge no political party."

Ben-Gurion did not in fact accept the Ministry of Defense until a few days later, when his conditions for the creation of a unified army had been met. He still had to fight against the hesitations of his colleagues, against the disapproval of the military leaders and the outcries from the Extreme Left. But he was never again so isolated and on his own as that May 6 when he had to fight hard to enforce his decision.

He had sought until the last to find some other means of convincing the people and *Haganah* that reorganization of the armed forces had become necessary. He had wanted his action to have a legal basis, and had also considered the effect his reforms might have on the conduct of the war. For that reason, he had not abolished the National Command when the Council of Thirteen had been formed on March 30, but had waited until the military situation turned in the Jews' favor. He could not, however, wait until the State was proclaimed, for then the existing institutions would have acquired a certain legality, and the opposition to his plans would have been even more forceful. He had acted during the short period of comparative calm after the victories over the Arab irregulars and before the greater trials of strength which could be expected when the Jewish state was proclaimed. Ben-Gurion was getting ready to meet the Arab regular armies with a regular army of his own.

He had decided to rid the armed forces of all political influences, and so had refused to accept any proposition which aimed at placing Galili between him and the Chiefs of Staff. He would accept him as an assistant, but in no event were Ben-Gurion's orders to the Chiefs of Staff to go through Galili.

Not until much later did Ben-Gurion's opponents realize that the dismissal of Galili was only the first stage in Ben-Gurion's great task of creating a unified army. It was perhaps because he was able to dominate his colleagues on that May 6, and so lay the foundations for a regular army, that he was able to dominate history by proclaiming the Jewish state on May 14.

II
THE
LEADER

SEVENTEEN

THAT DAY, MAY 14, 1948

"The Mandate will end officially at one minute past twelve on the night of 14th–15th May. His Excellency the High Commissioner will therefore leave Jerusalem for Haifa on 14th May and will sail on HMS *Euryalus* at midnight. The evacuation of our forces stationed in Jerusalem and elsewhere in Palestine will also begin on 14th May."

These lines were released to the press by a British official on the morning of May 12, 1948, ending thirty years of British rule in Palestine. The British were leaving a country which had caused them a great deal of embarrassment, leaving 650,000 Jews to face the millions of Arabs surrounding them.

It was now up to the Jews themselves to embark on the final and most risky stage of their long struggle and to establish the Jewish state.

Towards the end of March, when military disaster had yawned wide in front of the Jews, there were very few Zionist leaders who were prepared to proclaim independence. Then the panic subsided, but even so the numbers "for" and "against" changed from day to day. On April 10, the Zionist Executive meeting in Palestine had approved the partition project by a vote of 40–10, and had addressed a touching and naive appeal to the Arabs to cooperate with the future Jewish state.

At the United Nations there was a state of confusion, with pressure groups trying to get the partition decision annulled. The American delegation, after the reversal of policy on March 18, was putting forward one proposal after another—a cease-fire, an armistice, an international control, a provisional government, a truce . . . Trygve Lie threatened to resign, but even this did not lessen the flow of proposals and counterproposals. One diplomat cynically defined the attitude of Warren Austin and the American delegation by saying: "Of course we shall do nothing. But we shall do it immediately!" The United States put an embargo on the export of arms to the Middle East. And some delegates suggested that Jerusalem should be governed by the Red Cross!

The Jewish victories in April, important though they were, had by no means decided matters. The road to Jerusalem was again cut by the Arabs, but much more serious was the entry of the Arab Legion into the war. This intervention of a regular force commanded by British officers could well presage an attack by all the Arab armies.

Towards the end of April the President of the United Nations General Assembly had proposed an armistice between Jews and Arabs, and this was approved by several eminent Jewish leaders, among them being Moshe Shertok and Eliezer Kaplan. But to accept an armistice would mean abandoning all idea of establishing the State for some time to come. The Americans were still giving the same warning—"Don't proclaim independence!"

A final decision was to be made a few days before the British Mandate came to an end.

On May 11 the Ben-Gurion–Galili crisis was not yet over, and the Left-wing press was furiously attacking Ben-Gurion. The two adversaries, however, were drawn together by the urgent needs of the moment and were both present at Army staff meetings. There were heated discussions over the creation of an air force. Lists were made of the numbers of aircraft already bought, and either in the country or on the way. The question of priorities for the landing of arms was raised, and some officers demanded that mobilization be stepped up. No one seeing these men conferring in Ben-Gurion's office at the "Red House" could have any doubt that they were prepared to accept their responsibilities, to back up the declaration of independence and defend the Jewish state. But it was a different matter with the civilian leaders. Ben-Gurion hastened from the "Red House" to the meeting of the Central Committee of MAPAI. There was only one item on the agenda—the establishment of the State. And the end of the heated debate still left the issue uncertain. "It seemed obvious even at the beginning of May," wrote Eliezer Livne, "that the majority of the MAPAI leaders were hesitant about declaring independence."

Moshe Shertok was divided over the right course to take. At private gatherings and at meetings of the Jewish Agency he had expressed no definite opinion, and now he had gone to the United States to see General Marshall, and the latter, as was well known, would try to dissuade him from supporting Ben-Gurion. Secretary

of State Marshall was pressing hard for an armistice between Jews
and Arabs. The conflict might spark off a world war. The Jews
would be wiped out by the Arab armies, and they could not count
on any help from the United States, Marshall insisted. Shertok
presented the Zionist point of view, and emphasized that the Jews
had no intention of asking for American help. "All that we ask of
you is not to intervene!"

Marshall was not convinced. He did not believe in the Jewish
state, and it would seem that he communicated some of his doubts
to Shertok. No one in Tel Aviv was certain what Shertok's opinion
would be when he returned, but people who knew him well felt
anxious. Livne has reported a conversation he had with Ben-
Gurion which reveals the latter's opinion of his envoy in the United
States. "Only a few days remain before the end of the British
Mandate," said Livne. "Why don't you announce that the State will
be proclaimed on that date?"

"I don't want to do that until Shertok is back here," replied Ben-
Gurion.

"But he'll be against it?"

Ben-Gurion smiled. "Don't worry. I shall see to it that as soon as
he steps off the plane he'll be kidnapped by my military secretary,
Nhemia, and brought to my office. And I promise you that he'll
have a different opinion when he leaves!"

Whether or not this actually happened is not known. Several
persons claim to have had knowledge of it, but Ben-Gurion has
never admitted it. However, the fact remains that when Shertok
addressed the Central Committee of MAPAI he made a magnificent
speech in favor of proclaiming the State. His doubts and fears had
completely vanished, to the great surprise of the MAPAI leaders.

This important meeting broke up suddenly. Ben-Gurion was
handed a note which had been hastily scribbled by Golda Meyerson. He read it, then jumped up and hurried out to his car. A few
minutes later he was running up the stairs to his office at the "Red
House."

Golda Meyerson had been appointed head of the Diplomatic
Department of *Histadrut,* and she had fulfilled a number of
missions abroad with great success, the chief one having been to
obtain huge funds for the arming of *Haganah.* Ben-Gurion had
insisted most strongly that she should be a member of the Council
of Thirteen, which was destined to be the provisional government
of the new State.

He was not her only admirer. Abdullah, King of Jordan, had also
been greatly impressed by her qualities and intelligence. Although

usually scornful of women, the Arab monarch did not conceal his respect for this Jewish woman who had been sent by the *Yishuv* leaders in 1947 to have secret talks with him. If conflict with the country possessing the strongest and best-disciplined force of all the Arab states could be avoided, then the fate of the Jewish state would not be altogether hopeless. And Jordan was probably the one Arab country which could be dissuaded from taking part in the war.

Another Arab head of state, it was true, had sought to come to terms with the Jews. In December 1947 the Sultan of Morocco had sent an envoy secretly to the Zionists to say that in exchange for a good round sum—as a "present"—he was prepared to declare himself favorable to the partition of Palestine and would place the Moroccan Jews under his protection. Ben-Gurion had not even listened. At that time he was thinking of nothing but guns and rifles, and in any case Morocco was certainly not going to send an army to the Middle East.

Abdullah was the one Arab leader with whom there were hopes of reaching an understanding. But on May 8 some alarming news had reached Paris. The Jewish Agency's special envoy there, Maurice Fisher, heard that a secret article in the agreement between Britain and Jordan provided for the whole of Palestine coming under the Jordanian crown. Whether true or false, this news called for explanation. So on May 10 Golda Meyerson, disguised as an Arab woman, had gone to see the King of Jordan once again. It was an extremely dangerous undertaking, and the secret services were on the watch along her route.

Nevertheless she succeeded in meeting Abdullah. But his tone had changed, and all he would offer the Jews was a temporary autonomy within a Judaeo-Arab state.

"Last year I was alone and had freedom of action," he told her frankly. "But now I am just one head of state among five others. I have no choice—either you accept my new proposal or there will be war."

"Very well," replied Golda Meyerson, "then we'll meet again after the war!"*

She was courteously accompanied to her car and started on the long journey back to Tel Aviv. She saw in the distance a convoy of tanks and artillery crossing Jordan in the direction of Palestine. Iraqi forces were heading for the battlefront too.

* She did not know that she was seeing King Abdullah for the last time. Soon after the war some Arab fanatics assassinated him in the Mosque of Omar in Jerusalem, for having been sympathetic towards the Jews.

When she reached Tel Aviv she hurried to get a message to Ben-Gurion at the MAPAI meeting.

This was probably the crucial point in his determined struggle. Was it right for him to engage in a war which might lead to the massacre of hundreds of thousands of Jews? Shertok had been hesitant, Kaplan and Shprinzak were against it, the Extreme Left did not want a state at all, the Americans were pressing for an armistice. The organization of the Jewish armed forces was in no condition to meet regular armies, and hopes of Jordan staying out of the war had just collapsed.

Could he risk everything on *Haganah* in view of the doubts expressed by all his friends and colleagues? Had he the right to persist in proclaiming the State? The Army would back him up, but it was doubtful whether that alone was sufficient. He knew that, whatever his decision, it would carry other people with it. He knew, too, that a negative decision would mean an end forever to dreams of a Jewish state.

Nothing could shake his determination once his decision was made. He believed in victory. Never in his speeches, his interviews and his remarks jotted down in the black notebooks did he once admit to any doubts. Never did he ask himself "What will happen if we are beaten?"

This stubborn confidence in final victory was the source of his strength, of his power to influence and convince others.

A short while after reaching his office at the "Red House" he summoned an emergency meeting of the Chiefs of Staff. Golda Meyerson's talks with Abdullah and Shertok's report were things of the past—the future had to be considered now, and at once. The meetings and talks went on until evening. The military commanders were busy preparing for war.

The following morning, May 12, 1,500 men of the Arab Legion, supported by tanks and artillery, invaded Jewish territory. A few hours later, a British official calmly read out the communiqué announcing the forthcoming departure of the High Commissioner.

Accusations of totalitarianism and of sabotage were hurled at Ben-Gurion following his decision to relieve Galili of his functions. At the emergency meeting of the Defense Committee that morning, he made no attempt to parry these attacks by invoking the pressing dangers of war. He merely repeated that he would accept the Ministry of Defense only if he obtained satisfaction in the matter of a unified army. "A campaign of blackmail and lies is being directed against me over certain matters," he added. "I am not going to deny or refute these attacks. For security reasons I am obliged to remain silent."

The Galili affair followed him to the meeting of the Council of Thirteen. But it was soon deleted from the agenda. There were far more important matters to discuss, notably whether or not to proclaim the State when the British Mandate officially ended in 72 hours. After interminable discussions by all manner of committees, the decision had been left to the supreme body of the *Yishuv*. The Thirteen had to settle the question.

The Council sat for more than twelve hours. Three members were not present, others were uncertain or feared to defy the United States and the United Nations. Alarming reports had come in of American threats to block Zionist funds. Last-minute solutions—subtle combinations of armistice proposals and foreign protection—had been put forward by the United Nations, France, the United States and Britain. And the military situation in Palestine was grave—the Etzion group of villages was besieged by the Arabs and seemed likely to fall at any moment.

Golda Meyerson and Moshe Shertok reported on the outcome of their respective missions. The armistice proposition was placed before the meeting. To accept it meant renouncing the establishment of the State, and to reject it was almost tantamount to suicide. Galili and Yadin were called in to report on the military situation. Then Ben-Gurion gave a long analysis of the overall situation and drew the logical conclusions. "In my opinion," he said, "if we manage to increase our military forces by stepping up mobilization and from the arrival of immigrants, and if we speed up military training and can complete our armaments, then we shall be able to hold out and even to win. We shall have our losses, that is certain; but we can hardly expect to come through it all cheaply."

"The Etzion disaster does not shake my resolution," he added. "I expected such reverses, and I fear we shall have even greater ordeals. The outcome depends on our wiping out most of the Arab Legion. Destruction of the enemy forces is always the determining factor in a war."

Wipe out the Arab Legion! When all the other members of the Council were trembling at the thought that this crack force could sweep the Jewish defenses aside, Ben-Gurion was thinking not merely of stopping it or even throwing it back, but of wiping it out! He had nevertheless deeply impressed the Council. When a vote was taken, six of the ten members present were in favor of rejecting the armistice proposal. This meant that thanks to a majority of two the Jewish state would be proclaimed.

After a break, the discussions began again. How should independence be declared—and what name should be given to the state? Some members proposed Judaea, others suggested Zion. After much argument, the Council settled on Israel.

Another fierce argument broke out over defining the frontiers. One member wanted the declaration of independence to include an article which stated the exact lines of the frontier. Ben-Gurion did not agree. "Take the American Declaration of Independence, for instance," he said. "It contains no mention of the territorial limits. We are not obliged to state the limits of our State. The Arabs are making war on us. If we beat them, the western part of Galilee and the territory on both sides of the road to Jerusalem will become part of the State. If only we have the strength . . . Why tie ourselves down?"

Ben-Gurion did not intend to keep to the territorial limits for the Jewish state laid down by the United Nations. He was sure that opportunities for increasing the territory would arise, and that Israel would eventually attain her initial aims, even if it took centuries. Instead of making empty statements about the historic frontiers of the Jewish homeland, he said nothing. Later, he moved step by step towards his objectives. Was this imperialism—or a sense of history?

By five votes to four, the Council decided not to define the frontiers. The meeting ended late at night, but a small committee headed by Shertok began work on a draft of the Declaration of Independence.

On May 13 the Central Committee of MAPAI, exhausted by meetings and discussions, voted on proclaiming the State; one-third of the members was against it. The other parties also pronounced themselves favorable to it. The one leader who had made up his mind previously, and whose resolution had removed a number of hesitations, was Menahem Begin of *Etzel*. He had prepared two speeches—one was to announce his allegiance to the State, should it be voted, and the other was to proclaim the establishment of the State in the name of his own party. He kept his promise and made the former speech.

Ben-Gurion spent all morning in conferences with the Chiefs of Staff. Safed had just surrendered to Jewish forces and the leading Arabs in Jaffa were about to sign their capitulation, but the situation at Etzion was hopeless. Kfar Etzion had already fallen, and the Arab armor was concentrating on other sectors. In the south, Egyptian forces were attacking lonely outposts. There were reports from the United States of a state of confusion at the United Nations and in the State Department. In New York, the aged Weizmann sent a moving letter to President Truman in Washington asking for recognition of the State of Israel, when it had not yet been proclaimed.

In Tel Aviv there was feverish activity. The State had to be proclaimed on May 14 as the next day was Saturday, the Sabbath. On the evening of May 13 the text of the Declaration of Independence was placed before the Council. Ben-Gurion was not satisfied with it; he took it home in his briefcase and worked on it for some hours, deleting every "inasmuch as," adding a preamble here and there, so that the subtleties of Shertok gave way to Ben-Gurion's vigorous and direct style. At two in the morning, a telegram interrupted his work: "The inhabitants of Kfar Etzion, who had hoisted a white flag, have had their throats cut by the Arabs."

As the sun rose, the guard at Government House in Jerusalem presented arms to General Cunningham. The last British High Commissioner in Palestine was leaving. His car and escort sped through a deserted town and out to Kalandia Airport, from where the High Commissioner flew to Haifa. There he would go aboard the *Euryalus* and wait for midnight, when the British Mandate ended, then sail for Malta. From all the British Army camps, long convoys were heading for the frontiers which they were due to cross before midnight or were heading towards Haifa, where a small zone was reserved for the rearguard until June 30. The evacuating forces were leaving behind them a state of chaos.

Throughout the morning of May 14 Ben-Gurion was occupied with military matters. On this historic day, for which the Jewish people had been waiting two thousand years, Ben-Gurion showed no trace of emotion. He got up at his usual hour, seven, and had breakfast with Paula. Then a jeep took him to the "Red House," where his aides were already marking up the operational map. There had been fierce fighting in the north—the Arabs had repulsed an attack near Jerusalem and *Haganah*'s only field gun had fallen into their hands. Igal Yadin had been forced to evacuate two villages. Ben-Gurion discussed the mobilization plans and the agreement with *Etzel* which placed its forces under the command of the Chiefs of Staff. He heard the roar of a plane overhead. "So the British really are going," he murmured to himself. But they gave a parting shot before they left—invoking the authority they possessed until midnight, they stopped a ship off Tel Aviv which was bringing field artillery for *Haganah*.

When Ben-Gurion returned home he found Shertok waiting to

inform him of the international situation. "What we need to know," said Ben-Gurion, "is whether the threats of the Americans to use force will really come to anything. Either way, it's not terrible. If the United States does not use force against us, that's a good thing. If they do send army units to Palestine, that gives us a political advantage."

At one o'clock there was a final meeting of the Council of Thirteen prior to the proclamation of the State. Before leaving to attend it, Ben-Gurion had a brief conference with some of the *Haganah* leaders. General Dori, the Commander-in-Chief who was still ill, was replaced.

At four o'clock Ben-Gurion ran up the stairs of the art museum at Tel Aviv. Soldiers and police were having difficulty in controlling the large crowd which had somehow learned where the proclamation was to be made. There were 200 people, including journalists and press photographers, crammed into the picture gallery. The Council of Thirteen sat behind a long table on the platform. On the wall above their heads a portrait of Herzl was hanging between the blue and white of two large flags. The Tel Aviv Philharmonic Orchestra was ready in the upper gallery. Workmen had been busy arranging things until the last minute and had not had time to remove the pictures. The proclamation would be made under the eyes of Chagall's "Jew holding the Tablets" and the figures in Minkovski's "Pogrom."

Ben-Gurion rose, and read out the Declaration of Independence. There would be 37 signatures on the roll of parchment which proclaimed the State of Israel. One great name was missing— Weizmann, still in New York.

When the excitement had died down, when Rabbi Fishman had given his blessing and the orchestra had played the national anthem, Ben-Gurion hurried back to Army headquarters. The fighting was spreading.

In London, only a few MPs were in the House to hear the announcement of the end of the British Mandate. In New York, the United Nations Committee continued to discuss Palestine— although there was no longer a Palestine and the State of Israel had come into being.

Early the following morning, May 15, Arab armies crossed the Jewish frontiers in several places and their aircraft bombed Tel Aviv. No one could then tell whether the war would end in victory or disaster for the Jews. Nevertheless, for good or bad, on that sunny afternoon on May 14, 1948, Ben-Gurion took his place among the immortals of history.

EIGHTEEN

THE CONQUEROR

"On May 14, 1948, Friday 5th Yiar 5708, at four in the afternoon, Jewish independence was proclaimed and the State came into being. Its fate lies in the hands of the armed forces.

"Immediately after the proclamation ceremony I went back to Headquarters and we had a meeting to discuss the grave situation. Alarming reports mentioned armored columns of the Arab Legion and enemy concentrations in Syria. Enemy forces were reported at Lydda, less than fifteen miles from Tel Aviv. On the other hand, our forces had advanced into western Galilee at several points. We also held the police training center and a few key positions in Jerusalem.

"Nearly all the High Command was against my plan to make a strong thrust to seize the areas along both sides of the road from Tel Aviv to Jerusalem. They argued that we did not have enough troops and that we do not know the enemy's plans. Without a firm decision from the Thirteen, I did not want to give an order which went against the considered opinion of the High Command. But I feel that we have missed the opportunity to seize territory upon which the fate of Jerusalem depends, and perhaps the outcome of the war itself. Bad news came from the Negev too, in the evening. Will Tel Aviv be bombed tonight?"

Such is Ben-Gurion's entry in his diary for that historic afternoon of May 14. He makes not the slightest mention of his feelings at the moment when, by his own proclamation, the Jewish state became a reality. Some would say that this proves him a man of deeds, not words; others that he was unable to express his feelings. But at that time all his thoughts and energies were concentrated on the war. A friend who wanted to talk to him about the State received the reply: "So far as I'm concerned, the State does not exist so long as the war goes on." That was how the Arabs saw the situation. By attacking with their armored columns they would wipe the State from the map as quickly as possible.

On May 15 the Arab regular forces thrust towards Tel Aviv from the east, the north and the south. The dreaded invasion was well under way.

The first bombs fell on Tel Aviv at six in the morning. It was the Sabbath, and Ben-Gurion was at a small radio studio making a live broadcast to America. He had been awakened at two in the morning and told that the unpredictable Harry Truman, without consulting the State Department, had just recognized the State of Israel. Weizmann had done a good job there. The radio station shuddered as Egyptian bombers dropped their loads. "The explosions you can hear are Arab planes bombing Tel Aviv," Ben-Gurion coolly explained into the microphone. Then he continued with his prepared talk.

A few hours later he was at an Army conference. The situation was getting worse. Egyptian armor was advancing across the Sinai Desert. In the north the Lebanese forces were small and were making little progress, but Syrian and Iraqi aircraft were raining bombs on kibbutzim in Galilee and the valley of the Jordan. In the east, units of the Arab Legion were approaching Jerusalem, and they still held the Latroun strongpoint which commanded the road.

Events were proving that the campaign Ben-Gurion had been ceaselessly pursuing for the past few months was right. There was only one way to combat the Arab regular armies—with a Jewish regular army. Tanks and artillery were needed to meet tanks and artillery. Israel still had none.

During those first few days of its existence, the Jewish state seemed doomed. It had nothing with which to halt the enemy's onrush. A delegation from the kibbutzim in the Jordan valley came to ask Ben-Gurion for reinforcements, and he had to reply: "We haven't enough guns, enough planes or enough men. The whole country is in the front line. We haven't any reinforcements to send."

He did send help, nevertheless—four field guns, the first to reach Israel. Any war museum would have been pleased to have them.

However, real artillery was beginning to arrive in the country. The organization secretly built up by Ben-Gurion's special envoys all over the world worked well when D-Day came. As soon as independence was proclaimed, armaments bought in Czechoslovakia, France, Finland, Panama, Cuba or Mexico were hurriedly loaded into old ships and ancient airplanes which headed for Israel. It was a race against time. From every ship that docked, every plane that landed in Israel, there poured rifles, Stens and ammunition, field artillery and armored vehicles, and airplane parts which were assembled on the spot by a special team of Czech technicians. New agreements had been made for the purchase of Czech artillery, and a secret arrangement with France provided for a supply of Hotchkiss tanks and other wonders of bygone days. Men were hastily mobilized—some new immigrants found themselves going straight from the ship to training centers. Officers and men who had been trained surreptitiously at camps in Cyprus, France and Italy were sent to join the new Israeli Army. Several months passed before it was as well equipped as the Arab armies, but from the very beginning of the war, it was clear that the Jews would hold out. They had stopped the enemy and avoided being "thrown back into the sea," as the Arabs had predicted. The Syrian, Iraqi and Lebanese forces were held in the north, as were the Egyptian columns in the south—though only twenty miles from Tel Aviv. The Egyptians had boasted that they would raze Tel Aviv to the ground and overrun the whole country. Now they merely said they intended to cut the Negev from the rest of the country. The Arab Legion had predicted that Haifa would fall on May 20, Tel Aviv and Jerusalem on May 25, when Abdullah would be crowned King of Palestine with all due ceremony. No mention was now made of this program.

Ben-Gurion now felt able to state his war aims. They were no less ambitious than the Arabs' and showed an equal determination to expand. For Ben-Gurion, the 1,835 years of Jewish exile did not count, and the modern State of Israel was the natural successor to the ancient Kingdom of David. Its enemies were the heirs of ancient enemies—the Egypt of the Pharaohs, Assyria and Chaldea. The war was a continuation of the wars that Israel had always waged against her neighbors.

Ben-Gurion wrote in his diary on May 21: "The Achilles' heel of the Arab coalition is the Lebanon. Muslim supremacy in this country is artificial and can easily be overthrown. A Christian State ought to be set up there, with its southern frontier on the river Litani. We would sign a treaty of alliance with this State. Then, when we have broken the strength of the Arab Legion and bombed Amman, we could wipe out Transjordan; after that, Syria would fall. And if Egypt still dared to make war on us, we would bomb Port Said, Alexandria and Cairo. We should thus end the war, and would have settled the account with Egypt, Assyria and Chaldea on behalf of our ancestors."

Ben-Gurion had studied his military manuals well, and realized that in order to defeat a coalition he had to separate his enemies and eliminate them one by one. (He was later to use the same technique to overcome strong coalitions opposing him at home.) Meanwhile, his idea was for the first planes available to bomb Amman and Damascus, then Lebanon and Egypt. After holding the Syrians and thrusting into the Lebanon, the Jewish forces would launch an attack on the Egyptians. And in the end the Jews would occupy the Negev.

In short, neither the frontiers drawn by the United Nations nor those obtained by force of arms in 1948 were the definite limits of the State in Ben-Gurion's mind.

So absorbed was he by his conduct of the war that he almost seemed to forget that he was also Prime Minister of the State of Israel. Nevertheless, he had to preside at Cabinet meetings, where difficult and painful quarrels often broke out over ministerial responsibility. Many a time he left in the middle of a Cabinet meeting to return to Army headquarters, which had been moved to a picturesque house (previously a family hotel) perched on a green hillside overlooking Tel Aviv and the Mediterranean. From there, Ben-Gurion could see the ships laden with arms making for the port of Tel Aviv. He followed the military operations closely, and gave orders and instructions personally to the Chiefs of Staff. After the abortive revolt of May 6 there was a relative calm—but only on the surface. Galili's position was still not settled, the armed forces, which had been named "Army for the Defense of Israel," were still riddled with politics, *Palmach* still had an independent command. There were differences of opinion on matters of strategy—Ben-Gurion's could be summed up in one word: Jerusalem.

Acting against his generals' advice, he sent more troops to that sector. He was set on capturing the Old City, and was convinced that the key to the situation was the strongpoint of Latroun which commanded the road to Jerusalem.

Latroun was to become a symbol of heartbreaking defeats and bitter disappointments, a kind of Mount Cassino. Ben-Gurion threw his best troops and commanders against this strongly-held position—the hardened units of *Palmach,* Laskov's armored formations and the newly-formed Seventh Brigade, with the brilliant *Palmach* General, Igal Alon, and the American Colonel Markus to command them. But it was all in vain.

Latroun was a great personal setback for Ben-Gurion. The determination which had led to his most spectacular victories now made the defeat all the worse. Yet perhaps it was not entirely a defeat, for the commanders of the Arab Legion withdrew several units from Jerusalem to reinforce the defenders of Latroun. So the Jewish soldiers who died in attacks on that strongpoint may well have enabled the main battle to be won—the battle for Jerusalem.

Once again, however, the fate of the State and the Army, and Ben-Gurion's future, were to be decided in another battle. This time the battle was between Jews. It was a bloody fratricidal battle, the most tragic in the War of Independence, centering on a small American ship loaded with immigrants, arms and munitions—the *Altalena*.

NINETEEN

ON THE THRESHOLD OF CIVIL WAR

"Altalena" was the pen name of Vladimir Jabotinsky, who until his death had been the inspiration of the Revisionists and *Etzel*. It was given to an old vessel of the U.S. Navy purchased for $75,000 by a group of American Jews headed by filmwright Ben Hecht and novelist Louis Bromfield, who were supporters of *Etzel*. With this ship at their disposition, the *Etzel* leaders set about obtaining a large quantity of arms and munitions to send to Israel—a spectacular exploit which would make their organization the best-equipped fighting force in the country.

Gifts amounting to hundreds of thousands of dollars were placed in a central fund, and contacts were secretly made with the French Government. The French were already discreetly helping the Israeli Army, and they gave the *Etzel* project a sympathetic hearing. Through the good offices of Jean Morin, Undersecretary in Georges Bidault's ministry, *Etzel*'s request for arms was brought to the attention of the Foreign Minister. Bidault's attitude towards Israel was distinctly cool, if not hostile, but it seems that the French Government agreed to supply arms to the *Etzel* organization on condition that its troops saw to the protection of French Catholic institutions in Palestine.

The prolonged talks with the French and the difficulties of obtaining large quantities of arms in Europe caused the *Etzel* representatives to delay the sailing of the *Altalena* for Israel. She finally sailed on June 11, 1948, loaded with arms and munitions purchased by various means or supplied free by the French authorities. There were also 800 immigrants on board, volunteers for the *Etzel* armed forces and who had received some training in Europe.

However, the arrival of the *Altalena* off the Israeli coast at that time threw the *Etzel* leaders into some confusion. On May 14, just before the proclamation of the State of Israel, Menahem Begin had announced that he was placing *Etzel* at the disposition of the provisional government. On June 1, when fighting had been in progress for a fortnight, he had gone a stage further by ordering his armed forces to join the national army. Their own command would continue to function as a temporary measure until integration was completed. By this agreement, *Etzel* placed all its arms, supplies and contacts abroad at the disposition of the national High Command. Since Jerusalem was still an "international city," (Ben-Gurion calling it his capital did not bring it within the State of Israel), the *Etzel* organization there continued its activities separately from *Haganah* and *Palmach,* whose forces came under the orders of the Israeli High Command.

But the agreement signed by Begin and Ben-Gurion's representatives was not easy to define. Who except Ben-Gurion understood what was meant by a national army? Even the notion of a state was still novel to a people who had known only exile for the past two thousand years. How could the *Etzel* units become part of an army, formed by *Haganah,* which had acted against them in the past, and directed by Ben-Gurion had set in motion the hateful "hunting season?" The agreement did no more than create a temporary calm, easily followed by violent storms.

The arrival of the *Altalena* provided an opportunity to weigh the goodwill existing on either side. Begin had invited Galili and Eshkol, as representatives of Ben-Gurion to his headquarters to suggest that they buy the *Altalena* and her cargo. They had refused. At that time, the watchword for arms purchases was complete secrecy, but *Etzel* had given great publicity to this shipload of armaments. As common knowledge to all the secret agents of the Mediterranean region, it could serve no useful purpose.

Nevertheless, Begin had given orders for the ship to sail, and she had left Port de Bouc on June 11, heavily laden. That same day a four-week truce had been signed, through United Nations mediation, and one of the clauses prohibited the importation of armaments during this period. What was to be done with the *Altalena?*

The answer seemed simple—follow the same procedure as with other ships then approaching Israel loaded with war material, and discharge the cargo secretly at some lonely beach along the coast. The Jews had become adept at avoiding the vigilance of United Nations observers.

On this understanding, an agreement was signed between Galili and Begin. But then, on June 17, Begin pleaded that his associates were not of the opinion that the arms and munitions should be handed over to the High Command, but should go to the various *Etzel* units serving with the Army. "These are our armaments," said Begin. "It's only natural that we should equip our own men first."

The *Etzel* leaders were still imbued with a kind of feudal mentality, and decided to land the war material themselves and disregard the Government's instructions. Galili felt that the great amount of arms in the *Altalena,* in the hands of an aggressive minority like *Etzel,* could constitute a serious threat to the State institutions. Ben-Gurion's attitude was that the arms and munitions had to be handed over to the State authorities as soon as they were unloaded, and the *Etzel* units would receive supplies in the same way as other formations of the national army.

Events moved quickly. On June 20 the *Altalena* arrived in Israeli territorial waters and anchored off Kfar Vitkin, a village with a good beach. Hundreds of *Etzel* soldiers had left their units and were waiting on the beach; they had stolen a number of Army vehicles to transport the war material.

The provisional government met at Tel Aviv. Ben-Gurion said: "This affair is of the highest importance. There are not going to be two States, and there are not going to be two armies. Begin will not be allowed to do as he likes. I don't even want to discuss, just now, the political and international implications of this breaking of the truce; politics don't interest me in time of war . . . But we have to decide whether we are going to offer power to Begin or order him to cease his independent activities. If he does not submit, we will fire on him. . . . ."

The ministers tried to find another solution. Some wanted to temporize, others talked of arresting Begin. Ben-Gurion sent for Galili and Yadin, who said that two battalions were needed to put a stop to *Etzel*'s activities. Ben-Gurion demanded that force be used against the dissidents if they persisted in their action. "If it's true that they have five thousand rifles and two hundred and fifty machine guns," he said, "then what they are doing now is nothing compared with what they will do shortly. And then we shall have two States and two armies."

The ministers unanimously approved the use of force if the *Etzel* leaders refused to accept its warnings. A trial of strength seemed inevitable.

The following morning, Begin did reject the ultimatum. Dressed in civilian clothes, he was on the beach at Kfar Vitkin directing the work of his men. The *Altalena* had drawn close inshore, and they were unloading the arms and munitions onto an improvised pontoon bridge. "Don't worry, it's not serious," Begin reassured the captain. "Here we always talk in terms of ultimatums. Nothing will happen."

He was mistaken. At four in the afternoon, firing began from the hillside and the orange groves overlooking the pontoon bridge, and corvettes of the Israeli Navy appeared out at sea. Mortar shells and machine-gun bullets whined and fell among the crates of munitions stacked on the sands. The *Etzel* men tried to break through the semicircle of fire which was slowly driving them into the sea, but in vain. After a few hours of fighting they gave in, and one of their leaders signed a document of surrender whereby the armaments were to be handed over to the national army. The crates already unloaded were taken away and the *Etzel* men were made prisoners. Begin, however, had not surrendered. He had gone aboard the *Altalena,* which sailed along the coast. At two in the morning the ship hove to off Tel Aviv, a few hundred yards from the shore and opposite the luxury hotels. This was the setting for the final, tragic act in the *Altalena* affair.

Soon after daylight, people hurried down to the sea front from all directions. Groups of *Etzel* supporters arrived in great excitement from the suburbs. Boats began going out to the *Altalena* and returning weighed down to the gunwales with crates of munitions. *Etzel* was unloading its cargo despite everything, banking on the fact that the few Army units in Tel Aviv were under strength. The United Nations observers looked on incredulously from their hotel windows. In spite of the document of surrender, *Etzel* was not going to give up its arms without a fight.

An emergency Cabinet meeting was called. The atmosphere was very different from the previous day, fear, indecision, even panic, were present in the room. Blood had been shed at Kfar Vitkin, Jewish blood spilt by Jews—the supreme crime, which ought never to take place. Several ministers wanted to go back on the unanimous decision to use force, and to negotiate with *Etzel,* find some compromise solution. What mattered most was to avoid civil war, even if it meant a loss of prestige by the Government. Ben-Gurion thundered out, "No negotiating with *Etzel!*"

In the middle of the meeting a breathless messenger arrived with the latest news—the *Altalena* was discharging her cargo of war material and refusing to accept the authority of the State. Ben-Gurion once again succeeded in obtaining the unanimous approval of the Government for force to be used against *Etzel* if its leaders did not submit.

After several summonses to surrender, the fighting began on the seafront, the beach and in front of the hotels, under the astonished gaze of foreign visitors and journalists. The Army had called in units from the Tel Aviv district, including some of the *Palmach* brigade. The *Altalena* was stuck fast on a reef. Men aboard her had mounted heavy machine guns on the deck and were replying to the fire from the shore. A field gun was brought up, and, with Ben-Gurion's approval, the officer in charge gave orders to fire on the ship. There was grave risk of the ship blowing up, still laden with munitions as she was, and causing great damage to the buildings on the seafront. Nevertheless, the order was given. The first shot missed, the second was a direct hit, exploding in the hold. Fire broke out and rapidly spread through the ship. The men jumped overboard and swam for the shore. Begin was the last to leave her. A few minutes later the *Altalena* blew up, but with less serious results than had been feared.

That same day, by order of Ben-Gurion, all over the country the members of *Etzel* were arrested and the military units disarmed. These energetic measures removed all possibility of further action by *Etzel*.

In the evening, speaking over a secret transmitter, Begin made a virulent attack on Ben-Gurion, calling him a coward, an idiot and a dictator. But Begin ordered his men not to resist the Army. There would be no civil war.

The following day, two ministers, resigned in protest against the measures taken by Ben-Gurion. But the provisional assembly gave him a massive vote of confidence while clouds of smoke from the burning *Altalena* were still drifting over Tel Aviv.

By order of Ben-Gurion, *Etzel*'s units were disbanded (except those in Jerusalem) and the members were later enrolled into the national army. Civil war had been avoided but the grains of hatred had been sown.

Was there ever real danger of a *coup d'état* by *Etzel?* Ben-Gurion believed that if the *Altalena* had succeeded in discharging her cargo of arms and munitions, *Etzel* would have tried to seize power in Israel. Other people thought that the dissidents' aim was to make themselves masters of Jerusalem and there set up a government, proclaim a second Jewish state in the Holy City and surrounding district. Begin said he had no such intention. It is difficult to know what his thoughts were.

The *Altalena* affair and the crushing of *Etzel* at the risk of civil war has remained one of the most dramatic decisions in Ben-

Gurion's life. It roused the respect of the whole world for the young state and its institutions. They had proved themselves able to govern and put down attempts to overthrow them.

There can be little doubt, however, that Ben-Gurion had purposely used the showdown with the *Etzel* leaders in order to achieve his aims. The *Altalena* affair was not of his choosing, but he had made use of it to settle matters with *Etzel*. And by disbanding its armed forces, by playing on memories of the revolt, he was to attain what he had long been aiming for—the complete disappearance of the terrorist organizations in all their military forms and the enrolment of their fighters in the Army, an army which he wanted to be unified and nonpolitical. But that point had still to be reached. Only a week after the shelling of the *Altalena,* Ben-Gurion went to war again—another internal struggle, this time against the Army commanders, the men who had supported him in putting down *Etzel*.

TWENTY

BEN-GURION RESIGNS

On June 27, 1948, all was calm on the provisional frontiers of the State of Israel. The truce brought about by Count Folke Bernadotte, whom the United Nations had appointed as mediator, was due to last until July 9. In the garden of the Government offices at Tel Aviv a smiling group was having its photograph taken. There were the khaki-clad generals of the young "Army for the Defense of Israel," veterans of *Haganah* and *Palmach,* and, in the middle, three civilians in white shirts, Galili, Eshkol and Ben-Gurion, and Paula.

At a ceremony a few minutes earlier, the military leaders had solemnly taken an oath of allegiance to the Army and the Government. Similar ceremonies were being held in all the Army camps.

It seemed to be the end of an era—the end of *Haganah, Palmach, Etzel* and *Lehi* as separate forces and of political interference in military matters. The Army would in the future be the organization for which Ben-Gurion had been striving. So it seemed. But in fact the real struggle was only beginning. Several of the men were already bracing themselves for the final trial of strength.

When Ben-Gurion had successfully opposed the Chiefs of Staff on May 6 he had gained a victory but had not won the internal struggle. Galili had given way before Ben-Gurion's energetic measures but he had not given up his ambitions. The discontent among the military commanders had not disappeared, and there was still disagreement between them and Ben-Gurion over the strategy to adopt.

A number of serious incidents had occurred during the weeks following May 6. On several occasions, Ben-Gurion had discovered that his orders transmitted to the military commanders by Galili were not the same as he had given. His appointments to commands were not always carried out. *Palmach* units at Kiryat Anavim, near

Jerusalem, had seized arms, vehicles and rations being sent to other units, and despite orders from Ben-Gurion, the intercepted supplies were not given up.

Relations between the *Palmach* brigade and the commander on the Jerusalem front, Colonel Markus, an American, had reached the breaking point. A few hours before the truce, Markus was shot dead by a sentry. Tales were soon rife that he had been assassinated by order of the *Palmach* leaders. An inquiry ordered by Ben-Gurion concluded that the shooting was an accident, but this did not altogether clear the tense and suspicious atmosphere.

Day after day, the heads of MAPAM were pressing Ben-Gurion to restore Galili to his old position in the High Command. And reports from various sources all mentioned a lack of discipline among the higher ranks of the military.

When the truce began, Ben-Gurion decided that the time had come to reorganize the Army command. A few days after the proclamation of the State he had accepted the Ministry of Defense, in addition to being Prime Minister. This gave him power to direct the war effort and decide on the immediate aims. Throughout the month of June he prepared the changes he intended to make in the High Command. The promotions and postings were aimed at weakening the hold of those loyal to MAPAM, the leaders of *Palmach* and the supporters of Galili, and at giving military command to as many nonpolitical officers as possible, as well as to officers who were professional soldiers or had considerable military experience.

Ben-Gurion chose his time carefully, knowing his decisions were bound to arouse a storm of protest. He waited until June 29 before informing the High Command. There was violent reaction, a repetition of the revolt of May 6.

"I've had letters from all the members of the 'breakaway' group," Ben-Gurion noted down on July 1, only a week before hostilities were to start again. "Yadin, Galili, Ben-Hur, Ayalon—they have all handed in their resignations and made accusations against the present regime. They all ask me to bring their letters to the notice of the government. Galili has in fact already sent a copy of his to all the ministers, although he wrote on the letter addressed to me 'Personal and Secret!' "

Ben-Gurion immediately sent for Igal Yadin. He had a high regard for this young commander and did not want to lose him at any cost. But Yadin would not budge from his position. Ben-Gurion had to accept the facts and place the matter before the

Government. The thirteen ministers met the following day, and Ben-Gurion attacked at once. "The four letters I've received are a result of us not having accepted the proposals of three people—Galili, Yadin and Ayalon—for the reorganization of the High Command. I did not approve their plan as it appeared to me to be yet another attempt to transform the whole army into the army of a certain party . . ."

He informed the ministers of the changes he proposed to make. "Of the thirteen Brigade commanders that we have, eight are members of MAPAM, three have no political affiliation and two belong to MAPAI . . . " He attacked *Palmach* for its acts of insubordination, made a vehement speech against political interference with the Army, and offered to resign if his changes were not adopted and if Galili was still forced on him. "What this business really amounts to is an attempt at revolt by the army. A war is being waged on me . . . I demand that a committee of three ministers be appointed to examine the matter and draw conclusions . . ."

It was a struggle for power, for control of the Army, a battle between Ben-Gurion and those who questioned his authority and were even capable of ousting him. The risks for Ben-Gurion were great, but by accepting the challenge he added a dramatic element to the situation—there would be either a political army or a national army, an army belonging to MAPAM or to all the people, to Galili or Ben-Gurion.

MAPAM had been attacking Ben-Gurion continually, and a number of detrimental remarks about him were circulating: "Ben-Gurion hates *Palmach,* he's trying to starve it into submission"— "He wants to impose his dictatorship on the army"—"He's set against the MAPAM kibbutzim."

This malicious campaign supplied the sound effects to the struggle for power. The setting was provided by a committee of five ministers which sat to examine the matter. And Ben-Gurion was not to come out of it very well.

The first meeting of the committee was held on July 3, five days before the truce was to end. A general attack was launched on Ben-Gurion. Galili, called to give evidence before the committee, drew a dismal picture of the situation. He maintained that since his removal from the "National Command" there had been almost complete collapse of the army organization, due to lack of effective command. The interventions of Ben-Gurion in military matters were often disastrous. The Chiefs of Staff did not know to whom they were responsible, and there was no coordination between the various branches. The whole organization suffered from an excessive centralization.

Yadin, in his turn, was more restrained than Galili but was equally alarmed. He criticized Ben-Gurion's attitude, his general distrust, the tactics he was employing on the Jerusalem front, and his opinions of *Palmach*—which was a bold and disciplined force.

Nobody succeeded in refuting Ben-Gurion's accusations, but accusations were showered on him by staff officers. The impression given to the committee was that a crisis had broken out between Ben-Gurion and some of the senior officers.

On July 6, 48 hours before hostilities would start up again, Ben-Gurion made a last appearance before the committee. Some of the members conveyed their conclusions to him. The majority favored the appointment of two "directors" to assist Ben-Gurion, of whom one—in all probability Galili—would act as liaison officer between Ben-Gurion and the High Command. In other words, the position of "National Commander" was to be revived!

Ben-Gurion rose and left the meeting. He had been defeated. A few hours later, a letter was delivered to the committee which sent the members into a panic. The Old Man was resigning!

But was it a resignation or an ultimatum? A definite departure or a political maneuver? "I offer my resignation as Prime Minister and Minister of Defense. I am ready to place myself at your disposition as adviser on matters of security, without the right to vote . . . In order that the Government's time should not be wasted, I ask you to put aside your proposals for reorganizing the Defense Ministry, if you wish me to continue at its head. . . ."

The maneuver could not be more obvious. Ben-Gurion, having accepted the principle of a committee to decide on the situation, started to retreat as soon as he saw that the majority did not agree with him. He offered his resignation, but let it be understood that he was prepared to continue if his conditions were accepted, committee or no committee. It was in fact an ultimatum.

By then, only 36 hours remained before the war flared up again. And the man on whom victory depended, when all was said and done, had handed in his resignation.

What was to be done? Ben-Gurion was said to be ill. If his conditions were accepted, there would be an outcry and possibly trouble from the High Command. If they were not, it meant the loss of the creator of the State, the one man capable of leading the country at this decisive time.

The Cabinet meeting was one of indecision and confusion. The ministers protested that their hands were being forced, exclaimed indignantly against Ben-Gurion's dictatorial methods. They blamed him for not being able to work with men who displeased him, fumed against his centralization of power and criticized him for drawing up plans impossible to execute. And then they asked him to continue in power, and threw the committee's proposals into the wastepaper basket!

The most loyal supporter of Ben-Gurion at this meeting appears to have been Shertok, who had changed his name to the Hebrew style, Sharett. He defended Ben-Gurion, comparing him to a volcano which saves everything by erupting but in so doing throws up streams of lava which burn all they touch. Bernstein compared him to "an engine that backfires." The ministers who were members of MAPAM compared him to a dictator.

They all knew well that they could not do without him. Kaplan and the other ministers who belonged to MAPAI took Ben-Gurion's part, and this decided the matter. But it seems that Ben-Gurion could have lost everything at this meeting. Instead, he was victorious, and from then until his retirement in 1963 his authority was never questioned. He was the man sent by Providence, the leader chosen by History, who had to be retained at all costs—even at the cost of unconditional surrender.

That evening, Ben-Gurion agreed to continue. He would have a free hand in the conduct of the war and in transforming the Army. It was the end of revolts and political rebellions.

That evening, too, Galili retired to his kibbutz, bitter and defeated. For him, who had dared to oppose Ben-Gurion, it was the beginning of a long political exile.

And that evening fighting began again on the borders of the Negev. The truce had ended.

The road ahead was clear for Ben-Gurion to turn the Army into a united and nonpolitical force. In August, talks began with the leaders of the *Etzel* and the *Lehi* forces in Jerusalem, with a view to their integration in the national army. Ben-Gurion secretly had prepared a plan for suppressing *Etzel* by force, but there was no need to put it into operation. When mid-September, Count Bernadotte and his French deputy, Colonel Serrault, were assassinated by dissidents in the center of Jerusalem, Ben-Gurion seized the opportunity to put an end to the last of the private armies. Although he knew from reports that Begin's men had definitely had no hand in the crime, he insisted that the *Etzel* forces in the Jerusalem district be disbanded at once.

The last act came at the end of October 1948. The Israeli Army was then 100,000 strong and contained paratroop units and armored brigades, as well as having the support of an air force and a navy. *Palmach* was no longer the only well-trained force. On October 28, by order of Ben-Gurion, the Commander-in-Chief, General Jacob Dori, informed *Palmach* that its staff was to cease forthwith to operate as an independent command. In the future, all its brigades and their commanding officers were to come under the orders of the General Staff.

The MAPAM leaders made a national scandal of the incident. But nevertheless *Palmach* ceased to exist as such. The time for private armies had ended.

The War of Independence consolidated the State of Israel, wiped out the past and brought into being a regular, national army that was free of politics.

TWENTY-ONE

VICTORY

Ben-Gurion won his greatest victory during that first week of July, 1948, when a state of truce was in force. And this turning point in his career was also the turning point of the whole war. "After June 11, when the first truce began," wrote Ben-Gurion later, "the initiative passed to us." From then until the end of the war the Jews dictated the course of events, and the battles which took place in July showed that the fortunes of war had definitely changed sides.

During the truce the Jews had successfully hoodwinked the United Nations observers. Several ships from France and Italy had secretly landed hundreds of tons of war material in Israel. A large number of immigrants had found ways and means of slipping through the net which was strung to prevent any additions to the Jewish population during the truce. New brigades had been formed, equipped and trained in feverish haste, and squadrons of fighters and bombers were manned by volunteers who had come from all parts of the world. When the truce ended, the Israeli armed forces were much stronger than before and could go over to the attack.

The Jews no longer would be fighting a defensive war. In Ben-Gurion's hands, the Army was transformed into an offensive force whose aim was to extend Israel's frontiers. Ben-Gurion still clung to his method of *faits accomplis*. He had a ready answer to the proposals of United Nations missions and other mediators—the positions of the Israeli Army marked the real frontiers of the State.

The original partition plan, which gave the Jews much of the Negev, the coastal plain and eastern Galilee, was only the starting-point of Ben-Gurion's territorial policy. He wanted the rest of Galilee, to extend the coastal plain as far as the Jordan, to have Jerusalem as the capital, and to include the Judaean hills overlooking the Dead Sea. He would also have liked the rest of the Negev and the town of Gaza, which the Egyptians were using as a base for their invasion forces.

However, his policy was very flexible. He was prepared to renounce territorial gains if he could be assured of lasting peace with the Arabs. In any case, he had no wish to conquer areas which contained large Arab populations. He did all he could to persuade the Arabs not to return to areas already occupied by Israeli forces.

Another guiding principle concerned Great Britain—on no account were Israeli troops to clash with the British forces stationed in Egypt, and which were ready to aid Jordan under a defense agreement. Several of Ben-Gurion's plans, which might have given a different aspect to the Middle East, were abandoned as soon as there appeared any danger of British intervention.

The only country to support Jewish territorial designs at that time was Russia. The Kremlin wished to establish a claim to British preserves in the Middle East.

But President Truman was another friend. He had assured the Jews that America would strongly support the partition plan and would recognize the State of Israel as soon as possible. But foreign policy was not entirely in the President's hands, and the State Department was against partition from the outset. Truman sent James MacDonald, who was sympathetic to the Jewish cause, as Ambassador to Israel. But the State Department gave him a deputy, Knox, a gloomy busybody who acted as watchdog.

The British, whose attitude to the new state was openly hostile, sent no one. They had hoped that the United Nations would freely offer to extend their mandate over Palestine, and instead had found themselves with a nascent Jewish state on their hands. They had hoped that the Jews, scared by the Arab threat of extermination, would implore them to stay and give protection. They were now backing the Arabs, hoping that the invasion of Israel would eventually enable them to have the Middle East bases that they wanted.

The French did not want bases, but they appeared to be playing a double game. They secretly sent arms to Israel, allowed transit-camps to be set up on their territory, and ignored the fact that the airport at Ajaccio was being used by planes carrying suspicious loads to Israel. But at the government level Georges Bidault refused to recognize Israel, in spite of pressure by the Socialists, whose spokesman in this matter was André Philip. It was the Roman Catholics, alarmed by the destruction and requisitioning of their mission stations in Palestine, who were behind the refusal and the continual rebuff of Israeli overtures. The tone of French communications was often biting. At a Cabinet meeting on May 30 Sharett raised the matter of relations with France, referring to a letter he had recently received from the French Government and addressed to "The Jewish Authorities." Ben-Gurion said angrily: "If France wishes to write to us, she must address us as 'The Israeli Government.' The French Consul who delivered the letter cannot claim to be French Consul at Tel Aviv if he does not recognize the Government in Tel Aviv. If he wants something, he should know who to apply to. If he applies to the Prime Minister of Israel, I will receive him, but if he applies to Ben-Gurion I'll talk to him about the weather. 'Monsieur Sharett' is not the way to address this letter —it should be addressed to the Minister for Foreign Affairs. I refuse to reply to this letter. The French Parliament has passed a quite explicit resolution about us, and Bidault refuses to implement it. This might well bring about a conflict of opinion in France; we'll see whether Bidault dare risk it . . ."

But these were merely side issues. Ben-Gurion was concentrating on the war, and diplomacy was not his strong point. "When I'm engaged in war, I'm not interested in politics," he said more than once.

When the truce ended on July 9 he launched attacks on all fronts. But these battles came to a halt after ten days, when a second truce, of indefinite length, was declared. However, those ten days were enough to change the military situation completely. The Jews threw back the Egyptians advancing in the south, held the Syrians on the line of the Jordan and put Kaukji's forces to flight. Central Galilee was occupied, as well as a number of towns and villages on the eastern front. Lydda Airport was captured with the help of two Cromwell tanks that *Haganah* had stolen from the British a few hours before they evacuated the country.

An even more remarkable exploit was that of a young commando leader, Moshe Dayan, who later won renown in the Sinai Campaign. An attempt to take the twin towns of Lydda and Ramleh had been unsuccessful, when he arrived on the scene with a column of jeeps and drove straight down the main road and into the towns without waiting for orders. The Arabs were so taken aback by the "mad Jews" that they surrendered without a fight. In 37 minutes the two towns were captured!

An attack was mounted against Nazareth and the Old City of Jerusalem. Ben-Gurion gave strict orders that any Jewish soldier found desecrating the holy places was to be executed immediately. Nazareth soon fell, but only small forces were sent against Jerusalem and were easily repulsed by the Arabs. The cause of this setback, in Ben-Gurion's opinion, was the incompetence of David

Shaltiel, commanding the Jerusalem front. The fact remained that old Jerusalem was lost to the Jews. The Arabs held Latroun too, in spite of repeated attacks on that strong position. Egyptian forces occupied the northern half of the Negev, though they were being contained by the Israelis. The southern half was completely empty, without the presence of a single Jew to claim his country's right to the territory.

Such was the situation when the second truce was declared, which the United Nations and the great Powers intended should last until the official end of the war. On July 18 Ben-Gurion wrote: "Even if the front lines are in our favor at the moment of the truce being declared, this does not mean that we shall be allowed to retain the occupied territories, for now a diplomatic battle is about to begin. If, on the other hand, the front lines are favorable to the Arabs it is almost certain that they will be allowed to keep the territory they hold. So what happens during the truce is of the greatest importance."

The diplomatic battle began with Count Bernadotte putting his proposals for a settlement before the Israelis and the Arabs. They were: the return of the Arab refugees, an economic and political Judaeo-Arab union, the Jews to lose part of the Negev in return for western Galilee; and Jerusalem to be held by the Arabs, but with a certain autonomy for the 100,000 Jews living in the city.

Ben-Gurion and his ministers met to discuss the proposals. Sharett was prepared to accept an international status for Jerusalem provided the Jews were given a corridor linking the city with their state. He was definitely opposed to the return of the Arab refugees, but was attracted by the idea of exchanging the stony Negev desert for the wooded hillsides of Galilee.

Ben-Gurion blew up once again. Under no conditions would he give up the Negev, the Dead Sea and access to the Red Sea. With a wide gesture he swept aside the arguments of experts who maintained that the Negev was not even habitable. He insisted on Jewish Jerusalem becoming part of the State of Israel. As for the Arab refugees, "We must do everything to ensure that they never do return!"

Engineer units started to destroy abandoned Arab villages situated at strategic points. In August, the United States threatened to apply sanctions against Israel if the Arab refugees were not allowed to return to their homes. But Ben-Gurion had only one thing in his mind—the military preparations to extend the frontiers, to seize the Negev and the rest of Galilee and to obtain access to Jerusalem. Nothing could turn him from these plans. He knew that time was not on his side, and that once calm was restored the clauses of an armistice or a peace treaty would be the reproduction on paper of the front lines when the truce began. He had to strike quickly. The matter was to come before the Security Council of the United Nations in the second half of September, and that was the time, the military and the diplomats agreed, for the Israeli attack—the Americans would then be presiding and could prevent a too-severe resolution from being passed against their protégés, and the presidential elections in the United States would be too imminent for Truman to risk offending the Jewish electorate.

Ben-Gurion refused to accept the Bernadotte proposals, but they became a kind of creed of the whole of the United Nations after September 16, 1948. On that day, Count Bernadotte was assassinated. His proposals were then regarded as a political testament, the last wishes of the United Nations' first martyr. Ben-Gurion remained unmoved. At dawn on October 16, after a violation of the truce by Egyptian forces, the Israeli Army launched an attack to the south. The war had started up again.

The decision to reopen the fighting, with the risk of being treated as an aggressor, had not been taken lightly. In order to obtain agreement to it, Ben-Gurion had a hard struggle with his close associates and even with members of his own party.

Jerusalem, destined to become the capital of the "Third Kingdom of Israel," haunted Ben-Gurion's dreams and dominated his military plans. While the heights of Latroun were still held by the Arabs, Jerusalem could be brought within the Jewish state only by the capture of a large area. Ben-Gurion studied his war map— if access to Jerusalem could not be widened from the north, then let it be from the south. The area occupied by the Arab Legion extended across the Jordan, south of Jerusalem, and formed an enclave in the territory assigned to the Jews. It touched the border of the Negev in the south and reached the mountains of Judaea in the north; the chief town was Hebron. If this pocket could be eliminated and the area brought within the State of Israel, then the whole military strategy and political attitude of the Jews would be changed. Jerusalem would be isolated and soon fall to the Israeli forces, who could then occupy the heights overlooking the plain of Jericho. And the junction between the Egyptians in the Negev and the Jordanians would be cut.

The Israeli staff officers drew up a plan of attack in great secrecy. In their opinion, the objective required only ten days. A pretext for the offensive had to be found, but one was soon forthcoming—the Arab Legion had just blown up the water pumps at Latroun, contrary to the clauses of the truce. So an attack would be launched on Latroun and the offensive widened to include the whole of the pocket.

On September 26 Ben-Gurion put this plan of attack before the Cabinet. All went well at first. He obtained agreement on incorporating the Jewish part of Jerusalem into the State territory by stages. But the majority of ministers was against breaking the truce and attacking the Hebron pocket. Ben-Gurion commented in his diary: "The plan has been dropped. Fortunately for us, most of the offensives we've launched this year were not put to the vote of that lot!" From now on, Ben-Gurion was to qualify this vote as a reason for "wailing for generations."

His next plan was to attack the Egyptians and throw them out of the Negev. He was almost certain that the other Arab armies would remain in their positions and not support the Egyptians. In any case, the attack was becoming urgent. The American presidential elections were to be held in a few weeks. Any day, some precipitated move might result in the United Nations adopting several disastrous clauses of the Bernadotte plan. On October 5, having learned from his recent experience, Ben-Gurion first held a meeting of the MAPAI leaders and made sure of their support. On the following day he called a conference of Army staff officers and with them drew up a plan of attack. The fact that the Egyptians were preventing supplies from reaching the Israeli units in the Negev, which was contrary to clauses in the truce agreement, would serve as an excuse for the attack. That evening, Ben-Gurion raised the subject in the Cabinet. There followed a long and laborious discussion, but in the end all went well. Only Kaplan, of the MAPAI ministers, abstained. Remez, who had been against Ben-Gurion's plan at the party meeting, surprisingly spoke strongly in support of it. When a vote was taken it went in Ben-Gurion's favor, with one condition—Sharett, the Foreign Minister, who was away in Europe, had to be consulted. A cable was sent to him, and his reply arrived the following day. He agreed. The date of the offensive was fixed for the following Thursday, and a strong striking force of armor, artillery and motorized infantry was assembled. "We have just made the gravest decision since the proclamation of the State," wrote Ben-Gurion.

By October 15 all was ready. A supply column was sent south and the Egyptians obligingly opened fire on it. All along the southern front, the Israeli Army sprang into action. Operation Joab, or Ten Sores, had begun.

Although the advance was rapid, Ben-Gurion kept on harassing his generals to move faster. The United Nations had reacted swiftly, and all manner of pretexts had to be found for delaying the order to stop the fighting. The Egyptians were resisting strongly, and in some places the Israeli attacks had been thrown back. But, as Ben-Gurion had predicted, the other Arab armies took no action. In order not to provoke them, he called off an attack south of Jerusalem which had been planned by Dayan, although it had received the approval of the majority of the High Command.

The Jordanian forces had been given strict orders to observe the truce and refrain from any offensive action. On October 21 the Jews captured the capital of the Negev, the biblical town of Beersheba whose seven wells had provided water for Abraham's flock of sheep.

The tiny Israeli Navy had a great success off Gaza, where it sank the Egyptian flagship. On land, the Egyptians regrouped their forces, abandoning a number of strategic positions. But three days later the Israeli forces started a pincer movement from the south which developed into a spectacular tactical success. It ended with the bulk of the Egyptian expeditionary corps being encircled and contained within the "Falouja pocket," cut off from its lines of communication.

Sharett sent long enthusiastic cables from Paris. Celebrating crowds in Tel Aviv proclaimed Ben-Gurion "King of Israel."

The "King" saw the success in the Negev as a springboard for new offensives. He wanted to press home the attack and wipe out the Falouja pocket. At the same time he prepared to strike at the Iraqi forces on the central front, where they had penetrated into Israeli territory and were holding a triangular area which could be used as a base for an offensive to cut the country in two. However, he waited to see the international reactions to his offensive in the Negev.

The first sign was that, on Truman's orders, the Americans on the Security Council blocked an anti-Israel resolution by the British and the Chinese Nationalists. But the United Nations firmly requested the Israeli Government to withdraw its forces from Falouja and the Negev and to allow the Egyptians to install a governor in Beersheba. The Israeli Government refused.

At the United Nations, the sympathy for the 700,000 Jews courageously facing 27,000,000 Arabs turned to hostility when the Jews were no longer fighting to survive but to conquer new territory. Finally, the order was given to the Jews to withdraw immediately from the territory they had overrun in the Negev.

The Israeli Government met urgently and decided to refuse to withdraw. Would sanctions be applied? Truman, who had just been reelected President, told the Paris chief of the American secret service in a telephone conversation that he was opposed to sanctions. Secretary of State Marshall was furious and threatened to resign.

Ben-Gurion not only refused to withdraw from the Negev, he gave orders for another attack against the Falouja pocket. At the same time, other Israeli units advanced eastward and opened the road to the Dead Sea.

The situation in Galilee had been determined by military action. In the Negev too military action was to be the decisive factor, though other influences had their part. The Jerusalem situation, however, was dependent upon political and religious factors. For these reasons, Ben-Gurion did not renew attacks on the city. He might have captured it, but knowing the susceptibilities of the Western world he preferred the partition of the Holy City to the danger of being summarily ordered to withdraw from the whole of it. He gradually transferred government services to the new town, while repeatedly declaring that Israel had no intention of incorporating it within the State. Previously he had annulled the government's decision in favor of Jerusalem being an international city. His plan was gradually to install the capital of his country in the ancient capital of the Kingdom of Israel. He was walking a tightrope and a false step could have grave consequences.

A new road for vehicles was built, to link Jerusalem with Israeli territory by avoiding Arab-held areas as much as possible. To have captured the whole of Jerusalem would have been to defy the United Nations. But a Jerusalem divided into Jewish and Arab towns, based on an agreement between the two sides, was likely to be more acceptable—and the Jews would not be the only ones to brave United Nations' resolutions.

The stormy sessions at the United Nations did not deter Ben-Gurion from advancing several pawns on several boards at once. The fighting in the Negev continued; peace talks were begun in Jerusalem between Moshe Dayan and Colonel Abdullah Tal of Jordan; *Palmach* was disbanded. In the diplomatic field, Ben-Gurion attended a gala performance at the Tel Aviv Opera House with the Soviet ambassador on his left and the American ambassador, James MacDonald, on his right.

Ten days later, however, a grave situation arose between the United States and Israel. A new offensive had been launched against the Egyptians, but this time both Ben-Gurion and the Israeli forces went too far.

Operation *Horev* began on December 22, with the objectives of clearing the Egyptians from Israeli territory and capturing Gaza. The advance did not go according to plan at first. Torrential rain turned the Negev Desert into a field of mud, and Israeli armor and motorized infantry got bogged down in front of the Falouja defenses. A decision was made to attempt another pincer movement and to seize the Gaza Strip, in other words to mount an offensive in the direction of the Sinai Peninsula, which was Egyptian territory. The Israeli forces made a headlong advance and by December 29 were across the frontier. The Egyptians, taken by surprise, fled in disorder. Abu Ageila fell to the Israeli spearhead, and the following day the important military base of El Arish was reached. Igal Alon, the Israeli commander, was sure of victory. Ben-Gurion, who had allowed himself a short rest by the shores of Lake Tiberias, was kept informed hourly of the progress of operations.

At four in the afternoon of December 31, Foreign Minister Sharett was on the phone with Ben-Gurion. James MacDonald had called to inform him of a note from the United States Government, as the British were threatening to apply the clauses of a defense treaty with Egypt, dating from 1936, if the Israeli forces did not at once withdraw from Egyptian territory.

Sharett asked Ben-Gurion if he should order the Army to withdraw. "Before doing that," said Ben-Gurion, "get confirmation from Yadin that withdrawal will not weaken the chances of taking Gaza."

A few minutes later, Sharett was on the line again. "I've spoken to Yadin and Dori, and they believe it's all right to withdraw."

Ben-Gurion at once gave orders to evacuate the Sinai Peninsula. His orders were: "Immediate withdrawal. Destroy everything before leaving. Step up the attacks on Gaza and the Falouja pocket." At any moment, the British might attack the Israeli forces.

At eleven that evening, New Year's Eve in fact, James MacDonald and Knox arrived at Tiberias to see Ben-Gurion. MacDonald took a sheet of paper from his briefcase and read out to the Israeli Prime Minister:

"I have been instructed by the President of the United States to see you and inform you of the following circumstances.

"My Government has received a report from an authorized source that Israeli armed forces have invaded Egyptian territory after a premeditated attack.

"The British Government has informed my Government that it takes a serious view of the situation, and that if the Israeli forces do not withdraw from Egyptian territory the British Government will be obliged, in virtue of the 1936 treaty, to take action to carry out its obligations.

"The United States Government, which was the first to recognize the State of Israel and which is supporting its application to join the United Nations, wishes to draw the attention of the Israeli Government to the fact that its attitude could endanger peace in the Middle East. The United States Government would have to re-examine its attitude with regard to the Israeli Government's application to join the United Nations, which is presented as the application of a 'peace-loving' nation, and would also have to re-examine the character of its relations with the State of Israel.

"As proof of the peaceful intentions of the Israeli Government, and in order to avoid an extension of the conflict, it seems that the minimum requirement is for the Israeli armed forces to withdraw immediately from Egyptian territory.

"While awaiting a full reply from the Israeli Government the press will not be informed."

Ben-Gurion bitterly informed MacDonald that the order to withdraw had already been given. He protested against the attitude of the British Government and emphasized that it was not Israel, a "peace-loving" nation, who had violated peace and order in Palestine.

While a satisfied Knox was composing the cable to send to Washington, Ben-Gurion privately expressed to MacDonald his surprise at the firm, blunt tone of the American note. "Was it necessary for a great Power to address a small and weak State in such a manner?" MacDonald said that he too was surprised. It was obvious that the British had put considerable pressure on President Truman.

Britain and the United States had stopped Ben-Gurion, and Gaza was not captured. But a week after that dramatic New Year's Eve, the Egyptians collapsed. On January 7, 1949, the strongest of the Arab countries asked the Israeli Government for an immediate cessation of hostilities and for armistice talks to be opened.

The final fighting had almost led to the flare-up with Britain which had been so much on Ben-Gurion's mind. A few hours before the cease-fire, several unknown aircraft flew over the battle area. The Israeli ack-ack opened fire and shot down five—they were British planes. Was this to be a pretext for British intervention? Ben-Gurion anxiously hurried back to Tel Aviv from Tiberias to obtain the full details. The reports which came in were reassuring. The planes had crashed in Israeli territory, so the action had been legitimate. The British Government was obliged to explain the violation to the Americans, and was attacked at home for its intervention.

The King of Jordan and Colonel Tal, in his talks with Dayan, were claiming possession of southern Negev, saying that their troops occupied the area and that Jewish soldiers had not reached the Gulf of Aqaba.

Again—and for the last time in this War of Independence—Ben-Gurion acted in his own inimitable way. He launched Operation *Fait Accompli,* aimed at occupying the whole of the Negev. The code name had the stamp of Ben-Gurion. On March 10, after a lightning dash across the desert, Israeli forces entered Eilath (at the head of the Gulf of Aqaba) without a fight. The Jordanians had withdrawn before the Jewish advance. The British had not intervened. The whole of the Negev, except for the Gaza Strip, was in the hands of the Jews.

The Egyptians had already signed an armistice on February 24, at Rhodes. A month later, Lebanon, happy at getting back 14 villages, also signed. And on April 3 the Jordanian representatives, after an agreement had been reached, added their signatures. The last to admit defeat were the Syrians. Iraq, which had no common frontier with Israel, spared herself this humiliation.

Israel had won the war, had obtained all the territories conquered by her army—Galilee, the Negev and part of Jerusalem. Ben-Gurion's *faits accomplis* had prevailed over United Nations' resolutions.

The elections for a constituent asembly at the end of the winter had given his party more than a third of the seats. On March 10, at Jerusalem, Ben-Gurion presented his new government to the Knesset.

TWENTY-TWO

WHAT ARE YOU, BEN-GURION?

David Ben-Gurion, the Prime Minister and Defense Minister of the State of Israel, was 62 years old. He was probably the only man in the world who could justly boast of being the father of an army and a nation. He was a living legend, admired and detested, feared and respected, acknowledged by both supporters and opponents to be like some natural force.

What an odd phenomenon is this man who washes the dishes after dinner to save Paula the trouble; who never shows his feelings, but falls ill every time he has to take a decision on which depend the lives of thousands; who implacably launches wave after wave of soldiers to attack an impregnable fortress, and afterwards sends very tender letters, written in anguish, to the parents of the fallen; who does not fear to employ extreme measures when he believes his people are in danger; who can remain unmoved in the presence of an important diplomat but is enchanted by a magician's show; who is a prophet, but a prophet armed with a slide rule. And a man who, despite his love for the Hebrew language, the Bible and Judaism, remains a stranger to his people . . .

He is a small man, upright and firm on his feet, with a fine head expressing strength and willpower. His thin hair is snow-white, and he has lively, sparkling eyes, a thick nose and a thin-lipped mouth. A lion, a rock, tiger, prophet, wrestler . . . his friends and enemies have sought many comparisons over the years. Back in 1931, at Basel, a journalist said of him, "He's Danton and Beethoven in one!"

When relaxed his crafty eyes flash, his mouth smiles and his hands flutter and gesture all the time. He has a sharp, high-pitched voice, broken by little coughs now and again. When speaking at some working session his voice seems tired, but then it suddenly livens, the words spurt forth, accompanied by thumps on the table.

He invariably emphasizes the last word or last part of a sentence; his words never flow gently. He does not know how to talk entertainingly, but he animates what he says. For instance, when telling of his encounter with an Arab brigand during his early years at Sejera his face lights up and he acts the whole scene.

In the summer he usually wears an open-neck white shirt, in the winter a dark suit. After attending a brilliant reception given by the Soviet ambassador towards the end of 1948, he felt most uncomfortable in his dress suit and tails. "You must excuse me, comrades," he said, "but I'm in working clothes."

His giddy rise from the hungry farm laborer at Petah Tikva to the position of Prime Minister and all-powerful leader of the State of Israel had in no way changed his character. He avoided honors, detested ceremonial occasions—it would anger him to learn that a colony of new immigrants had given his name to a street of their village.

His tastes remained simple and almost ascetic. Paula was there to see that the stove in his room was kept burning during the damp winter, to run after him with a scarf, and even to interrupt a Cabinet meeting or an Army staff conference to give him a hot drink or some fruit. She was much better than her husband at judging people, and was disconcertingly frank. Her opinions, though formed in a matter of seconds, often proved to be right. It was not unknown for her to rush out of the Prime Minister's official residence, broom in hand, to chase away children whose shouting was disturbing the siesta of her "great man." And when she decided that "Ben-Gurion," as she called her husband, needed rest, even generals, ambassadors and ministers had to give way to her. Years later, when Ben-Gurion was over seventy, he still wrote love letters to his faithful companion.

Although Ben-Gurion can write well and movingly, he cannot express his feelings in direct personal encounters when it comes to love, friendship, human warmth. His relations with his children and grandchildren suffer from a certain remoteness. He rarely sees his brothers and sisters who emigrated to Israel. One of his brothers, Michael, had a soft-drink stand for several years under the acacias along the Boulevard Nordau in Tel Aviv, and was a complete outsider to the elder's rapid career. "David was always crazy," he would tell his customers. "Besides, at Plonsk, I was thought to be the more brilliant. . . ."

It is easier to admire than to love Ben-Gurion. He has had only four real friends in his long life—Berl Katznelson, Shmuel Yavnieli

Itzhak Ben-Zvi, and Nhemia Argov, military secretary to the Prime Minister. Nhemia was a small man too, young, intelligent, sensitive, and devoted to Ben-Gurion who spoke freely in front of him. And Nhemia listened, never turning the monologue into a dialogue. He could not have made a reply, for his art was in being a good listener, in carrying out orders, keeping quiet and loving. Loving to the point of being jealous.

Ben-Gurion's enemies were legion, on the Left and on the Right, at home and abroad. The late leaders of *Etzel* and *Lehi,* the spiritual heads of *Palmach* and some leaders of his own party never forgave him for having succeeded where they had failed or had made mistakes.

He, too, could hate with tenacity and passion, right to the end. His hatred for *Etzel* and its leader, Begin, had been enduring. He waged a holy war against these men by keeping them out of all positions of command. He was convinced that his way was the right way and was implacably opposed to all those who dared to block his path. In 1948 he stood out against the nomination as President of the Knesset of his old associate, Joseph Shprinzak. Ben-Gurion had never forgiven him for being opposed to the creation of the State. For similar reasons, Ben-Gurion was against Weizmann being elected President of the State. Ben-Gurion had probably been right to decide that the Declaration of Independence should be signed only by Jewish leaders actually in Israel on that May 14, but his attitude to Weizmann savored of revenge.

He never forgives, never forgets. To him, men are either good or bad, white or black, to be trusted or distrusted. Once he puts his trust in someone, he will not refuse that person anything—until he finds he has been mistaken. And, unfortunately, he has always been a poor judge of character and often mistaken in his choice of associates.

Nevertheless, Ben-Gurion has not persecuted his opponents simply because they disagreed with him. He did not break Galili until a choice had to be made between them. He did not force Sharett to resign, despite their many differences of opinion and opposing policies. Nor did he take revenge on the five generals who had dared to rebel against him at one of the most dramatic moments in the history of Israel. In fact he even later chose Igal Yadin, who had been among the rebellious generals on two occasions, to be his successor.

Ben-Gurion can be hard even on his best friends. For his enemies, he is a ruthless opponent, a man who can drive them out of their minds, who humiliates and insults them. At the end of verbal battles which might have lasted days or even weeks, when each side is worn out and lays down its arms, rarely can anyone remember the exact moment when Ben-Gurion set the discussion alight and sidetracked the real issue between himself and the opposition.

His aggressiveness is legendary. "You must always distinguish between essentials and trifles," he once said. He has applied this principle excellently in pursuing his policies and conducting his campaigns, but has failed to do so in this personal battles. He has often attacked an insignificant opponent with as much fury as he directed against his greatest enemies. He has poured out articles, hurtful, biting, slashing articles, with equal rage and fury whatever the subject. Perhaps it is because he loves a fight, or because he never feels any contempt for his adversary.

Although capable of descending from his Olympus to crush an ant, he has a very thick skin. No attack or insults ever really harm him. He returns blow for blow without ever feeling their effect himself.

Other great men have had their recreations and hobbies. Not Ben-Gurion. The books he reads are all connected with his work. He has not been to a movie for twenty years, and the theater and the arts have never interested him.

He has read all he could find about Palestine, the history of the Jews, the civilizations and religions of the world. He has delved into the literature of ancient Greece, studied numerous works on political science, military theory, philosophy and theosophy. In later years he embarked on a new subject—biology and natural science. All the time he was an avid reader of the Bible and the Talmud, and became an authority in all fields of Judaism. He constantly added new books to the thousands lining the walls of several rooms of his house at Tel Aviv. This private library is now one of the finest collections of books in the Middle East.

One morning in 1940 Ben-Gurion left by car for Haifa. With him was a boy of seventeen, proud of having been invited to accompany the great man, already a legendary figure. It was the first time he had been alone with Ben-Gurion, and he kept silent. Ben-Gurion, full of his own thoughts, did not even look at the boy. But suddenly he said: "You know, Trotsky was not a statesman. At Brest-Litovsk he declared 'Neither war nor peace.' It wasn't a good thing to say. He ought to have made a decision one way or the other—war or peace. He was not like Lenin, who called for peace.

But then Trotsky was not a true Russian, he was a Jew; he was not a statesman. He did not understand, he hadn't grasped the deep truths of Soviet Russia. . . ."

The astonished young man, who was Shimon Peres, made a mental note of every word and later thought deeply about them. "Those few sentences give the key to Ben-Gurion's character," he said many years later, when he had become one of the prominent figures in Israel and was Ben-Gurion's deputy at the Ministry of Defense. "They show his liking for the trenchant decision and reveal his nonconformity. I saw him, even then, as a man who does not accept secondhand ideas, even if they come from the great and famous."

Another characteristic revealed by that tale is Ben-Gurion's continuity of thought in all circumstances. He reflects over a particular matter, examines it from all angles. Although he sometimes consults his associates and advisers and asks for their opinions, he never draws his own conclusions from the ideas and advice given. He is a lone thinker and decides alone. His best counselor is himself. Enclosed within four walls, he thinks things out at length, puts his ideas on paper, walks up and down the room with short, quick steps. At such times he is tense and peevish. Once his decision is made, nothing can shake him from it. Then he relaxes, smiles and becomes calm again.

Over the years he has trained himself to examine fully every possible outcome of an action he wishes to embark upon, to think all around it and sum up with calculating shrewdness. He tackles a problem by paring it down, like peeling the leaves off an artichoke. He has never hesitated, when necessary, to make a complete about-face, to change his political tactics if the situation seemed to demand it. Until 1939 he had always opposed illegal immigration into Palestine and had rejected the views of extremists such as Jabotinsky who wanted to use armed force to achieve independence. But after the St. James's Conference he went on the other tack, supported illegal immigration and declared war on the British, using the same terms as his opponents. The greatness of a statesman resides not only in his ability to produce some magic formula, but in knowing the right moment to use it.

Ben-Gurion has often shown courage verging on folly, but his action has always been based on a cool calculation of the consequences. His opponents maintained that when he made the lone decision to establish the State he was taking a chance and luck was with him. To this, he simply replied: "I thought we could stand up to the Arabs."

It is noticeable that over the years there has been a constant change in his teammates, that his associates have dropped by the wayside after a time, and others have accompanied him for a while until they, too, have had to stop, gasping for breath. His early companions in his Sejera days have, for the most part, stayed in agriculture and community life. The men who formed *Histadrut* with him have remained immersed in the trade-union movement. His Left-wing associates continued to follow the idea of an international mandate in Palestine, and the leaders of *Haganah* and *Palmach* stayed in the background when he created the national army. He alone has forged ahead, drawing friends and associates in his train but at a pace that proved too fast for them. In such circumstances it was almost inevitable that he should be accused of treading on corpses. It was the objectives, not the men, that mattered: he was not battling for men, but for history.

"Dictator," "Autocrat," "Utter tyrant" . . . Such accusations were showered on him from all sides. And indeed, by his liking for concentrating power in his own hands, by his grim determination to have his decisions accepted, Ben-Gurion does seem to have been inclined to dictatorship. However, it is an illusion that he was ever a dictator. He has an innate sense of democracy, and while it is true that when he wanted something done he employed every means to impose his views, he never went beyond the limits of legality. When, in a time of crisis, one of his close associates suggested setting up a military dictatorship, he not only refused but excluded the man from his circle. He always submitted to the decisions of the majority, though with bad grace, and would return to the attack as soon as an opportunity occurred. And he nearly always succeeded in getting his views adopted. Whenever he opened a debate in the Cabinet, the majority almost automatically took his side. This was not dictatorship, but rather an example of what happens to democracy in the hands of a man of strong personality.

He has often been capable of exercising an almost irresistible charm, and, deliberately or not, of putting a spell over his opponents. "I'm scared of going to see him," confided one of his political enemies. "On leaving, I always have the feeling that I've been possessed . . ."

Ben-Gurion once said to Haïm Guri, one of Israel's finest poets and a *Palmach* officer: "We've freed a vast amount of territory, much more than we had hoped. We've work for two or three generations now. After that, we'll see . . ."

These remarks are characteristic of him. Some Israeli Army officers accused him of lacking the courage to occupy the whole of

Palestine. But he had good reasons for calling a halt to a campaign which was looked upon with increasing disfavor abroad. The risk of foreign intervention, particularly British, became greater each day. Ben-Gurion was also worried by the presence of hundreds of thousands of Arabs in the areas which remained to be conquered. Not that he has any sentimental feelings about the Arabs; he had no hesitations over ordering the destruction of their villages and the turning back of the trickle of refugees trying to return to their homes when the fighting had ceased. Nevertheless, at meetings of specialists on Arab affairs he was the most ardent defender of their right to vote and to take part in the democratic life of the country. The moral and human principles which guided him had also caused him to refrain from provoking massacres of the innocent.

His attitude towards the Arabs was rather unusual—apart from his short flirtation with Moussa Alami, he had had practically no relations with their leaders. Some of his associates, Sharett for instance, had lived among them for some time and had won their confidence. But in Ben-Gurion's world, in his State, there was no place for Arabs. He never made speeches exalting the friendship and the common interests of Jews and Arabs. He wished for peace, for an alliance between the Jewish and the Arab states, but no more than that.

He feared a revival of Arab attacks. "Let us face realities," he said at a conference of the Army commanders after the end of the War of Independence. "We have beaten the Arabs, but are they likely to forget it? Seven hundred thousand men have beaten thirty million Arabs. Are they going to take that insult? They must certainly have some self-esteem. We shall try to bring peace, but two are needed to make peace. Let's be frank—it wasn't because we were able to perform miracles that we won, but because the Arab armies are rotten. What will happen to us if an Arab Mustapha Kemal makes an appearance one of these days?"

Such a redoubtable leader already existed, in the person of Captain Nasser.

The duel with Nasser, the final battle with Weizmann, the tussle with Sharett and the struggle against giant Russia—these were still awaiting Ben-Gurion after the end of the War of Independence.

He had gotten his State. Now it was up to him to prove that the accursed seed of the Wandering Jew could bring forth a nation.

TWENTY-THREE

THE UNITED NATIONS DEFIED

"I am following the activities of the young government very closely, and although several of the measures it has taken seem rather amateurish, in general it is doing well in very difficult circumstances. Ben-Gurion, as Prime Minister and Defense Minister, has had great success. He reminds me of Winston Churchill, who is good in time of war but not so good in time of peace. He is very deliberate, calm and determined, and endowed with great boldness . . ."

This was Weizmann's evaluation in October 1948. And it might have proven accurate had the State of Israel been like any other state, and had the end of the war meant the beginning of peace. But Israel's neighbors had by no means renounced intentions of wiping her off the map at the earliest opportunity. The humbled Arab armies and the defeated kings, the swarms of refugees, were all thinking of revenge. For many years to come, Israel would live sword in hand—hated, alone, awaiting the next onslaught. She would have to justify her existence, forge the people into a state, absorb thousands of Jews from all parts of the world, and reestablish the ancient realm to which she claimed to be heir. The War of Independence, that defiance of the Arab world, was only a small part of the whole challenge to history contained in the advent of the Jewish state.

The period following the War of Independence was the time of a glorious epic—"the gathering in of the exiles." They came from the four quarters of the world, 700,000 of them in four years, thereby doubling the Jewish population of the new state. They came from DP camps in Germany, from Morocco and Tripolitania, from the far corners of India and South Africa, from villages in Poland, Romania, Bulgaria, Persia, Turkey . . . Ships and planes by the hundreds spilled out multitudes of Jews speaking dozens of different languages—dark Jews, fair Jews, some with blue eyes and others with almost black skins; distinguished scholars from the West and whole tribes which had emerged from medieval strongholds of the East. "Operation Babylon" brought Jews from Iraq by air, while "Operation Flying Carpet" lifted tens of thousands of Jews from the Yemen. In America and Europe, university chairs were vacated and research institutes lost their directors; engineers and tradespeople, jewelers, cobblers, all converged on the Holy Land by various means and from various places.

Israel had to absorb them all, then change their outlook and ways of thought. Tradespeople and clerks had to become pioneers and farm laborers, members of the middle classes found themselves in collective settlements. This modern Tower of Babel had to be replaced by a new structure founded on the Hebrew language. Eastern or Western traditions and national customs had to give way to an Israeli way of life. This could not be done overnight.

These early years saw a period of austerity, with severe rationing and heavy taxes. Protests rose from all sides—immigration must be slowed down to prevent famine and economic disaster. But Ben-Gurion stuck to his policy of "the return to Zion" against the advice of his committee of experts, in spite of the outcry of financial specialists and against all logic. His view was that Israel had been created with the one aim of receiving all the Jews in the world and giving them a homeland.

Everyone in the land had to take part in the struggle. These hard years were also the most heroic. Many new villages sprang up in the desert, on the hillsides and amidst the bare countryside. Rows of government housing appeared around the large towns, for giving a roof to new arrivals was more important than preserving the beauty of the countryside. Factories were built and new industries created. When Ben-Gurion was told that, according to experts, the Negev was uninhabitable and that nothing would grow there, he angrily exclaimed: "And who are these so-called experts? An expert is a man who has tried to grow something once, twice, three times, four times, and finally succeeds. Having succeeded, he's an expert; if he doesn't succeed, he isn't an expert, because he still hasn't found the right way of doing it."

These early years of the Jewish state appear now to the biographer of Ben-Gurion like a series of snapshots in a family album: Ben-Gurion laying the foundation stone of a new kibbutz, Ben-Gurion visiting a village of immigrants, holding forth in the Knesset, acting as godfather to the baby of a pioneer couple. These activities, to him, were part of history.

Most of his activities, nevertheless, were connected with the Israeli Army. He had succeeded, after the hardest struggle in his career, in making it the only nonpolitical organization in the State. He considered its leaders the best and most selfless pioneers. The Army built roads and frontier villages. A special force, *Nahal*, consisted of units which founded new settlements and cultivated land on the edge of the desert, in view of the enemy and ever ready to meet an attack. The Army also organized classes in Hebrew, general studies and civics, and taught a trade to new immigrants.

Ben-Gurion was happiest when among the young officers and soldiers. He could often be seen visiting Army camps, having long conversations with young recruits, taking part in night exercises, crossing large uncultivated areas at the head of a convoy of jeeps, visiting soldiers wounded in skirmishes. . . .

In Ben-Gurion's hands, the Army had become a powerful and democratic force. Yet he conducted the last battle in the War of Independence alone, unaided by guns or tanks. It was the battle which, several months after the fighting war had ended, crowned the successes of the army—the battle for Jerusalem.

This time, Ben-Gurion did not just defy the Arabs, but the United Nations, France, Britain and the United States. The New City of Jerusalem was held by the Jews, but the United Nations' resolution that it should be an international zone still applied. Ignoring this, Ben-Gurion launched his offensive to make Jerusalem the capital of Israel.

On May 11, 1949, Israel became a member of the United Nations. Foreign Minister Moshe Sharett and others responsible for foreign polity were at pains to show their great respect for the international organization. Not Ben-Gurion. This was a major point of disagreement between him and Sharett. Ben-Gurion contended that the United Nations had forfeited any rights it had as creator of the State of Israel by not following up the decision of November 29, 1947, and refusing armed support to the Jews against Arab aggression. He had already defied the United Nations several times during the War of Independence by refusing to withdraw from territory he had occupied and not permitting Arab refugees to return to their homes. He and Sharett were now to have the most serious clash in their long association.

Towards the end of 1949 the General Assembly decided to put Jerusalem under the jurisdiction of the United Nations. Ben-Gurion reacted swiftly. "We consider it our duty to assert that Jewish Jerusalem is an integral part of the State of Israel, as well as being permanently linked with the history and religion of the Jews. We are proud that Jerusalem is a holy city to the followers of other religions, and we wholeheartedly offer them freedom of worship there. But we cannot admit that the United Nations should attempt to separate Jerusalem from the State of Israel or to infringe our country's sovereignty over Israel's eternal capital."

Ever since the creation of the State Ben-Gurion's ambition had been to establish the capital in Jerusalem. When he had been obliged to leave in 1947 he made a symbolic gesture. He slipped the key of his office into his pocket, murmuring to one of his assistants, "I think I'll keep this key—I'm sure I'll be back again."

However, he had had to wait. After capturing Jerusalem he had transferred a few minor administrative offices there, but he had not dared to wave the flag of Israeli sovereignty too brazenly in the face of the United Nations. However, in view of the recent decision of the General Assembly, he had to act quickly.

"Jerusalem is not safe enough to have as our capital," said Sharett.

"On the contrary," retorted Ben-Gurion, "by having our capital in such a forward position we shall be making the Arabs feel unsafe!"

Tension mounted in the days that followed. Ben-Gurion was weighing the political risks of such a plan. Sharett had left for the United States, from where he kept sending cables asking for the plan to be canceled or at least to await a more propitious moment. Moreover, a strong note from Washington informed Ben-Gurion that the United States Government wished Israel to abstain from any "inflammatory initiative."

Time was pressing. Any day, the United Nations might put the resolution to internationalize Jerusalem into effect. Ben-Gurion, as usual, made the decision himself. Early in December he obtained Cabinet approval, despite objections from Sharett. Buildings in Jerusalem were hurriedly prepared for the various ministries. Only the Defense Ministry remained in Tel Aviv, for security reasons. On December 13, 1949, Ben-Gurion publicly announced that the State capital had been transferred to Jerusalem. The following day, trucks loaded with office furniture and files began their interminable pilgrimage to the Holy City.

Foreign countries thundered their disapproval. France, eldest daughter of the Church, placed a resolution of censure before the United Nations. The Vatican fumed. But the fact remained—Jerusalem had become the capital of the Jewish state. Ben-Gurion had added another *fait accompli* to the series in his career.

Sharett, back from the United Nations, found that reaction and pressure from abroad had not been excessive, and he was greatly impressed. He offered his resignation, but Ben-Gurion refused to accept it, and Sharett adapted himself to the new situation. However, the foreign ambassadors had been instructed to disregard the transfer of the capital and not to move to Jerusalem, so Sharett's Foreign Ministry would remain in Tel Aviv for the time being. Later, in 1953, Sharett moved his ministry to Jerusalem, and then the foreign diplomats were obliged to travel back and forth every day.

Ben-Gurion established his headquarters in Jerusalem in the old, pink stone building which had been the offices of the Jewish Agency.

He had won his last battle. Henceforth, things would never be the same with him. The spectacular transfer of the capital was the last initiative he took on his own and carried to a successful conclusion by obliging others to follow in his steps. With one exception, he was never to act again in that way. In the future, he gave his assistants and colleagues much more freedom of action, leaving it to them to conceive bold plans and then submit them to him. As in the past, however, his was the decisive vote, and he controlled the plan's execution. But he was no longer the lone horse drawing the plough.

In the future he shared his great burdens with others, and this enabled several talented young men to show their powers, working in the shadow and under the protection of the old leader. But freedom of action in the hands of less gifted men could lead only to disastrous consequences for the country. It was a luxury that Israel could not afford.

Ben-Gurion was beginning to show signs of fatigue, too. He was 63, and the conduct of the war had taken full toll of his energy.

A final tussle took place between Ben-Gurion and Weizmann. During the previous thirty years the character of world Zionism had been shaped and fashioned by the agreements and disagreements, the quarrels and mutual admiration of these two men. Towards the end of the British Mandate their relations had reached the breaking point. But in 1948 Ben-Gurion had made another approach to Weizmann. A cable signed by Ben-Gurion, Kaplan, Sharett, Remez and Golda Meyerson was sent to him on May 15 (the day after the proclamation of the State) to say that the Jewish nation would like to have him as head of the State as soon as possible. Weizmann at once saw himself as President holding Cabinet meetings, appointing ambassadors and generally exercising great influence on foreign policy. He was soon disillusioned. He would be a head of state without any real powers, he was informed, fulfilling purely representative functions like the then President of the French Republic. Weizmann showed his disappointment by delaying his arrival in Israel and spending time in Switzerland and Paris.

Ben-Gurion's attitude was clear. Weizmann would be elected President, with Ben-Gurion himself putting the proposal to the Provisional Assembly, but only on condition that the aged Zionist leader had no say in the conduct of State affairs. Weizmann spoke of refusing such a titular position, and told journalists "I hope I am more than a simple holder of a title," but it made no difference—in a state with a head of government like David Ben-Gurion, its President could never be more than the symbolic representative.

As President of the State of Israel, Weizmann spent the last few years of his life at the Institute for Scientific Research at Rehovoth. They were bitter years for this monarch of Zionism. He came forth only to preside at official ceremonies and to lead the salute at military parades. He was called "the prisoner of Rehovoth," and it was there that he died in December 1952. This great man possibly did not deserve the fate that Ben-Gurion had reserved for him. But despite all his exceptional qualities, Weizmann had never learned Ben-Gurion's magic formula—a sense of reality and *faits accomplis*. The brilliant monarch-scientist had been defeated by the pioneer-builder.

TWENTY-FOUR

THE END OF A CAREER?

Israel's foreign policy was stated officially as a desire to collaborate with both East and West, and Sharett proclaimed his intention not to be dragged into the conflict between the two major Powers. But this was just window dressing. From the very beginning of Israel's existence she had shown herself to be pro-Western. Her flirtation with the Soviet Union lasted no more than a year, the year of the War of Independence.

Ben-Gurion did not intend to ally himself with the Communists. He admired Britain's democratic institutions, and the United States —the powerful Jewish organizations there, a Democratic Party sympathetic to the Israeli cause, and President Truman in the White House had played a decisive part in the battle to establish the State. American Jewry, five million strong, was going to be of the greatest support, the source of funds and immigrants for Israel.

The Soviet change in attitude to Israel became evident before the young state had taken up a pro-Western position. There were two reasons for the Soviet reversal of policy: the Left-wing parties in Israel had been unsuccessful in obtaining power, and the Arab countries were in a ferment and offered more fertile ground for Communist penetration. Moreover, the Judaeo-Arab war had increased the hatred between the two races. In such circumstances, the Soviets had no interest in courting a small state. That would only kindle Arab hatred for Moscow. It seemed far better to change horses and support the Arab nationalist and revolutionary movements.

The Soviet change of policy was probably influenced, too, by a demonstration which remains in the memory of all who witnessed it. In September 1948, when the War of Independence was at its height, the Jewish New Year was being celebrated in Moscow and Mrs. Golda Meyerson, Israel's first Ambassador to the Soviet

Union, visited the synagogue in the Russian capital. She was greeted by a delirious crowd, shouting and weeping, singing songs in Hebrew and waving flags. During the next few days, the Jews packed the streets around the Israeli Embassy, demonstrating their pride and joy in the new Jewish shate, alarming the Soviet Government. This mass demonstration showed that the official claims that there was no Jewish problem in the Soviet Union were lies. The creation of the State of Israel could prove to be a cause of dangerous agitation by the three million Russian Jews.

At the end of December a letter written by a Soviet citizen reached Ben-Gurion: "A complete change in Soviet policy towards you is under way."

On March 7, 1949, Ben-Gurion wrote in his diary: "Moshe Sharett read out some reports from Romania. They contained bad news. The Communists have ordered the immediate elimination of Zionism and its pioneering organizations."

Emigration from some of the Communist countries was allowed to continue for a time, but only against payment in dollars by the State of Israel as a kind of heavy fine for each Jew permitted to leave. There could be no doubt that Bucharest's change in attitude, dictated by Moscow, was the beginning of a policy which would show the Soviet Union to be an outright enemy of the Jewish state.

In 1950, after many hesitations, Israel proclaimed her support of the Western nations in the Korean War. The following year, Ben-Gurion visited the United States and received a great welcome which demonstrated more than anything the strong bonds existing between the State of Israel and American Jewry—and the White House. That same year, 1951, Israel began secret negotiations for her first military pact with the West.

Soundings were made by General Brian Robertson, Commander-in-Chief of British Middle East Forces, when he paid an official visit to Israel in the spring of 1951. His first meeting with Ben-Gurion, at which Moshe Sharett and General Yadin were present, got off to a bad start.

"What are your plans in the event of war with the Soviet Union?" asked Ben-Gurion.

"The Russians would certainly attack the Middle East from the north," replied Robertson. "To stop them, our forces would advance across the Middle East from the south, through Israel, Jordan and Iraq."

Ben-Gurion's eyes opened wide in astonishment. "But what gives you the right to talk in that way? Do you think you have Israel in your pocket—that we're a British Colony? Or that we're a State like Jordan, always sponging off you? Israel is a sovereign State, and before deciding to treat her as transit territory for your army you would do well to consult her government."

Robertson was taken aback. Sharett looked anxiously at Ben-Gurion.

"I'm sorry," said Robertson. "I don't understand those things. I'm a soldier, and what you talk of is a political matter."

However, the conversations continued, and Robertson did not conceal the advantages of closer relations in the military sphere between Britain and Israel. In the course of detailed talks with Israeli senior officers he revealed that what he had in mind was the signing of agreements which would give British air and naval forces the right to use Israeli airfields and ports. Moreover, as Britain possessed no military base in the Middle East, she would like to see Israel construct the arsenals and repair workshops needed by the British forces.

Negotiations developed in a friendly way. Morrison, the British Foreign Minister, sent Ben-Gurion letters which made no mention of Israel as "transit territory" but spoke of efforts to bring their two countries closer together. Ben-Gurion replied in similar tone: "I think our entry into the Commonwealth is out of the question, but we should like to establish relations with you on the lines of those between you and New Zealand."

The two sides got down to details, and it seemed that Israel would become Britain's first ally in the Middle East, thus assuring the security of the Jewish state as well as increasing her economic resources.

But the fine dream was soon shattered. The general election in the autumn of 1951 brought Churchill and a Conservative government back to power. One of the first acts of the new British government was to base its defense policy on that of the United States. Moreover, the Foreign Ministry was again given to Anthony Eden, who promoted friendship with the Arabs, and showed a cold reserve towards the Jews. He sent a military mission to Jerusalem, but the keenness had gone from the negotiations. The leaders of the Jewish state were soon obliged to admit the fact that Eden had filed away the project of a military alliance which could have assured Israel's security. A few years later, Ben-Gurion proposed a similar alliance to the United States, but this also came to nothing. In Middle East politics, Israel was like a piece of red-hot coal, and none of the Western statesmen desirous of Arab friendship wanted to get burned.

Israel had at one time been close to reaching a friendly understanding with her Arab neighbors. Ben-Gurion had not given up hope of a peace treaty after the War of Independence had ended. The moderate and westernized Lebanon was prepared to make peace, provided it was the second Arab country to do so. Which would be the first? King Abdullah of Jordan had secret peace talks with Moshe Dayan in 1949 and 1950. Abdullah's terms were that Jordan should have the Gaza Strip, where many Arab refugees were living, and also an access to the sea at Haifa. On his part, he was prepared to make many concessions. The Israeli Government was favorable to the proposals, especially as one of the concessions by Jordan was free access to the Old City of Jerusalem.

The Gaza Strip was in any case held by the Egyptians, and its transfer to Jordan was purely a matter for the Arabs. The Israeli Government, Ben-Gurion in particular, preferred the presence of a small state like Jordan on their frontiers to that of Egypt, which, with a population of twenty million, seemed bound to become the most powerful Arab country in the Middle East. Ben-Gurion was ready to give Jordan access to the Mediterranean, though if it had been proposed in the southern part of Israel he would have refused, for the danger of having the country cut in two would then be much greater. In the north, however, the Jewish population was very dense, and there would be no risk in giving Jordanian convoys a right-of-way.

However, it was the question of this right-of-way which caused the negotiations to collapse. Ben-Gurion proposed that the corridor should be so many yards wide, but several Jordanian ministers wanted it to be so many miles wide. The Jordanian Prime Minister even threatened to resign, and King Abdullah became uneasy, withdrew his proposals and abandoned a project which was on the point of being successfully concluded. Nevertheless, he continued seeking an understanding with the Jews, aware that with their aid he would be able to develop and modernize his country. But his government was much more nationalistic than he was, more conscious of Arab unity and alive to the opinion of the British. And it seems that just then, because of her own selfish interests in the Middle East, Britain would not have been overjoyed at the prospect of a peaceful settlement between Israel and Jordan.

King Abdullah paid with his life for having dared to reach agreement with the Israelis. A few months later he was assassinated in the Old City of Jerusalem. Only a few days before, the same fate had befallen the Lebanese Prime Minister, Riyad el Solh, who shared Abdullah's opinions. Henceforth, no Arab leader dared to make peace with Israel.

Attempts had also been made at Lausanne in 1949 and at Paris in 1951 to negotiate a peace settlement, but had come to nothing. From 1952 onwards, tension grew between Israel and the Arab countries, culminating in the Sinai Campaign in 1956.

The vise was slowly but surely tightening around Israel. Arab refugees were becoming restless, skirmishes developed into frontier incidents. The great Powers discovered that the creation of the State of Israel had turned the Middle East into a barrel of gunpowder liable to blow up at any moment. In 1950 the three Western Powers, in a joint declaration, guaranteed the *status quo* of the Middle East and tried to establish some kind of military balance of power there.

In March 1951 there was fighting between Jews and Arabs on Israel's northern frontier. Later that year, the Security Council called upon Egypt to allow Israeli ships to pass through the Suez Canal, but to no effect. Egypt had, moreover, occupied the two islets of Tiran and Sanafir in the Gulf of Aqaba, which ships had to pass in order to reach the Israeli port of Eilath. In 1952 Israel's eastern frontier blazed up, embittering relations with Jordan—and Britain, that country's faithful protector, refused Israeli requests for war supplies. So Ben-Gurion's envoys turned to France.

In the Soviet Union and the Communist countries, anti-Semitism was at its height. The trial had begun in Moscow of the Jewish doctors accused of attempting to assassinate Red Army generals.

Ben-Gurion, writing under a pen name, made barbed attacks on his MAPAM opponents in anti-Communist newspaper articles. The Left Wing never forgave him. Not long afterwards, following the throwing of hand grenades at the Soviet Embassy in Tel Aviv, diplomatic relations between Russia and Israel were broken off for a long period. At the United Nations, Russia supported the Arab countries which were demanding a stop to the Israelis' work on changing the course of the River Jordan. In short, the situation of the State of Israel grew worse, both at home and abroad.

Huge sums were needed to pay for arms and munitions; millions were desperately being sought to meet the immigration costs. The State had obtained loans from many sources and had received funds from American Jewry, but this was not enough. Financial collapse seemed imminent. Capital was needed for development, consolidation and defense. Where was it all to come from?

Ben-Gurion had to make a difficult and painful decision, for the money and equipment so badly needed could be had from Federal Germany. Heated discussions and fierce arguments broke out in Israel when it was learned that Germany would pay reparations to the Jews. In September 1950 Chancellor Adenauer had agreed that reparations would be paid to help Israel absorb the Jews among the displaced persons in Europe.

"Israel will never become an accomplice of the Nazis by accepting money from these monsters!" proclaimed spokesmen for political parties and organizations.

Ben-Gurion, though, was prepared to accept. He had two arguments: the German reparations were not to compensate for the millions of murdered Jews, but for their possessions which had been seized by the Nazis; and Israel's security was Ben-Gurion's paramount aim. In order to obtain it he was ready to do anything, even to turn to the country which was still reviled by hundreds of thousands of Israelis.

The painful dilemma rocked public opinion. A tragic struggle for power was to mark the final decision.

By the end of December the negotiations with Bonn were concluded, and the Knesset (the Israeli national assembly) met to vote on the matter on January 7, 1952.

That morning, in Jerusalem, the national assembly building was surrounded by barbed-wire barriers and six hundred police were ready to deal with demonstrations. Begin, the ex-*Etzel* leader who had become head of the Opposition party, *Heruth,* and the Communists and other Left-wing elements were all determined to fight Ben-Gurion's plan.

He took his seat in the chamber at four-thirty in the afternoon, and then formally proposed that negotiations over the payment of reparations be opened with the Federal German Republic. At once the storm broke. Members made impassioned protests from all sides. Worse yet, outside, a few hundred yards from the building, Begin was haranguing a crowd of several thousand. They began to march on the assembly. Excited young men broke through the police cordon, hurled stones at the building and set fire to cars.

Begin had got into the chamber and was making a furious verbal attack on Ben-Gurion from the podium, calling him a fascist and a hooligan. The President of the Assembly sharply called him to order, telling him not to speak in such tones. "If I don't speak, nobody shall!" roared the leader of the Opposition. Outside, the crowd was defying the police and threatening to break into the building.

As a last resort, Ben-Gurion called in the Army, and shortly afterwards troops arrived to break up the crowd and restore order. The scene of the clash looked like a battleground, with burnt-out cars still smoldering, the ground strewn with tiles and stones and broken clubs. All the windows of the parliament building had been smashed and more than 100 police injured.

Would it lead to civil war? Begin told the assembly that he and his supporters would no longer respect members' immunity. A wave of anxiety swept the country.

Ben-Gurion broadcast to the nation the following evening. "Yesterday, the hand of evil was raised against the sovereignty of Knesset, and the first steps were taken to destroy democracy in Israel . . . I want to reassure the nation—all necessary measures have been taken to safeguard democratic institutions, law and order . . ."

His energy and calmness had great effect. Members of the parliament who were considering abstaining or of seeking a compromise found reassurance in his confidence, and decided to support him. On January 9 the Knesset gave him a vote of confidence by 61 votes to 50. There would not be a civil war.

Towards the end of 1953 the German reparations started to arrive in the form of machinery and industrial equipment, gasoline, trains and ships. The country's development in the years to come, its security and well-being were assured.

That year, tired and exhausted, Ben-Gurion resigned from his political posts. He had been feeling their heavy burden for some time. He had been Prime Minister not for five years but for twenty—ever since he became head of world Zionism. For a man who found his natural element in warfare and struggle, a time of peace brought bitter disappointments. He greatly disliked coalition government. His own party was unable to obtain an absolute majority at the general elections, and he had immense difficulty in breaking down the partitions between political parties, and also in establishing a single educational system. People voted for Ben-Gurion in spite of the party he belonged to. He had become the one personality considered to be above party politics, a leader who belonged to the nation and was not subject to the interests of a particular group.

He did not intend to retire definitely from public life, only for two or three years, he told his friends. But he was not going to bury himself among his books in his house at Tel Aviv. His eyes were fixed on the stony desert of the Negev.

Some months previously, while crossing a particularly wild region of the Negev at the head of a convoy of Army jeeps, he had seen a group of young men erecting prefabs and pitching tents. He stopped his jeep and asked what they intended doing.

"This is the kibbutz of Sde Boker," they told him. "We founded it last year."

A kibbutz in the heart of the Negev! What tremendous appeal for a man who had been dreaming of settlements in the Negev since 1935! And now he could make his dream come true. There were no politics here, no intrigues—only work, real work. He could set an example to his people, to the youth of the nation. Perhaps he would be able to revive the pioneering spirit, which seemed to be vanishing from the heart of the Israeli nation.

It was on December 13, 1953 that Ben-Gurion and Paula set off to join the Sde Boker kibbutz. A wooden prefab became their home. At the age of 68, Ben-Gurion spent his days planting young trees, carrying hay and tending sheep. They were happy months.

But he failed to arouse the nation. Despite his appeals, the speech he made to a youth meeting at Tel Aviv and his articles for the press, the people remained indifferent. It was a profound disappointment for him.

Meanwhile, the new Prime Minister, Moshe Sharett, was running into a grave crisis revolving around "the Lavon Affair," a top-secret security incident.

TWENTY-FIVE

WHEN SECRET AGENTS TAKE A HAND

In mid-July, 1954, Israel was suffering from a heat wave. Britain had just announced her intention to withdraw from Suez, and even the Egyptians were surprised. If the British left the Canal Zone, Israel could expect an aggressive policy on the part of Egypt. The presence of British forces had hitherto acted as a powerful brake on Egyptian aggression.

From his primitive kibbutz in the heart of the Negev, citizen David Ben-Gurion had just sent an article entitled "By Absorbing Immigrants We Can Develop the Desert" to the publication *Davar*. It was a statement of faith and hope expressing the old prophet's vision of the resurrection of the Negev.

In the stifling heat of the afternoon of July 16 there was no one about in Jerusalem to notice an officer hurrying from an imposing building near the Ministry of Defense. He was Colonel X, head of counterespionage, and he had just been talking with the Minister of Defense, Lavon. His next step was to send secret instructions to his "man in Cairo" which would set off a terrorist campaign. Thus began the most disastrous and scandalous secret-warfare episode ever known in the Middle East, "the Lavon Affair."

"It all began with Lavon entering the government," Levi Eshkol, who was a minister at the time, said later. This was true. Lavon was the most dreaded man in the government, a strange character, whose sarcasm was feared by his opponents. Pinhas Lavon, who had changed his name from Lubianiker, was a brilliant, intelligent man with a strong personality, that could have made him a great man. But his arrogance and cynicism created a barrier between him and his colleagues. He had suffered a cruel disappointment in his youth which had sowed the seeds of bitterness in him.

As a young man, Lavon had been an active member of the MAPAI moderates headed by Shprinzak and Kaplan. On several occasions he had criticized Ben-Gurion's activist policy, and had always supported Kaplan and other leaders in their contention that it would be a mistake to risk everything by proclaiming the State. But afterwards he had been appointed Minister of Agriculture, and in Ben-Gurion's last government he served as minister without portfolio.

Lavon's colleagues did not like him. Army officers spoke of him with hostility, his antimilitarism being well known. The MAPAI leaders looked upon him as a dangerous man, scheming and aggressive. Nevertheless Ben-Gurion saw to it that Lavon succeeded him as Defense Minister, a move which caused many people to see Lavon as Ben-Gurion's heir presumptive, the future head of government. When Ben-Gurion had proposed to the new Prime Minister, Sharett, that Lavon be appointed Defense Minister, Sharett had promptly done so. Yet Golda Meyerson, Eshkol and Avigur had all warned Ben-Gurion against "this danger called Lavon." But the Old Man was impressed by the newfound activism which Lavon was flaunting, as well as by his abilities in economic and financial fields, and remained steadfast against the attacks on his protégé. Before leaving for Sde Boker he had handed him the keys to that great military and political power which was the Ministry of Defense.

It would appear that Lavon began to justify the fears of others from the very start. He was determined to prove to the army that he could be just as much of an activist as Ben-Gurion, but he went too far. Even before Ben-Gurion's departure, when only interim Minister, Lavon had issued irresponsible orders which had serious consequences. Once in power, and eager to demonstrate his firmness and ability, he approved several ill-conceived actions, covered up for officers who were overzealous and boasted to the High Command of having carried out more reprisal raids than his predecessor, and with greater success. He was arrogant before the Knesset and to the press, taking credit for all military successes. Questioned about a particularly brutal action in an Arab village, he said scornfully: "There's no need to get upset—there was no fine mahogany furniture in the village." He made no attempt to hide his disdain for certain Army officers, and tried to make himself a hero through publicity. Instead of gaining the Army's confidence, he soon made himself generally disliked. And the Army was not his only enemy. His arrogance and lack of tact caused the MAPAI and government leaders to shun him. Sharett himself, humiliated and made to look ridiculous by Lavon's sarcasm and insubordination, had almost been driven to resign.

Sharett, an intelligent and cultivated man and a shrewd diplomat, was too weak a prime minister to discipline this colleague who had no respect for him. Lavon did not keep him fully informed and gave him modified accounts of military activities, even keeping some matters from him entirely. Lavon was protected by the facts that he held a key position and that MAPAI and the public in general believed (though wrongly) that he was Ben-Gurion's heir. Admittedly, the activist policy he adopted was often more in line with Ben-Gurion's opinions than the diplomatic pirouettes of Sharett.

Nevertheless, Lavon's attitude caused a whole procession of MAPAI ministers and leading officials to visit Ben-Gurion at Sde Boker. In June, July and August 1954, Ben-Gurion confided in his diary a number of conversations he had with these prominent people who came to protest to him about Lavon and to warn him of the danger to the country if Lavon continued in charge at the Ministry of Defense.

Relations between Sharett and Lavon became increasingly embittered, but instead of bringing matters to a head the Prime Minister took a step which, in itself, went against democratic procedure. He set up a select committee of MAPAI ministers to deal with security matters, which were thereby kept from the Government. By this means Sharett hoped to be spared a clash with Lavon in the Cabinet. The move did not bring him honor.

In addition to the Army and the MAPAI leaders, a third front was soon opened against the Defense Minister by the "fair-haired boys" of Ben-Gurion, whose leaders had key positions in the country's defense organization. Two of them, Moshe Dayan and Shimon Peres, had been appointed by Ben-Gurion, just before his departure, to the positions of Army Commander-in-Chief and Director-General at the Ministry of Defense respectively. They both enjoyed Ben-Gurion's full confidence, they were used to his methods and to being allowed wide freedom of action by him. This soon changed. Lavon was suspicious, and wanted to know everything they did. He refused to allow them to make decisions without his knowledge. Against this, they rebelled. Peres and Dayan were not at all alike. The former, who had come from a Galilee kibbutz, had shown his worth in military missions abroad. The latter, the elder by eight years, was a war hero, a man who thought and acted like a soldier. "Shimon knows how to build up strength, Moshe to make use of it," one of their friends once said.

They both became involved in the open opposition to Lavon, who brought the first negotiations with France for the purchase of tanks to the brink of rupture. He suspected everyone, intrigued against Peres, and tried to cause trouble between him and Dayan. Even Ben-Gurion was not spared: "I don't read his articles," Lavon told a professor, "they're just a lot of blah." To another person, he boasted: "Before, the Minister of Defense was only a semblance of one. Now you've got a real Minister!"

Dayan, the first to give vent to his feelings, in June 1954, sent in his resignation. Only after long talks with Ben-Gurion were he and Lavon reconciliated. Peres and Lavon no longer spoke to each other—they communicated through notes and messengers.

Dayan and Peres went to see Ben-Gurion more and more often. The "fair-haired boys" were preparing a MAPAI campaign against Lavon. Ben-Gurion listened but made no comment.

Meanwhile, the Western Powers were supplying arms to the Arab countries but not to Israel. The British were getting ready to leave the Canal Zone, and tension was mounting on the Israeli-Jordan frontier. The morale of the Israeli Army dropped alarmingly. Sharett and Lavon clashed in the Knesset. The MAPAI leaders admitted to Ben Gurion that they did not know what to do. General elections were due within a year.

Such was the atmosphere when "the Lavon Affair" broke.

The plan conceived by the Israeli secret service was stupid, although old hands at secret warfare had known far worse. The aim was to prevent the British from leaving the Canal Zone—or rather, to make them change their minds. The Israelis were quite sure that Egypt, under the young and ambitious Colonel Nasser, would soon become their greatest enemy in the Middle East. But while the British remained in Egypt they served as scapegoats for the hatred of the masses. However, during recent months, coded messages from London had been causing anxiety in Tel Aviv. In early July it appeared that Churchill had made his decision. The British, under pressure from the Egyptian Government and with their troops in the Canal Zone being subjected to terrorist attacks, had definitely decided to pull out of Egypt after obtaining guarantees from the Government.

In mid-July 1954, it was known at Tel Aviv that the signing of the agreement was only a matter of days. The Israeli secret service realized that the time for desperate measures had arrived. Since 1951 it had been organizing a spy and terrorist network in Egypt, but this was still incomplete and amateurish. The members were young men in their twenties living in Cairo or Alexandria, all of good family and known to one another. They left compromising papers and photographs lying about at home, and it would only take the arrest of one of them for the whole rickety structure to collapse. There was little danger as long as the group had not been active. The intention was to use it as a secret unit behind the enemy lines in the event of war with Egypt. However, despite the lack of training of the members, and against all common sense, the Israelis decided to use the group to try and convince the British to remain in Egypt after all.

In May and June the two young Israeli leaders of the group had been in Europe under false names and been given their instructions. When the order was given, the group was to start a wave of terrorism in Cairo and Alexandria, attacking public places such as movie houses, post offices and railway stations, but especially to be directed against British institutions, information services, cultural centers and embassy buildings. These bomb attacks would be attributed, it was hoped, to the Egyptians, to the "Muslim Brotherhood," thus proving the weakness and incapacity of the central authorities and the little trust that Britain could place in Egyptian promises. The plan was naive to say the least.

All was ready in early July, only the word had to be given. And Colonel X gave it immediately after his talk with Lavon that hot afternoon of July 16.

It has never been known just what was said between Lavon and Colonel X; no other person was present. Apparently Lavon, although approving the application of the plan in general terms, did not give an explicit order for it to be carried out. Long afterwards, in private conversations, Lavon did not deny having approved the operation. But at the time he said in public that he had not given his approval.

Unknown to Colonel X, the members of the group in Cairo and Alexandria were doomed in advance. His man in Cairo, the brilliant secret service Agent Y, was a counterspy in the pay of the Egyptians.

Operation Egypt had in fact begun a fortnight before Colonel X gave the word. Agent Y, acting under the direction of the Egyptian counterespionage service, had set a trap for the members of the "Egypt" network. On July 2 some of their rudimentary bombs—tin cans and eyeglass-cases filled with a chemical compound—went off in a post office and a railway cloakroom. They did very little damage. There was a small fire and some smoke. On July 14 a number of similar incidents occurred in the American Information

Centers in Cairo and Alexandria, in the United States consular offices in the two cities and in the United States Embassy. Damage was again slight, but the Egyptians could congratulate themselves on having achieved the exact opposite of what the Israelis sought. These incidents provoked a grave crisis in relations between Israel and the United States. For some years, until the treachery of their Agent Y became known, the Israeli secret services were unable to understand why their bomb attacks on British institutions had in fact been carried out against the Americans.

Another series of bombings which did little harm occurred in Cairo and Alexandria during the days following July 16. On July 23, according to the official Egyptian report, a security officer arrested a young man of European appearance at the entrance to a theater in Alexandria. Wisps of smoke were coming from his trouser pocket and he was twisting about in pain. One of the "terrorist bombs" had burst too soon.

The whole network was burst wide open. A mass of compromising material—documents, a printing press and radio transmitters—were found at the homes of the arrested man and his accomplices. Operation Egypt had ended in a fiasco.

Colonel X learned of the arrests and sent a report to Lavon on July 26, informing him that the operation had been put into effect—and had failed. Lavon read the report and initialed it. At that time he did not deny having given his approval to the operation. But two months later he learned that it had actually begun a fortnight before his talk with Colonel X, and he got the impression that his approval had been asked to cover the failure of the first part of the operation and that his orders had applied only to the second part. He was furious with Colonel X, and afterwards changed his story and denied that he had even seen the Colonel on July 16.

Ben-Gurion noted in his diary on August 24: "Moshe Dayan arrived at Sde Boker this afternoon. He told me about a stupefying order given by Lavon during his absence, to do with an operation in Egypt which failed (they ought to have known it would fail!). It's criminal irresponsibility!"

On October 5 the Egyptians publicly announced the discovery of "a network of Israeli spies," and on October 10 the names of the accused were given by the public prosecutor in Cairo. On October 16 Ben-Gurion celebrated his sixty-eighth birthday at Sde Boker. Eshkol was present and had a long talk with Ben-Gurion about Lavon. The Old Man was furious, not only over the operation itself, but also because Lavon gave the order without consulting the

Government. "I think today Ben-Gurion has at last seen Lavon for what he is," wrote Nhemia Argov.

Sharett was even more dumbfounded. At first, he declared that the Egyptian accusations were "slanders intended to harm the Egyptian Jews," until he was quietly informed that the slanders were based on facts. He then demanded explanations from Lavon and the senior army officers involved. A series of dramatic meetings led to Lavon breaking completely with Colonel X. Meanwhile, in Egypt the charges against the arrested men had been made public, and the trial opened on December 7. Another of a different kind was held in Tel Aviv. Lavon, having been unable to prove his innocence, asked Sharett to hold an inquiry into the origin of the fateful order. On December 12 the commission of inquiry gave its findings—and Lavon was not cleared of blame. Some doubtful testimony by members of Colonel X's staff gave the impression that Lavon had been the victim of a plot. Dayan and Peres had not been required to give evidence, as they were never involved in the affair, but they had been called to testify as to the current feeling at the Ministry of Defense and in Army circles.

Meanwhile, in Cairo, the trial was coming to an end. One of the accused committed suicide in his cell. The prosecution was asking for the death penalty on some of the men. Pleas for clemency came from many parts of the world, and prominent people made approaches to the Egyptian authorities. The French were particularly active as some of the accused were of French nationality, and the Foreign Minister, Edgar Faure, sent a personal letter to Colonel Nasser.

The military court pronounced sentence on January 27. Two of the accused were acquitted, two were given seven years' hard labor, two fifteen years' and two hard labor for life. The two leaders were sentenced to death, and were executed four days later in the courtyard of Cairo prison.

Lavon was furious over the findings of the commission and demanded that Sharett transfer Colonel X to another post, recall Peres and completely reorganize the Ministry of Defense. Sharett, hesitant as usual, summoned Colonel X and asked him to resign. "That is unjust," he replied with dignity. "If I am to be asked to go, I have the right for the reasons to be made public. But I'm not going to resign of my own accord."

The MAPAI leaders were in a state of confusion. Those who knew the truth about the affair were under the seal of secrecy and could say nothing. The party, deprived of its leader, who was away reclaiming the desert, was incapable of reaching a decision. The majority had realized that Lavon must quit the Government. But with the parliamentary elections coming in the summer, and being involved in political maneuvers, they were afraid. So they turned to their last hope. Sharett, Golda Meyerson, Eshkol and others took the road to Sde Boker. "What's to be done?" they asked Ben-Gurion in effect. He heard them out in silence. Then he said firmly "He must go!"

But who was to replace Lavon? Ben-Gurion suggested Shaul Avigur, in whom he had complete confidence. But Avigur refused. The delegation returned to Tel Aviv in some dismay.

In the early hours of February 17 the faithful Nhemia was heading towards the sandy wastes of the Negev. Sharett had had several talks with Lavon, and the latter had resigned. The Prime Minister had given Nhemia the vital mission of persuading Ben-Gurion to come out of retirement and to take up the reins again as Minister of Defense.

The Old Man listened to Nhemia's pleas with lowering brow. The decisive moment came in the evening. Ben-Gurion's diary tells of it in the usual laconic but precise manner: "Golda and Namir arrived at the end of the afternoon. The country's security is in danger. Lavon is definitely leaving and there is no one to replace him. They proposed that I should take over again. I was thrown into confusion. I have decided to accept and to return to the Ministry of Defense. Defense and the army matter more than anything."

At eleven that night a radio announcer gave the news of Ben-Gurion's return. The following morning, telegrams of congratulations and relief began to arrive at Sde Boker. On February 21 Ben-Gurion was in Jerusalem and took the oath of office.

The abscess had burst, and Operation Egypt had been the needle. Ben-Gurion reluctantly came out of retirement. "If the crisis had not been so serious," he wrote to a friend, "a hundred bulldozers would not have dragged me away from Sde Boker."

He prudently refrained from having any more inquiries made into "the Lavon Affair." But he moved Colonel X to another department and refused him promotion because of the suspicion surrounding him. As for Lavon, Ben-Gurion raised no objections to his appointment as General Secretary of the labor federation, *Histadrut*. The Lavon Affair was closed, as far as Ben-Gurion was concerned.

However, five years later even greater violence was to erupt. Ben-

Gurion's return to the Ministry of Defense had marked only the end of the first act.

At the end of February, a reprisal raid on Gaza resulting in forty Egyptian casualties marked the turning point in Nasser's relations with Israel. It was also an opening shot in the Suez affair.

TWENTY-SIX

THE PINCERS CLOSE

A bronzed Ben-Gurion, glowing with health, came back from Sde Boker. In his desert clothes he made a sharp contrast with the other members of Parliament in their white shirts and dark suits. He had come back, too, with his iron fist, which was soon heard thumping the desk to emphasize his words to the Knesset. Aggressive, impetuous and determined as ever, it was not long before he started his "reprisals campaign" which caused fighting to flare up along Israel's frontiers.

The reason for his decision was obvious. The State of Israel was in a graver situation than at any time since the War of Independence—its very existence was at stake. The creative impulse of 1948 had petered out, and the honeymoon with the outside world was over. Other nations were beginning to realize that this Jewish state was quite a problem. Hopes of a peaceful settlement to the conflict were fast disappearing. Either through the fault of the Jews, those uncompromising victors, or the Arabs, who were eager for revenge, the dove of peace seemed to have flown from the Middle East. Secret peace talks between Jews and Arabs had been broken off, and mediators had met with nothing but failure. Iraq, tainted by all her oil, was strutting with importance, and hostile. Syria was going through a period of revolutions and military *coups d'état*, and Lebanon was consequently anxious about her own internal stability. Jordan was in the grip of a war of succession, made even more bitter by outside influences, which was leading to raids along her frontier with Israel. In Egypt, the army junta was jubilant at its newly-won power. The Israelis had thought for a time that General Neguib, a moderate, cultured man, might hold out the hand of friendship. But Neguib had proved to be a puppet skillfully manipulated by the giant figure looming over the Arab world—Gamal Abdel Nasser.

A general pro-Arab policy was increasing Israel's isolation. The

Soviet Union had long been betting on the Arabs, and obliging the Communist countries to do likewise. Britain and the United States were also paying open court to the Arab potentates. Modern armaments were being delivered to Iraq, and were soon to be extended to Jordan. The Western Powers did not wish to see Israel disappear from the map, but Truman's influence on American foreign policy had disappeared with the advent of Eisenhower, and there were many pressures—from oil kings, diplomats and the imperatives of the cold war—all insisting on wooing the Arabs, even at the cost of weakening Israel. The British had forgotten their short flirtation with the Jews. France, weakened by the war in Indo-China, engaged in fighting in Algeria and torn by political strife at home, was in no position to make herself felt in the Middle East.

Now that Britain had decided to withdraw from Egypt it was only a matter of time before the Suez Canal fell like a ripe plum into the hands of Egypt's new rulers. And Egypt would undoubtedly become the dominant Arab country. The Israelis had followed anxiously the various stages of the British disengagement, for this stabilizing influence would not easily be replaced. They had tested Egyptian intentions by sending a fishing boat to pass through the Suez Canal. As could be expected, the Egyptians captured the vessel. Sharett had hoped that this act, which was contrary to the Constantinople Convention, would cause the British to reconsider. But it did not. The Security Council and international jurists could condemn Egypt for this breach of international law, but common sense had to admit that there was nothing absurd in the Egyptians refusing to allow their enemies to pass through their territory.

Israel was increasingly isolated and abandoned. When her envoys protested to the State Department about the enormous quantities of arms being supplied to the Arab countries, they received the curt reply: "You must get used to it. These armaments are not intended to be used against you." Israeli delegates were again obliged to roam the world in search of tanks and aircraft, as in the days before the creation of the State.

Israel was not at a disadvantage only in the military and international spheres. The country was also suffering from lack of proper leadership. Moshe Sharett was a capable and intelligent man, much like Weizmann in character, but was no Ben-Gurion.

A sentence in a speech made by Ben-Gurion soon after his return showed the difference between his attitude and that of Sharett: "Our future does not depend on what the Gentiles will say, but on what the Jews will do."

Sharett might have been the right man in peacetime, but Ben-Gurion has always been the war leader.

David Ben-Gurion's opinions were diametrically opposed to Sharett's, and the outcome of the duel between the two was never in doubt. While to all appearances restricting himself to defense matters, Ben-Gurion really acted as though he alone were master—not as someone who had returned to office, but as future Prime Minister.

"I have decided that from time to time I shall publicly announce my opinions on the main problems of our foreign policy," Ben-Gurion wrote to Sharett on April 12, 1955. "My reasons are that the elections are drawing near, and I may be asked to form a government. This I should do, and I therefore feel that I must tell the nation the principles on which my policies will be based. As you know, I am not in agreement with the policy that the present government has carried out since I gave up the Premiership."

Their first dispute came a week after Ben-Gurion's return, when he had ordered the reprisal raid on an Egyptian Army camp at Gaza which resulted in the death of forty Egyptian soldiers. Sharett had authorized the raid, but was angry when he heard the proportions it had reached. Ben-Gurion replied that a truck carrying Egyptian reinforcements had blown up on a mine. "How were we to know that would happen?"

Ben-Gurion's new policy had three basic principles: to react strongly against Arab provocation, to make intensive efforts to obtain arms abroad, and to seek military alliances with Western countries in order to guarantee Israel's security. The Gaza raid was the first step. The next was to obtain arms from abroad, and here he found a glimmer of hope in the French.

"Who are your contacts?" Peres had asked his agents when he arrived in France. One said he knew Paul Reynaud, who was then Deputy Prime Minister, and another claimed to have contacts with the heads of Nord Aviation. Meetings were arranged, at the Israeli request. Peres was received by Reynaud, who kept the conversation general. But it was apparent that closer relations were possible. At the Nord Aviation offices Peres met Piette, who had at one time been secretary to Léon Blum. He was prepared to sell some Nord 2501 (cargo and paratroop) planes, to which Peres replied: "I want Mystère fighters—if you can get me some, I'll buy some Nord planes as well . . ."

In time, Peres met all his French agents' contacts, made new connections and widened his circle of acquaintances. The French, with the Algerian War on their hands, became convinced that they and the Israelis had similar missions in the Arab world—France in North Africa, and Israel in the Middle East. At the end of 1954, Peres had signed an agreement with Catroux, Minister for Air in Mendès-France's Government, which covered the purchase of arms, aircraft, guns, tanks and radar equipment.

General Dayan, visiting France for the first time, also obtained the promise of bazookas from General Guillaume. "The Arabs are our common enemy," he said. "You're at the rear, and we're in the front line. When the front blazes up, ought not the weapons be sent to the forward positions?"

However, officials at the Israeli Foreign Ministry were not at all pleased at Army chiefs playing at diplomacy and negotiating directly with the French Government for the purchase of arms. Sharett, who was a stickler for formalities and jealously guarded his ministry's preserves, strongly opposed these direct negotiations. In the spring of 1955 there was a clash over this matter too.

Ben-Gurion was somewhat skeptical of any real results from his assistants' efforts to establish friendly relations in France. But his confidence in his colleagues caused him to give them every support.

Soon after the Gaza raid a decision had to be made on whether to seek armaments from France or the United States, and whether or not to make a conventional approach. Ben-Gurion followed the advice of his go-ahead lieutenants and chose France. He realized that the United States would not offend their Arab clients by supplying arms to Israel. In view of the French Foreign Ministry's cautious policy towards Israel, Ben-Gurion was also of his aides' opinion on the second point. The French ministries of War and of the Interior, as well as the Army, which was deeply involved in the Algerian war, were far more likely to listen sympathetically to Israel's requests.

Ben-Gurion felt that he could go ahead, and in spite of Sharett's doubts he wrote a personal letter to the new French Minister for War, General Koenig, who had a warm regard for the Jews since their valiant conduct at Bir Hakeim. Peres met him in Paris, and things began to move. Peres also made contact with Abel Thomas, and became friendly with Bourgès-Manoury, who was Minister for Home Affairs. Dayan and his Air Force commander also went to Paris and opened negotiations for the purchase of armaments. Edgar Faure showed much goodwill towards them, and altogether the Israeli representatives established a combination of friendly contacts, useful to the official relations between the two countries.

But it was still not enough. Pressure from the French Foreign Ministry and the cautious policy of Britain and the United States held back the delivery of armaments to Israel. And in the stark realities of the Middle East, only armaments mattered.

Soliciting France's aid did not mean neglecting other possibilities. The United States had helped Israel once, and might do so again. With the boldness born of despair, Israel made approaches for a military alliance.

This was not a crazy idea, considering it was 1955, when American policy was to make agreements with every country that could give military bases and help strengthen the strategic encircling of the restive Soviet giant. In the greatest secrecy, the Israeli ambassador in Washington made tentative advances. The Americans did not turn down the proposition outright. They listened, asked questions and put forward suggestions. Israel was prepared to give military bases, but in exchange wanted guarantees for her frontiers and her security. In the end, the United States proved to be lukewarm about guaranteeing the security of a country which might keep having clashes with Arab forces on its frontiers, for this could provoke a wave of anti-Americanism in the Middle East. What the Americans really wanted was some unilateral agreement which would give them the bases they required and the right of intervention in Israel's military policy.

On Israel's Independence Day, Ben-Gurion gave a reply: "We are a small nation and a tiny State, but we have the same rights as any other sovereign State; and our relations with other States can only be on the basis of mutual equality . . . And, just as we have no right to interfere in the affairs of another State, small or great, so no other State shall have the right to interfere in our affairs."

The talks continued, nevertheless, throughout 1955. In spite of the secrecy maintained in Israel, word reached some of the Left-wing parties and they strongly objected to an alliance which would draw the country into the anti-Russian camp. And they had very real fears over the nature of the control which the United States would have over Israel.

Then in September 1955 Egypt signed an agreement with Czechoslovakia for the delivery of great quantities of tanks, fighter and bomber aircraft, guns and army vehicles. The Communist bloc was crashing into the private preserves of the Western Powers. And Israel felt the pincers closing on her.

TWENTY-SEVEN

THE END OF SHARETT

Nasser had attended the Bandoeng Conference, where he met Chou En Lai and spoke to him about Egypt's need for armaments. Nasser had been greatly alarmed by the Gaza raid, and was far more concerned about Egypt's military situation than the problems of the emergent countries which were being discussed at this Afro-Asian conference. Chou En Lai listened to him sympathetically. China had no arms for sale, but did have good friends. Peking would have a word with Moscow. It was a perfect moment—the Russians were still gnashing their teeth over the news of the Baghdad Pact. This pact, signed in February 1955 by Iran and Turkey, blessed by the West, was intended to create a military menace against the "soft underbelly" of Soviet Russia. The Western Powers had drawn the Middle East into the Cold War, and now there was an opportunity for Russia to pay them back. The Soviet ambassador in Cairo was informed of Egypt's request, and this led to the signing of the armaments agreement, which was made public in September 1955. An armaments race in the Middle East had begun, and another stage was reached along the road which led to the Suez affair.

Parliamentary elections were held in Israel that summer, and MAPAI lost five seats. This was taken as a sign of dissatisfaction with Sharett's appeasement policy. It was clear that Israel was going to adopt a much firmer line. However, it was Egypt who took aggressive action. She prevented ships sailing up the straits from the Red Sea to the Israeli port of Eilath. This was interference with an international sea route and tantamount to piracy.

Matters were desperate, for Washington had just turned down the Israeli proposals for a military agreement. Ben-Gurion was ill and had still to form his government. Sharett, head of the caretaker government, left for Europe to buy armaments with which to face the Arab menace. Peres flew to Paris too. Sharett obtained from

Edgar Faure the promise of 24 Mystère planes, while Peres and his aides began negotiations with General Billotte, the new War Minister. In addition to aircraft, the French promised tanks and artillery. The final agreement was to be signed on November 12, but only a few days later the Faure Government finally fell and Parliament was dissolved. There could be no certainty that the new government would respect agreements made by the old, and in any case the small amount of armaments promised was far from equaling the huge Soviet consignments to Nasser.

Ben-Gurion prepared for the worst. He sent for Dayan, and they decided that the Egyptians would probably mount an offensive as soon as their army was strongly equipped and trained in the use of the new weapons. The obvious strategy for Israel was to take preventive measures. Ben-Gurion told Dayan to prepare three plans—an attack on the Gaza Strip, an advance into the Sinai Peninsula and an operation to clear the Egyptians from their positions controlling the sea approaches to Eilath. The date envisaged was in three months' time at the latest.

Ben-Gurion had still not entirely recovered from his illness when he presented his government to the Knesset. In his speech, he gave a stern warning to Egypt: "Egypt is trying to prevent Israeli shipping from using the Gulf of Aqaba, contrary to international law. This unilateral war must end, for it cannot remain unilateral for long . . ." He went on to refer to Egyptian armed incursions. "If saboteurs and murderers continue to cross the lines established by the armistice, then the lines will not stay closed to the defenders on this side of the frontier. We are prepared to make peace, but not to commit suicide."

Little notice was taken of another sentence in his speech, which occurred in every speech he made: "I am prepared to meet the Egyptian Prime Minister or any other Arab leader at any time and in any place, to negotiate a peaceful settlement." This sentence, which aroused no comment, was probably the most important in the whole speech, for he was then secretly engaged in the most promising peace negotiations with the Arabs since 1950.

A certain American had arrived in Israel incognito. He was a prominent Democrat, a clever and persuasive negotiator and an outstanding economist. Eisenhower was later to give him a high position, but at the moment had sent him on a difficult, top-secret mission—to try to reconcile Jews and Arabs.

The American President was feeling very guilty after the breakdown of the talks on a military agreement between his country and

Israel, and realized that there was an explosive situation in the Middle East. He foresaw, after the Czecho-Egyptian armaments agreement, a bloody struggle for power that he wanted to prevent at all costs. So he had given his friend and colleague the task of finding a miraculous solution to the problems of the Middle East.

He was soon to discover that there was no miraculous solution. The start of the mission, however, was encouraging. Eisenhower's envoy was welcomed by Ben-Gurion. Nasser greeted him warmly too, and assured him that his sole desire was peace between Jews and Arabs, and said that he was ready to negotiate with Israel through the American. The latter, delighted with this promising start, flew back to Washington and then left again for Tel Aviv to obtain a basis for negotiation. He proved to be the most able and devoted mediator that Israel had known in her short existence.

However, he was not then aware that the charming Egyptian colonel was concerned only with assuring the United States of Egypt's peaceful intentions and maintaining friendly relations as in the past, not with actual negotiations with the Israelis. When the American returned to Cairo for the second round of talks, Nasser realized that he had underestimated him. Nasser had thought that this amiable American, like so many others, would report back to Washington and consider his mission accomplished. But this mediator had returned with detailed plans for a settlement.

Nasser found himself in a difficult position, and to get out of it he put forward as a condition to any settlement that Arab refugees must be allowed to return to Israel. The American at once left for Jerusalem. In order to maintain secrecy, Ben-Gurion did not receive him in the Prime Minister's office but at his hotel (Ben-Gurion did not then have a private residence in Jerusalem). The American gave an account of his talks with Nasser, but when he spoke of the return of Arab refugees Ben-Gurion stiffened. For two hours he explained why he thought the return of the refugees could threaten the existence of the State of Israel. A population of a million and a half Jews could not consider absorbing a million Arabs all full of enmity, a perfect fifth column for the future. Ben-Gurion was adamant. He rejected Nasser's proposal of giving a "free choice" to the refugees, of returning to Israel or being compensated. He was prepared to pay compensation to all of them, but would agree to the return of Arabs only in certain specific cases, notably those who had been separated from their families by the tragic fighting in 1948. The reunion of these families had in any case been under way ever since the signing of the armistice. Moreover, added Ben-Gurion, many Arabs had left the country before the proclamation of independence, following appeals by the Mufti and the Arab Council. Since then, half a million Jews had entered Israel from Arab countries. So that, in effect, a change of population had taken place.

The American listened to Ben-Gurion. "You're quite right," he said at the end.

He flew back to Cairo again. Nasser was getting tired of these negotiations, which were not really of his seeking. If the arms agreement with Czechoslovakia had not already been signed he might have been more inclined to listen to the American overtures. But with Egypt strongly armed and his own prestige with the Arab leaders soaring, he no longer feared Israel and thought increasingly of revenge. Nasser told the American with disarming frankness: "I would have been prepared to meet Ben-Gurion, as you propose, if I weren't scared of being assassinated an hour afterwards. It's too much of a risk."

Nasser claimed that the Arabs would revolt against the traitor who dared to negotiate with the Jews, and declined to proceed any further. This was the end of the American's hopes and of his mission.

At the end of November 1955 Ben-Gurion put before the Government the plan prepared by Dayan and his staff, to clear the Egyptians from their positions controlling the approaches to Eilath. But the majority of ministers, including the pacifist Sharett, voted for it to be shelved. Ben-Gurion had to give in, although convinced that it was the only way of breaking the blockade of Eilath.

Although deploring the Government's decision, Ben-Gurion was no longer sure that a preventive war was the only answer to the fundamental problem of Egypt's increasing war potential. He came to the conclusion that if Israel could obtain armaments in sufficient quantities to neutralize the effect of the Czechoslovakian deliveries to Egypt, then the situation in the Middle East would return to its *status quo*. Once Egypt's supremacy had been canceled out, war might be avoided.

During the next few months, Ben-Gurion's chief aim was to obtain armaments at all cost, wherever they could be had. He first conferred with Army leaders and his chief assistants at the Ministry of Defense. "We must obtain arms," he said in substance. "If we don't, why go to war?"

It was clear to all that the moment was not propitious for going to war. The first aim was to acquire arms and munitions. After a number of study sessions, the Army chiefs gave figures and details of the armaments needed to counterbalance the Egyptian purchases. The greatest need was for several dozen jet fighters equal to the Russian "Mig" and for a considerable number of tanks. Those required were all of French or American manufacture.

The next step was to act, and Ben-Gurion set things in motion. Urgent instructions were sent to Israel's ambassador in Washington, Abba Eban, who was then preparing a detailed memorandum for the United States Government. The list of armaments required was added to it, although the chances of obtaining them were slight. At the same time, an offensive was launched in the financial field to gather without delay the huge sums necessary for all these purchases. The third front—and the right one, as it turned out—was opened in France. Dayan was skeptical at first, but Ben-Gurion's optimism prevailed. Peres flew to Paris, arriving in the midst of yet another Parliamentary election.

"I think we shall be able to help you," said Guy Mollet, General Secretary of the French Socialist Party, to Peres. Then he hastened to add: "Haven't you been told that I'm anti-Jewish?"

"I have heard something of the kind," Peres replied.

"I want you to know that there's not a word of truth in it. I've had differences of opinion with Daniel Mayer, it's true, but that was over Socialist affairs and had nothing to do with anti-Semitism."

Peres, referring to this conversation in his book *The Next Stage,* comments: "It was quite obvious that Mollet was most grieved by this accusation, as though he had been called a traitor."

The conversation continued. "The opposite is true," said Mollet. "I myself have suffered from Nazi persecutions. The greatest Frenchman I've known was my chief, Léon Blum. As you know, Blum was a brave man and proud to be a Jew. Believe me, my dearest wish is to visit your country, where several of my friends live, and to help you as much as I can. I think it's a country where socialism is practiced to the letter."

"I replied," wrote Peres, "that I did not doubt his attitude as a Frenchman towards the Jewish people, but that certain Socialists had often disappointed us in their attitude towards Israel. It sometimes seems that a Socialist movement gives expression to an aggressive ideology only in peacetime, and in time of war it slides into a liberalism which threatens the very existence of free society. I added, with a touch of insolence, that the young workers in Israel would like to know if every Socialist was bound to become a Bevin as soon as he reached power."

"I shan't become like Bevin," retorted Mollet. "There'll be other occasions for me to give proof of my friendship as a Socialist as well as a Frenchman."

In January 1956, a few months after this conversation, Guy Mollet became Prime Minister.

On April 12 Peres arrived at the Hotel Matignon, the French Premier's official residence, bearing a letter from Ben-Gurion.

The situation in the Middle East had been steadily deteriorating. In December the Egyptians had made more raids into Israeli territory. The Syrians had fired on Jewish border settlements and on fishing boats on Lake Tiberias. In January and February tension had increased. General Burns, head of the United Nations mission, tried in vain to persuade the Egyptians to cease their armed raids. The Jews had hit back, shelling Gaza and causing much damage, and had gone into action with artillery and infantry on the southern frontier, in the "demilitarized" zone of Oujda.

War seemed certain, and the United Nations' attempts to prevent it were having little effect. In the Knesset the Opposition pressed the Government to take preventive measures while there was still time. Fighting flared up again on the frontier with Syria. There were street patrols in Tel Aviv, where Arab killers had been reported.

On April 11 Ben-Gurion held an Army staff meeting and gave instructions for everything to be ready to meet an attack. The Secretary-General of the United Nations arrived from New York to try to prevent an outbreak of hostilities. At the same time, Ben-Gurion sent Peres to Paris with an urgent request for help. And so, on April 12, Peres was closeted with Guy Mollet.

The French Premier read Ben-Gurion's letter attentively. "There is still a chance of saving the peace," Ben-Gurion had written, "but only if Egypt be no longer sure of her supremacy in armor and aircraft, and so refrains from unleashing her forces. The small and young Republic of Israel is in grave danger and turns to the great and long-established French Republic, in the hope that her request will not meet with refusal."

Guy Mollet replied to Ben-Gurion immediately, and discussed with Peres the details of the Israeli request. He repeated the phrase he had used some months previously: "I think we shall be able to help you."

He kept his word. Although friendly relations existed between the Socialist Governments of Ben-Gurion and Mollet, it was the Algerian War which had brought them closer together. Each was convinced that they were up against a common enemy.

In May, France sent two consignments of a dozen Mystère IV fighters and a number of tanks to Israel. These deliveries had the secret blessing of the United States, who preferred to see a European country arming Israel and drawing Arab barbs. But in June and the following months huge quantities of armaments flowed towards Israel, under a top-secret agreement, all unknown to Washington and to the French Foreign Ministry, which was opposed to favoring Israel because of fear of offending the Arabs and harming what remained of French connections and interests in the Middle East.

France now saw that the one way to end the Algerian problem was to smash the instigator and agitator, Nasser, who was believed in Paris to be behind the Algerian rebellion. Once he was crushed, the rebellion would collapse. And a sure means of wearing down Nasser was to arm Israel.

This success of the Israeli Defense Ministry coincided with a grave crisis at the Foreign Ministry. Moshe Sharett found himself in complete disagreement with Ben-Gurion and resigned. The inevitable rupture between the two was complete.

They had been together for a long time, but when Ben-Gurion had retired in 1953 the differences of opinion between them had already been considerable. Ben-Gurion had wanted Eshkol, not Sharett, to succeed him as Prime Minister. In 1954, when the return of Ben-Gurion was in the air, Sharett had let fall a significant remark: "If Ben-Gurion comes back from Sde Boker, the only thing for me to do will be to leave the government and go off with my wife to Beer-Sheva to teach the children of Israel . . ." He felt that cooperation with Ben-Gurion was almost impossible. However, with an integrity from which he never swerved, he had welcomed Ben-Gurion's return like that of a Messiah, although he feared it would eventually mean the end of his political career.

Only a few days after Ben-Gurion had taken over the Ministry of Defense again, he and Sharett clashed over the policy to adopt in the matter of Arab raids. Ben-Gurion was all for hitting back, whereas Sharett wanted to play down the incidents and refer the matter to the United Nations mission, even if it meant making some concessions. Ben-Gurion was against any concessions, however small, and was convinced that the Arabs would regard it as a sign of weakness.

By April 1955 the conflict between the two was common knowledge. It was not of the kind which had embittered relations between Sharett and Lavon. The political differences dividing Sharett and Ben-Gurion, both straightforward men of integrity, never led them into base intrigues or resulted in humiliating public clashes. Nevertheless, Ben-Gurion never missed an opportunity to criticize Sharett.

During the electoral campaign that summer, Sharett had supported Ben-Gurion and worked for his return at the head of the government. After the elections he had wanted to resign from office, but Ben-Gurion had insisted that he remain at the Foreign Ministry.

The political and military situation had forced Ben-Gurion to take an even firmer stand. Sharett continued to lead a group which was opposed to military action and sought despairingly to find a political means of reaching a settlement. In December, Sharett had succeeded in getting a majority vote against the plan to attack the Egyptians in the Sinai Peninsula. Later that month, while in Washington trying to get arms from Dulles, he had been shocked by the reprisal raid that Ben-Gurion had ordered on the Syrian positions overlooking Tiberias. On his return to Israel he had made an issue of it, and the Cabinet decided that in the future the Defense Minister was not to order reprisal actions without the approval of the Foreign Minister.

In February and March there had been another clash between the two over the policy regarding the Egyptian pressure on the Oujda zone. The United Nations, in order to appease the Arabs, had requested the Israelis not to create any more kibbutzim in this zone. Sharett agreed, but Ben-Gurion, ever conscious of Israel's sovereignty, did not. And the Government, influenced by Sharett, had not supported Ben-Gurion. In exasperation he had written to Sharett: "My conclusion, seeing how things stand, is that once the danger of war has disappeared I shall leave the Government . . . I have publicly stated my policy, supported by all its members. You yourself did not raise any objections, and you know quite well that I don't like saying things which I have no intention of carrying out. The situation at present is that the majority of ministers now oppose a policy that they had approved."

So in June 1956 the inevitable happened. Ben-Gurion's policy, consciously or not, was inclined towards a trial of strength against the Arabs, while Sharett sought to avoid this at all cost. Ben-Gurion saw that the decisive moment had come. On the evening of June 3 the two men, who had hardly addressed a word to each other for several weeks, met for a long and frank talk. "I can't work with you any more," said Ben-Gurion. "It's either me or you." Sharett offered to resign, but Ben-Gurion asked him to stay for a few more weeks. Then he informed the MAPAI leaders and said that he wanted Sharett to be replaced by Golda Meyerson, whose opinions were more in line with his own. On June 18 Sharett announced to the Cabinet that he was resigning. Ben-Gurion and the MAPAI ministers looked away and said nothing. The others tried to persuade Sharett to change his mind, but in vain.

An impassioned debate followed his departure. Neither Sharett nor Ben-Gurion had revealed the true state of affairs which had caused the resignation. But Ben-Gurion, in an important speech, said: "Recently, when Defense problems hardened and the dangers in foreign policy increased, I reached the conclusion that, for the good of the country, complete coordination between the Defense Minister and the Foreign Minister had become imperative. A harmonious relationship between the two Ministries, which in fact deal with the same matters, was most necessary. Although differences of opinion can be beneficial, a close ideological outlook and a more intimate understanding between the two Ministers are required. These are the reasons which must have led Sharett to resign."

In a personal letter to Sharett, Ben-Gurion's tone was harsher and even offensive: "I fear I'm going to cause you pain," he wrote, "and God is my witness that I don't want to hurt you, but I believe it my duty to give you my opinion on this painful subject—that I've come to the conclusion that your presence as Minister for Foreign Affairs is not beneficial to the good of the State . . ."

Sharett never forgot this humiliation. His departure provoked a public scandal, with the Opposition and other parties shooting venomous darts at "Dictator Ben-Gurion." And for the first time MAPAI members themselves expressed doubts.

Ben-Gurion said nothing. If Sharett had stayed, the Suez affair might never have happened. But with Sharett gone, the way was open for the war on Egypt which Ben-Gurion had long envisaged. The French were sending great quantities of armaments, the Israeli Army was ready, and the danger of an Egyptian attack seemed greater than ever.

International pressure on Israel to accept another Munich and appease the Arabs was still possible, especially after Anthony Eden's recent visit to Cairo. Israel had to strike quickly. All that was lacking was assurance that she would not be isolated, that foreign armies—Russian, European or American—would not intervene. And Ben-Gurion was assured on that score, a month after the end of Sharett—assured by the good offices of Gamal Abdel Nasser, when he announced to the world on July 26, 1956, that Egypt had nationalized the Suez Canal.

III
THE
WOUNDED
LION

TWENTY-EIGHT

DESTINATION SUEZ

Ben-Gurion saw Nasser as the man he had been dreading ever since the War of Independence—a great leader who would unite the Arab armies and launch them in a holy war against Israel.

Nasser was elated after his dramatic speech at Port Said in which he had dared to defy the great Powers, the Suez Canal Company and world opinion. A vigorous, athletic man, he was the son of a post office employee and had been one of the first of the lower-class Egyptians to take advantage of the new facilities for entering the Officers' Training College. As a very young man he had organized a secret group of army officers, "the free officers," who plotted against King Farouk and the British. He had a fanatical hatred for the British, and hoped that Hitler would win the war. In 1952 his "army junta" had thrown the corpulent King Farouk out of the country. In 1954 a bloodless struggle for power had ousted Neguib, an honest man but weak and lacking in authority. Thus, at the age of 36, Colonel Nasser found himself the leader of 22,000,000 Egyptians. In July 1954, with the backing of the Americans—who seem to have the peculiar gift of always backing their future enemies—Nasser secured the departure of the British from the Suez Canal Zone. Luck favored him; several attempts on his life failed. He had charm and impressed visiting foreign politicians. In a booklet with the grandiose title of *The Philosophy of the Revolution* he expressed his vast ambitions, promising the Arabs dominion over huge territories extending from the Atlantic coast of Africa to the frontier of India. His Ministry of Information published maps showing Spain, half of Africa and Israel as parts of the Arab world. Nasser's agents were busy everywhere stirring up revolts and plotting assassinations. Terrorist commandos were sent into Israel.

When the United States refused to sell Nasser $27,000,000 worth of armaments he promptly bought $200,000,000 worth from the Soviet bloc. Insolent and self-confident, he believed he could draw profit from both sides, and he showed his independence by recognizing Communist China.

The United States curtly refused to finance the Aswân Dam and Russia also declined, so Nasser, then at the height of his power, produced a trump card—the nationalization of the Suez Canal. The revenues from it would pay for the dam. Army trucks sped through the streets of Cairo and soldiers armed with Stens burst into the offices of the Suez Canal Company. There was no resistance. An exultant Nasser saw himself as a giant in the Arab world. The bombshell he dropped in Port Said set in motion the series of events which were to end with warfare in the arid wastes of the Sinai Peninsula.

The news flashed round the world—"Nasser has nationalized the Suez Canal." The French and the British decided to hit back at what they called "the insolence of an apprentice dictator." Britain was particularly affected, for the Canal was a maritime shortcut to the East and the Commonwealth, and she could not afford to lose control of it. France welcomed the opportunity to smash Nasser and eliminate the chief ally of the Algerian rebels. There was a great deal of talk about the unfortunate people who had invested their savings in the Canal Company, and much consideration was given to the threat to Israel, but when France talked about Suez, her thoughts were chiefly on Algeria.

In London, there were many conferences between the French and British, with the Americans invited to some, with the hope of dragging them into the undertaking. There was every chance for swift action. The French assembled a naval task force at Toulon, and paratroop units were put on the alert. French residents in Egypt were warned to be prepared to leave the country at a moment's notice. Britain called up reservists, and naval reinforcements were sent to Malta. By early August, the invasion of Egypt by a Franco-British force could have been announced any day. But nothing happened. John Foster Dulles had taken a hand in the affair.

The United States, far from joining in the attack, was strongly opposed to any military operation which might start up another world war. Eisenhower wanted to stand at the next presidential elections as a champion of peace. And however regrettable the "Suez coup" might be, in the eyes of the Americans it did not warrant action. Dulles had flown to London and succeeded in getting the attack postponed.

Anthony Eden then called an International Conference to try to find a peaceful solution to the problem. The British, and even more so, the French, doubted if this was possible, but they yielded to American wishes. On August 22 the conference adopted the Dulles plan for international control and management of the Canal. Nasser could breathe again—this organization conceived in London was never dangerous.

Dulles had another idea—the "Suez Canal Users' Club," which Egypt would be made to accept; it would collect the dues from ships passing through and use them to maintain the Canal. But when Dulles added "We do not envisage using force to allow ships to pass through," Egypt realized that the "Users' Club" would be short-lived. They would simply defy it, knowing that the United States was against the use of force. And in fact when a convoy of ships was sent as a test, with hardly any protecting escort, it did not even get as far as the Canal.

This was the end of French illusions. Eden kept giving way to American pressure, and it seemed clear that he was going to let the plan of combined action die. The British merely spoke of a military operation in the winter or perhaps in the spring.

Matters were at that stage when Shimon Peres, in Paris, received a cable from Ben-Gurion which gave a new turn to the affair. Israel had entered it officially. She had in fact been greatly in the minds of the French from the very beginning. Soon after the nationalization of the Canal, the indefatigable Peres was in Paris having secret talks with the French. A combined attack on Egypt was not mentioned, only the stepping-up of arms deliveries to Israel. However, early in August the French sprang a surprise on Peres. Bourgès-Maunoury sent for him, and he was ushered into the map room where some high-ranking officers were gathered. Bourgès-Maunoury said to Peres: "We're discussing the matter of the Canal. How long do you think it would take the Israeli Army to cross Sinai and reach the Canal? Our Staff reckon about six weeks."

"I think we could overrun Sinai and reach the Canal in one week," Peres replied. Then one of the officers put the vital question. "If we make war on Egypt, would Israel be prepared to fight alongside us?" Without hesitation Peres answered "Yes."

That was all for the time being. The French were then preparing for a military intervention in Egypt with the British. It was only towards the end of August, when the British hesitations became evident, that the French turned to the Israelis. The latest date for an attack was in the first two weeks of November, before the rainy season began in Egypt.

In September, Bourgès-Maunoury again asked Peres if Israel

would attack Egypt in conjunction with France and Britain. Peres replied that he would have to refer the matter to Ben-Gurion, and he sent off an urgent cable. Days passed, but no reply came. Another cable brought no better result.

Ben-Gurion's silence by no means indicated that he disapproved of the initiatives taken by his chief assistant. But he did not declare himself. When Peres or Dayan reported to him on their talks, he listened in silence, occasionally asked a question, but made no comment. He still hoped to avoid war, so he waited.

But by mid-September it was no longer possible to wait, as the French were well aware. Bourgès-Maunoury again raised the matter. "Apparently the dates that we and the British have fixed do not suit you. You must tell us definitely what you think." Peres sent yet another cable to Ben-Gurion, and this time there was a quick reply. "Tell them that their dates suit us." The old warrior had decided to throw in his lot with the French.

He had been influenced by the state of affairs on the Israeli frontiers. The Judaeo-Arab conflict during the past three years had been characterized by Arab provocations and Israeli reprisals. But things had reached such a pitch that it was impossible to tell whether Arab killings were provoking Israeli reprisal raids or whether the latter were the cause of the intensification of terrorism. It was time for a wide sweep. As General Dayan wrote: "I have given my opinion; we can no longer tolerate this state of affairs which is neither war nor peace. We must make our Arab neighbors choose between putting a stop to these acts of terrorism or going to war against us. This we can do in two ways: by carrying out reprisal raids in broad daylight, using armor and aircraft, or by crossing the frontier and seizing key positions in enemy territory. The objective could be the Gaza Strip, where the Fedayin Headquarters is located. At the moment, Egypt has no defense treaty with any European country, so we could seize frontier positions in that area . . ."

Everything pointed towards war. There was the blockade of Eilath, the Canal affair, the Czecho-Egyptian arms agreement, the failure of the reprisal tactics and the deterioration of the general situation in the Middle East. So Ben-Gurion broke his silence late in September and sent the cable to Peres.

When Peres informed Bourgès-Maunoury, the latter at once made a number of propositions on the form that Franco-Israeli collaboration could take. Peres replied that the first conditon was the supply of great quantities of armaments to enable the Israeli

Army to confront the Egyptians. A conference of French and Israeli Ministers and Army staff officers was arranged for September 29. At the same time, the British would be informed of the possibility of a military operation in conjunction with Israel.

Peres flew back to Israel on September 25 and General Dayan met him. They went to the small airfield at Ramla, where an airplane landed with only one passenger—Ben-Gurion, returning from his kibbutz in the Negev. They drove together to Jerusalem, discussing on the way the reprisal raid which was to be made that night on the frontier strongpoint of Houssan, in the mountains beyond Jerusalem. Ben-Gurion agreed that the attack should go in, then turned to Peres and asked, "What's the latest from France?"

Peres reported on his mission, mentioning the disappointment felt by Pineau, the French Foreign Minister, after the second conference in London had come to nothing because of the Americans, and the doubts that Pineau had about Eden engaging in a military operation. Peres also spoke of the attitude at the French Ministry for War, where there was increasing feeling in favor of an attack on Egypt even if France were alone at first. Britain, they thought, eventually would join in. Ben-Gurion listened with great interest.

On September 28 four Israeli representatives flew to France in a French bomber. They were Dayan, Peres, Mrs. Meyerson (who had changed her name to the Hebrew form *Meir*) and Moshe Carmel, the Minister of Transport. The same day they began talks with the French about the delivery of arms to Israel. Nothing was said concerning political matters or the projected attack on Egypt. The four returned to Israel on October 1.

The following day, Dayan revealed his plans for an offensive to his staff. He instructed his officers to prepare to seize the Sinai Peninsula and to clear the Egyptians from their positions controlling the approaches to Eilath. The offensive was to open on October 20.

In the meantime, Ben-Gurion remained silent, not revealing his thoughts even to his closest colleagues. In the whole of his long career he had never been so uncommunicative. He read dispatches, listened to reports and asked questions. He had still not made up his mind. He wanted to avoid open conflict in the Middle East if possible, and he was apprehensive about world opinion, but the question continually on his mind was the attitude of Britain in the event of hostilities.

A report from Paris informed him that Pineau had had talks in

London about the joint military action. The future Defense Minister, Sir Anthony Head, sent the following message to Ben-Gurion: "It would be most opportune for Israel to attack at the same time as Britain opened the offensive on Suez. Britain would strongly denounce the Israeli aggression, but at the peace talks which followed she would help Israel to obtain the best possible terms."

Ben-Gurion made no comment, but smiled skeptically. He could not believe that Britain would ever take joint military action with Israel. On the other hand, he was convinced that no attack could be made on Egypt without Britain's participation. France needed the British bases on Cyprus in order to launch her attack. But the British were quite capable of persuading France to abandon the attack at the last minute, leaving Israel alone against Egypt and with the whole of world opinion against her.

Ben-Gurion wished he knew what the British intended to do; but it appeared that the British themselves did not know. Eden kept changing his policy.

Tension was growing on the Jordanian border, for the Egyptian terrorists were entering Israel by way of Jordan. In spite of this, in October Ben-Gurion put a stop to reprisal raids in those areas. He explained his decision in a letter to Dayan. "I think that Eden will eventually join in 'the Cyprus action.' In my opinion, France will not act without Britain, so we must not give the British any pretext just now to slip out of the affair; and it would not be wise to step down from our position at the United Nations of a country demanding its just rights."

These sentences indicated that Ben-Gurion intended to go to war, and wished to have France as his ally. He was convinced that France would not fight without Britain, so it was essential that the British should come in too. But he had no confidence in them.

He rejected the idea of military action by France and Israel alone. It was paradoxical for him to be suspicious of the British and yet in favor of their participation. But it was his fear of their influence on the French that caused him to agree to Israel joining in the attack only if Britain also took part. Later events proved him right.

Nouri Saïd visited London and on October 8 revived the plan of restoring peace in the Middle East by a return to the United Nations' partition plan of 1947, and by allowing Arab refugees to return to Israel. The British Foreign Secretary gave wholehearted support to Nouri Saïd's proposals. On October 11, while Israeli forces were carrying out a reprisal raid on the strongpoint of Kalkiliya, King Hussein of Jordan invoked the defense treaty with

Britain and asked for the RAF to attack the Israelis. Britain refrained from doing so, but did not fail to inform Israel of Jordan's
request. The implied threat was obvious. There was a fresh alarm
the following day, when Israel was officially informed that an Iraqi
division was being sent to Jordan, where elections were about to be
held. Iraq had never signed an armistice with Israel, and the British
chargé d'affaires told Ben-Gurion that if Israel made this a reason
for engaging in military action against her neighbor, then Britain
would feel obliged to intervene on the side of the Arabs. Ben-
Gurion was furious and protested strongly, telling the British representative that Israel reserved her freedom of action.

An outbreak of hostilities seemed imminent, but Ben-Gurion's
eyes were fixed on Egypt. As he said in a speech on October 15
which greatly surprised observers: "Let us not forget that Israel's
most dangerous enemy is still Egypt." While reminding his listeners
of recent altercations with the Jordanians, he devoted most of his
speech to the dangers emanating from Cairo.

Eden's idea concerning Jordan was already dead. King Hussein
had rejected the help of an Iraqi division, and the Jordanian elections looked like an overwhelming victory for the pro-Nasser candidates. Eden would have to look elsewhere.

General Challe* brought the solution when he arrived in London on October 14 and saw Eden and Selwyn Lloyd. The day
before, the Russians had applied the veto in the Security Council to
a Franco-British project for a peaceful settlement of the Canal
question. The way was thus open for France and Britain to use
force, all peaceful means having failed. A conflict between Israel
and Egypt would provide the opportunity. Israel was to open an
offensive towards the end of the month, and then France and
Britain would intervene to separate the enemy forces and to occupy
the Canal. Eden and Selwyn Lloyd, who had been previously
informed of the plan, though somewhat vaguely, listened to General Challe, who moved to the large map of the Middle East which
was spread in front of them. "The Israelis will be here," he said,
pointing to the Sinai Peninsula, "and the Egyptians there." He
indicated the part of Egypt west of Suez. "Where is our place?"
And he at once gave the answer by placing his hand on the Canal.
"Here!"

Eden and Lloyd went to Paris on October 16. The decisive

* Deputy Chief of Staff, French Air Force. Mr. Anthony Nutting has recently revealed that these talks took place on October 14, and at Chequers—
for secrecy. (Translator's note.)

meeting between the British and French has been described in Terence Robertson's detailed book on the Suez affair:

"The four statesmen sat facing each other amid the ornate splendour of the Hotel Matignon, once the home of the Monagasque princes and Talleyrand, and now the official residence of the prime ministers of France. The wall behind a grimly determined Eden and Lloyd was covered by a magnificent tapestry showing Don Quixote tilting at his windmill; behind Mollet and Pineau was a portrait of the archconspirator, Cardinal Richelieu, who gazed down upon this intimate gathering—austere and sardonic."*

Who would prevail—the cunning Cardinal or the candid Quixote? The four discussed the matter for five hours. They felt it was now or never, that the pretext to be provided by the Israeli offensive was the only plausible one. They thought that if London and Paris gave way now, it would be another Munich. The international situation was propitious. Pineau did not believe that the Russians would intervene, and Eden thought that, in the end, the Americans would not let their allies down.

The decision being made, Eden carried out drastic changes at the Foreign Office and the War Office. The French sent naval units to sea with sealed orders marked "Egypt." The military machines of both countries were set in motion. A reassuring cable was sent to the still-skeptical Ben-Gurion by his French friends: "You can have complete trust in the British."

But that was just the moment when Israel chose to say "No!"

The reason could have been a United States plane on a secret reconnaissance flight over Israel, which reported having spotted 60 Mystère aircraft on the ground instead of the 24 given in official figures, and which caused Eisenhower to send a strongly-worded warning to Israel. Or the reason could have sprung from Dayan's repugnance to be associated with foreign armies. But in fact the reason was the British attitude. Although they had given their agreement to the French plan, they wanted the Israeli Army to advance in great strength and on a broad front—to mount a heavy attack which would threaten Cairo. It would be a real war, and the French-British forces could present themselves as saviours of the peace. Moreover, reports had reached Ben-Gurion from French sources that Selwyn Lloyd, with the approval of the British High Command, had proposed bombing both Israeli and Egyptian forces, on either side of the Canal, thus showing the world that the

* *Crisis*, by Terence Robertson (Atheneum, 1965).

one desire in intervening was to safeguard the international water-way.

Israel, however, had never had any intention of waging full-scale war, of aiming to conquer territory, and even less of exposing her forces to the "impartial" fire of the British and pay with her dead for improving British prestige in the Middle East and the world. Israel's only aim was to clear the Egyptians from the Gaza Strip and break their control of the sea approaches to Eilath. This was proved by General Dayan's Army Order Number One, which he quoted in his *Diary*. The order stated that the Israeli objectives were to seize control of the northern half of Sinai, to clear the Egyptians from the Gaza Strip and to seize the coastal strip below Eilath. There was no mention of conquering the Sinai Peninsula nor of threatening the Canal. But that was not at all what the British wanted.

So Ben-Gurion, convinced that he had been right to distrust the British, had refused to take part in the plan as it stood. He was in a very strong position—whether or not there would be a Suez war depended on him, on his decision, so he could dictate his con-ditions.

TWENTY-NINE

THE SÈVRES SECRET

On the evening of October 21 a private car with drawn blinds was driven to Lydda Airport. In it were Ben-Gurion, Peres, Dayan and Nhemia Argov, recently promoted Lieutenant Colonel. In a following car were a few senior Israeli Army officers and two staunch French friends—Colonel Mangin and General Challe. These two had come to ask Prime Minister Ben-Gurion to go to France. A French DC-4 was on the runway at Lydda, its propellers churning the hot night air of a lingering summer. The little company went on board. The crew were used to secret missions and showed no curiosity. The great silver bird took off, but met with strong winds in the higher altitudes and was several hours late in reaching its destination. Mist patches hovered about the wet runways at Villacoublay, creating an eerie atmosphere, when Ben-Gurion set foot on French soil the following morning. All preparations had been made to receive these secret visitors. They stepped from the plane into black cars without any official markings and were whisked away. Contrary to some published accounts, the French Prime Minister was not present to greet Ben-Gurion. On that October 22 another important person, the Algerian rebel leader, Ben Bella, was flown to France in no less dramatic circumstances—his plane having been diverted while on the way from Morocco to Algiers.

The black cars followed twisting country lanes, while the passengers anxiously wondered what Ben-Gurion was thinking. Would he go to war? Would he agree to the Franco-British plan?

A sign that might have encouraged those in favor of the Suez offensive was a book tucked under his arm and which he had been reading on the journey. It was the *History of the Wars of Justinian* by Procopius, a sixth-century Byzantine historian, in the original Greek. Ben-Gurion was particularly interested in the account of an ancient independent Jewish kingdom said to have existed on the island of Tiran until the fifth century. And this island is in the approaches to Eilath that Ben-Gurion had been wanting to clear by force of arms since November 1955.

The cars took the travelers by a roundabout route to Sèvres, where a villa standing in its own grounds had been prepared for them. Bourgès-Maunoury has described the arrangements to Terence Robertson: "This villa belonged to private friends of mine who were in no way involved in government business. I asked them for the loan of it and they agreed without knowing the purpose for which it would be used. Mangin and I arranged the details of the meetings and were responsible for security precautions. Nothing was done to draw attention to the fact that something important was going on. The old servants remained to look after the guests as they would do normally. They were accustomed to house guests, mostly English, so the visitors were treated as usual without any suspicion that they might be very out of the ordinary."*

Ben-Gurion was to sleep at the villa, but the other members of the Israeli delegation were less fortunate—they had to sleep at hotels in Paris. For three days they went in fear of being recognized by one of the many Israelis in Paris. But they escaped notice. So did Christian Pineau. He has told me that to get to the Sèvres villa, which for sixty hours was the nerve center of Franco-British diplomacy, he drove his car himself and took many detours along little lanes. The meeting was kept a closely-guarded secret by all those present—ministers, high-ranking officers and senior officials—and nothing transpired of it until many years later.

Even today, all is not known of what happened at Sèvres during those three fateful days. Ben-Gurion and the other Israelis refuse to talk about it. Guy Mollet, Selwyn Lloyd and others are equally reticent. But from what certain other Ministers and officials both in London and Paris, told me, and from statements made by the same people to two other writers, it is possible to reconstruct a fairly complete picture of what was said and done.

In going to Paris for a secret meeting with representatives of Imperialist Powers—a meeting later dubbed "collusion"— Ben-Gurion was compromising the international prestige of his young country. Yet he had sound, logical motives. He was determined to free the Eilath approaches by force. But in the prevailing political climate he could not do it alone, for then Israel would be condemned by all the Powers and be obliged—perhaps by the interven-

* *Op. cit.*

tion of foreign troops—to cease hostilities. But by opening an offensive in conjunction with France and Britain, Israel would acquire powerful allies who could veto any anti-Israel resolution by the Security Council. Also, their participation in the action would probably receive greater condemnation than that of Israel, whose motives could be more easily explained. Moreover, the danger of foreign intervention was greatly diminished, as the Power most likely to have taken action against Israeli aggression—Great Britain—would be already committed.

On the military side, Ben-Gurion's motives were of a different order. Both he and Dayan were certain of an overwhelming victory in a Sinai campaign, even without help. But, according to Pineau, Ben-Gurion was "obsessed" by the fear of Egyptian air attacks. Most of Israel's population is concentrated in the large towns—Tel Aviv, Haifa, Beersheba and Jerusalem—and the Egyptians had many squadrons of Russian Ilyouchine bombers that they could send over Israel without any fear of their own civilian population being bombed in return, for the Israeli Air Force had no bombers. Ben-Gurion was haunted by the thought of a murderous rain of fire and steel turning Tel Aviv or Haifa into another Dresden, so he was determined to obtain effective protection of the Israeli cities from the French and British in return for the "pretext" he would be supplying. This protection could take the form of an air "umbrella" combined with an intensive bombardment of Egyptian airfields. But he put a limit on the price he was prepared to pay—he would not wage the all-out offensive the British wanted. He was going to have discussions with them, ask for definite assurances and consider what was required from him. Only then, and at the last, would he make his decision. Throughout the Sèvres talks he was to keep changing tactics, and no one was ever sure what he was really thinking.

On that first day, October 22, Ben-Gurion went to bed on arrival. In the afternoon he and his aides, Pineau, Bourgès-Maunoury and senior French officers held a preliminary meeting. Apparently Ben-Gurion felt very relaxed that day. He explained that on no account would Israel embark upon a real war with Egypt. Another pretext must be found.

In the evening, General Challe flew to London and reported on Ben-Gurion's attitude. The British had no choice but to yield, Ben-Gurion held all the trumps.

On the second day, the Old Man began to reap the benefits of his attitude. Reports arrived from London in the morning that the British were prepared to forego their plan of playing their familiar role of world policemen.

The first visitor of note to arrive at the villa was Guy Mollet. He looked strained and tired, having had to face a rowdy Chamber of Deputies the previous evening, when the Ben Bella scandal had broken. However, he had managed to slip away for a few hours, leaving Paris by the same roundabout means as his colleagues. Pineau introduced him to Ben-Gurion, who was obviously greatly moved. Apparently Ben-Gurion was in very good form; he was wearing a well-cut dark blue suit which set off the splendid halo of white hair above his pink face and lively, twinkling eyes. He quickly became engaged in an informal conversation with the French, darting from one subject to another, but chiefly subjects which interested Ben-Gurion—history, philosophy and philology. He asked about the teaching of Greek and Latin in France, and the French explained the system in their schools.

However, they soon turned to more serious topics. The French and Israelis sat around the long, solid table in the dining room and listened to Ben-Gurion as he reviewed the situation in the Middle East. He spoke at length of the danger of destruction which hung over Israel, of Arab aggression and the Egyptian terrorists, of the blockade of the Eilath approaches and of Soviet penetration in the form of armament supplies to Egypt. He explained the reasons for Israel launching an offensive against Egypt—"More than a raid, less than a war"—and then put his request for air and naval protection of the Israeli cities. Guy Mollet, usually cold and calm, was visibly moved by Ben-Gurion's review and promised his support for Israel.

They passed to the details of the military protection, and Mollet agreed to send air squadrons and warships to Israel. This put the official seal on arrangements provisionally agreed upon between Peres and Abel Thomas, who was Bourgès-Maunoury's "Gray Eminence" and one of Israel's best friends. Thomas had also promised Israel great quantities of arms and that French planes would drop supplies to Israeli armored columns as they advanced across the Sinai Peninsula.

The next point discussed was the "pretext." Someone proposed sending an Israeli vessel to pass through the Suez Canal. The Egyptians were bound to turn it back, or possibly even seize it—and the Israeli attack would begin. But this idea did not meet with much support. Pineau, who was the most cautious of the French, would have liked a Franco-British action directed at the Canal, independent of the Israeli offensive. But he was in the minority. Finally, the forumula adopted in general terms was that the Israelis should carry out a limited offensive which threatened the Canal and justified Franco-British intervention to safeguard it. This was the formula which was put to Selwyn Lloyd when he arrived accompanied by Patrick Dean, head of the Middle East Department at the Foreign Office.

The two Englishmen, who appeared ill-at-ease, had flown across in a RAF plane and landed at Villacoublay too, at the end of the morning. The atmosphere of the talks, which had so far been friendly and relaxed, became stiff and formal. The handshake between Ben-Gurion and Lloyd was a cool, fleeting touch "for the record." Everyone present noticed their mutual distrust. Selwyn Lloyd seemed furious that he, Her Majesty's Minister for Foreign Affairs, should be obliged to prepare in secret with the Prime Minister of tiny Israel, the enemy of Britain's Arab friends, a concerted attack against those friends. Ben-Gurion, shedding none of his distrust of the British, peered searchingly at the other's ruddy face.

The decisive stage of the conference began, each side giving its point of view on the details of the offensive. Remarkably, Ben-Gurion spoke very little, and left these final negotiations to Peres and Dayan. In fact, at no time during the Sèvres talks did he really "negotiate." At the most, he seized on a detail from time to time, then sat back and started discussing his favorite subjects, history and philosophy. "He's a philosopher," a French minister confided to a friend, with a trace of criticism.

The Old Man remained philosophic and somewhat aloof throughout this session, although deliberating in asides with his aides when they consulted him on some point. But in general he avoided entering into operational details, either because he was conscious of his position or through dislike of the "give-and-take" tactics.

The evening shadows were creeping into the large dining room when the session came to a close. The main lines of the action had been agreed: Israel would strike first by dropping paratroops in the Canal area, and would announce the raid over the radio. Britain and France would then address a joint ultimatum to Israel and Egypt, demanding that each country withdraw its troops ten miles from the Canal on their respective sides of it. Israel would accept, but Egypt was almost certain to reject the discriminatory Franco-British conditions, and the RAF would then attack Egyptian airfields, destroying the fighters and bombers on the ground, thus removing all fear of the Israeli cities being bombed and the Israeli columns attacking in Sinai being subjected to air attack. Finally, Franco-British forces would land and seize the Suez Canal.

The British did not know of the French agreement to give air and naval protection to the densely populated coastal regions of Israel, and to drop supplies to advance Israeli units in the Sinai Peninsula. This was in keeping with their policy of feigning ignorance of any anti-Arab collusion.

Selwyn Lloyd, who had been like a cat on hot bricks all afternoon, left with a sigh of relief to fly back to London. Pineau went with him, wanting to be sure—as he confessed later—that Lloyd gave a proper report to Eden and that the latter was in agreement. Guy Mollet returned to Paris and the stormy Parliamentary debate. Patrick Dean remained behind to sign the agreement on behalf of Britain the next day.

The sun rose in a clear blue sky, giving every promise of a fine day. Pineau was back early from London, triumphantly bringing Eden's agreement. The dining table was used again on the third morning of this top-secret conference. Gathered round it for the final session were Ben-Gurion, Dayan and Peres, Pineau, Bourgès-Maunoury, Mangin, Challe, Patrick Dean and another Foreign Office official who had arrived from London earlier in the morning. They fixed the dates of the operation and arranged the details of the landings and the paratroop drop, as well as matters such as the bombing of the Egyptian airfields and the attitude to adopt at the United Natons if the Security Council met and condemned Israel's action. On this last question, differences arose between the British and French. The former were not inclined to give open support to Israel. There was still deep distrust between the British and Jews. The latter were satisfied when Pineau added a paragraph in his own writing to the final document, stipulating the assistance that the French would give to Israel.

That day the others saw a different Ben-Gurion. "This isn't the philosopher," someone murmured. He was his old decisive self, getting to the bottom of problems in his usual way, analyzing the different points and clearly expressing his position in well-formed and succinct phrases. Only when something under discussion did not meet with his approval did he talk about philosophy or history again. He did not negotiate—he said "yes" when he was in agreement, but otherwise he just ceased to pay attention to the point under discussion and took refuge in his "historiosophy." The others knew that this meant "no."

In the evening, Dean, Pineau and Ben-Gurion signed a provisional document which was sent for Eden's approval. Ben-Gurion signed another "secret document" that evening. During a private consultation of the Israelis, Dayan wanted to draw a rough plan of the Sinai offensive, but had no paper. Someone produced an empty cigarette pack, and Dayan drew a rough map of the Sinai Peninsula on the back and put in arrows to show the direction of the offensive. Afterwards, Dayan and Peres signed this top-secret cigarette pack, and Ben-Gurion did the same, laughing freely. The "document" was carefully preserved.

The final signatures were to be given to the "Sèvres protocol" the following morning. There was still time for Ben-Gurion to change his mind. Some hours of inner debate were ahead of him, as Peres alluded to in his memoirs: "More than once I have seen David Ben-Gurion faced with a fateful decision, but I shall never forget that evening and night of October 24, 1956 . . . Great numbers of officers and men risked their lives during the Sinai campaign; many showed great courage. But the decision had to be taken, in a certain place and by a certain person, while several of the factors for and against were still obscure and some elements were missing, frighteningly so. We were sitting under the trees with Ben Gurion—Moshe Dayan, Nhemia Argov and myself. None of us envied him the long, lonely hours ahead. But in the morning we found him fresh and ready as ever. His decision was made—once again, and for the good of Israel."

The following morning, October 25, after the final signing, a French plane took Ben-Gurion and his party back to Israel. Peres went at once to his office, which became the liaison center with the French. Dayan, at Army Headquarters, revised the operation order dated October 5, which had the limited objective of the northern part of the Sinai Peninsula, and fixed the aims of the new offensive as being the proximity of the Suez Canal. Ben-Gurion went home. The traveling and change of climate, and so much emotion, had had their effect on him. He was soon in bed with a high fever.

In four days' time Israel was due to go to war.

Mobilization was in full swing by Friday, October 26. At Army Headquarters the tireless Dayan held meeting after meeting of his staff officers. The Commander-in-Chief was full of confidence. Unlike Ben-Gurion, he did not fear Egyptian bombers. Army signals were almost jammed by a record number of coded messages and secret dispatches from France. At the Paris end, an Israeli Army officer was acting as interpreter at the War Ministry. At Tel Aviv, the Defense Ministry was already ordering railroad ties for extending the railway to Gaza. Swarthy-faced soldiers with an Oriental appearance—immigrants from Arab countries—were drawing up propaganda appeals directed at the population in the Sinai Peninsula. The elections in Jordan had been held on October 20 and, as expected, had resulted in overwhelming victory for the pro-Nasser party. Consequently, Jordan proclaimed her readiness to join the military alliance proposed by Egypt and Syria, through which the Arabs had long dreamed of crushing Israel. The counter-espionage services of the Israeli Army kept putting out false reports of Iraqi troops having crossed into Jordan. The tension this created on the eastern borders of Israel led to a belief that if there were war it would be in that direction.

The Russians were involved with the Hungarian Revolution and would find it difficult to intrude elsewhere at this time. It was consoling. Ben-Gurion received the MAPAI ministers and informed them of the imminent offensive. Golda Meir had of course known what was afoot for some time. Eshkol had heard about it vaguely, as Ben-Gurion had approached him for funds to purchase aircraft. Aran showed some anxiety. The Minister for Trade, Sapir, said in an aside to Ben-Gurion: "I heard in Switzerland that important deposits of oil have been discovered in Sinai." The Old Man pricked up his ears. He had his own ideas about Sinai, but he said nothing of them to Sapir. "You're against the offensive, aren't you?" he flung at him instead. "I'm in favor of extending Israel's frontiers," retorted the wily and ebullient Sapir, "without connecting it with some action or other." Ben-Gurion smiled, and said, "I pity the traders who have to put up with replies like that from you."

The following day, Saturday, some French ships that had been renamed and hurriedly painted a different color, to confuse observers, discharged two hundred heavy trucks at a port in the north of Israel. It was manna from heaven for General Dayan. He allocated this transport to the units ordered to advance rapidly across the Sinai Peninsula. The naval protection promised by France was approaching Israeli waters, formed by the trio *Surcouf, Kersaint* and *Bouvet*. In the evening, a number of big Nord Atlas French planes arrived from Cyprus with equipment and technicians. Two squadrons of Mystère fighters and Sabre F-86 bombers, which had been withdrawn from the French forces with NATO, landed at military airfields and Lydda Airport. The Israelis had never seen so many military aircraft. Troops were sent to the Jordan frontier to add to the belief that Israel might be about to invade her eastern neighbor. Eisenhower became alarmed and prepared an urgent message for Ben-Gurion. But the head of the CIA ; Allen Dulles, in his office a few hundred yards from the White House, knew the truth of the matter, that the United States Army had obligingly organized an airlift from Florida to France in order to supply the French Sabres with extra fuel tanks. But he never informed Eisenhower of what was really behind the preparations in Israel, and he has never given any reason for not doing so. In London, Abel Thomas asked the British to speed up their timetable. He was certain that the Israelis would beat all records and occupy the Sinai Peninsula earlier than planned. And he had a long talk with Selwyn Lloyd about remarks made by some of his Israeli friends that there were intentions to annex the Sinai Peninsula.

In Jerusalem, Ben-Gurion saw the ministers belonging to other parties in the coalition government, although he still had a fever, and informed them of the imminent offensive. He was assailed with questions, but evaded all reference to cooperation with foreign powers and made no mention of the Sèvres conference. The ministers belonging to MAPAM, the Extreme-Left United Workers' Party, were opposed to the offensive.

On Sunday morning, October 28, there was a Cabinet meeting. Afterwards, a vaguely-worded statement was issued, referring to "tension with the Arabs" and "the urgent necessity to call up reservists." Dayan already had nearly 90,000 reservists under arms. The Government had, by a large majority, given its approval to the Sinai offensive. This was not enough for Ben-Gurion. That afternoon he summoned the leaders of the parliamentary groups (except the Communists) to his bedside and told them of the plan to attack. For the first time in years, his greatest enemy on the political scene, Menahem Begin, was there in his company. After receiving one party leader after another and talking to them of preparations for war, he obtained their complete support.

In the early evening one of his aides arrived breathless, the bearer of a sealed envelope. It contained a message from Eisenhower. He had sent one to Ben-Gurion on October 16, through the Israeli ambassador, Abba Eban, and Ben-Gurion had replied on October 20, emphasizing the grave situation arising from Iraqi troops having crossed into Jordan. Eisenhower's latest communication, dated October 27 and headed "Secret," repeated his warning to Israel but was moderately worded:

". . . I cannot say that I am in agreement with your present position, but in any case Iraqi troops have not crossed into Jordan, so far as I am aware. I hope that you consider the suspension of this troop movement to be a contribution to peace in the region. I must frankly express to you the anxiety I feel on learning of the mobilization taking place on your side; this is a move which, I fear, can but increase the tension that you say you would like to see reduced.

"These are days of great strain . . . I am sure that only a peaceful and moderate attitude can really bring an improvement in the situation, and I am renewing the appeal made to you by Secretary Dulles, notably that your Government should take no initiative in the use of force, which would threaten the peaceful relations and growing friendship between our two countries."

At eight o'clock that evening Ben-Gurion, having returned to Tel Aviv, sent for Jacob (Jacky) Herzog, one of Israel's best diplomats and the son of the Chief Rabbi. This highly intelligent and resolute man had recently been appointed head of the American Department at the Israeli Foreign Ministry. In the battle to come he was to be a member of Ben-Gurion's inner Cabinet with special responsibility for international relations. For the moment, Ben-Gurion wanted him to draft a prudent reply to Eisenhower's letter.

Nothing could now stop the Israeli war machine.

Earlier that day a messenger had been sent to Washington with a sealed envelope containing all the secrets of the imminent offensive to deliver into the hands of Abba Eban. But the messenger did not arrive in time.

Monday, October 29, was D-Day. It began at five in the morning, when the sentries outside the Ministry of Defense at Tel Aviv saw a man get out of a car with Diplomatic Corps license plates and hurry towards the entrance to the Ministry. They stopped him. He was a counselor at the United States Embassy and had a thick envelope in his hand—another message from President Eisenhower, for the urgent attention of Prime Minister Ben-Gurion. At seven o'clock Jacob Herzog took the letter to Ben-Gurion, who had had a restless night and was again feverish.

"My dear Prime Minister," Eisenhower had written, "yesterday I sent you a personal message . . . This morning I have received new reports indicating that the mobilization of Israel's armed forces is continuing and is almost complete. This new message is motivated by the seriousness of the situation as I see it.

"In view of the wide repercussions which might result from the present grave state of tension in the Middle East, and also in view of the intentions expressed by the United States in the Tripartite Declaration of May 25, 1950, I have given instructions for the situation to be discussed with the United Kingdom and France, the other signatories to the above-mentioned Declaration, and for them to be asked to exercise all possible efforts to improve the situation. I have also given orders for other States in the Middle East to be informed of my anxiety, and to be urgently requested to abstain from any action which might lead to the opening of hostilities.

"Once again, Mister Prime Minister, I feel obliged to emphasize the dangers arising from the present situation and to request most earnestly that your Government do nothing which might threaten peace."

At first Ben-Gurion had been dismayed on receiving the letter, fearing that it contained an ultimatum or was intended to bring great pressure to bear on Israel. But when he had studied it carefully, he saw that the tone of the letter was not too disconcerting. But there was something sad in seeing the head of a great Power with a completely erroneous idea of the situation, believing quite candidly that the seat of the fire was to the east of Israel and thinking of appealing to the very countries which, at that moment, were in collusion with Israel. The smoke screen drawn over the operation had obviously been most effective.

Ben-Gurion disliked deceiving the Americans, whose country had played a decisive role in making the State of Israel a reality. But he had no choice. And Eisenhower's reference to the Tripartite Declaration of May 1950 explains to some extent the bitterness felt by the American President when he discovered, a few hours after sending his letter to Ben-Gurion, that he had been taken in by all concerned.

At eleven-thirty Herzog brought Ben-Gurion the draft of the reply to Eisenhower. The Old Man approved the general tenor. It indicated that Nasser was chiefly responsible for the tension in the Middle East because of his expansionist policy, subversive activities and purchase of armaments from the Russians, and enumerated the Egyptian aggressions against Israel, and referred to the creation of the "united Arab command" by Syria, Egypt and Jordan, the fresh incursions of the Fedayin and the closing of the Suez Canal and the Aqaba Gulf to Israeli shipping: "Considering the presence of large Iraqi forces on the Iraq-Jordan frontier, the creation of a united command by Egypt, Syria and Jordan, the growing Egyptian influence over Jordan and the fresh raids into Israel by Egyptian gangs, my Government would be failing in its essential duty if it did not take all necessary measures to ensure that the Arabs do not succeed in their declared aim of eliminating Israel by force. My Government has appealed to the people of Israel to remain calm and vigilant. I am confident that with your vast military experience you will fully appreciate the crucial danger in which we are placed."

Ben-Gurion did not promise Eisenhower that he would not go to war. In the afternoon, after informing the French ambassador of the imminent attack on the Egyptians, he went back to bed. The book by his bedside—his reading during the forthcoming campaign—was entitled *The Intellect of Prehistoric Man*.

That afternoon, a few Israeli planes took off and flew across the Sinai Peninsula at very low level, ripping away telephone wires with hooks attached to their fuselages, thus cutting the communications of several Egyptian Army bases with their headquarters in Cairo. When the hooks proved ineffective, the pilots went even lower to cut the wires with their propellers.

Dayan went to see Ben-Gurion at a quarter past five. At that moment, nearly four hundred paratroops were being dropped on the Mitla Pass, a score or so of miles from the Suez Canal. The news was flashed around the world that Israel had gone to war. In Washington, Abba Eban was assuring Undersecretary of State Rowntree of Israel's peaceful intentions when one of the latter's staff brought him a hastily scribbled note. He glanced at it, then sharply interrupted the Israeli Ambassador: "I think this conversation has become somewhat academic . . ." Moshe Sharett heard the news while in New Delhi, on his way to an appointment with Nehru. At last the Israeli Ambassador in Paris knew what was happening.

The Suez War had started.

THIRTY

THE INVASION OF SINAI

"I have no idea what will be the fate of Sinai. What interests us is the Eilath coastal strip and the straits. I imagine that if we occupied the Sinai Peninsula a certain number of Powers would force us to evacuate it. France and Britain are with us, but they are not everyone. There's America and Russia, there's also the United Nations and Nehru, Asia and Africa, and I'm thinking more of the Americans than the others, because they would force us to withdraw. The United States wouldn't need to send troops; it would be enough for them to announce that diplomatic relations were being broken off, that collections for the Jewish funds were forbidden and loans to Israel blocked. The United States are going to calculate which is more important to them—us or the Arabs. I don't know what they will decide. I'm not making you a present of the two Yotvat islands . . .

"If a passive peace were offered us, I would accept it. What we are most concerned about is free movement for our shipping. We have a sentimental interest in Yotvat, but I'm prepared to give way on that point as it's not essential to us. What is essential to us is free movement for our shipping, even if we don't stay in the Sinai Peninsula . . . The Gaza strip is a hindrance; we've got to take it, but it's a burden to us. If I believed in miracles, I would like it to sink beneath the sea. . . ."

Ben-Gurion was speaking to the Cabinet, on October 28, 1956. He did not want the Gaza Strip; he would be forced to withdraw from the Sinai Peninsula; the islands of Tiran and Sanafir were not essential . . . But did he reveal all of his thoughts? Some of the remarks he made after the campaign indicate that he may have been hoping that Israel would be able, after all, to keep the Sinai Peninsula. What a wonderful diplomatic and strategic advantage

224

that would have been—the Israeli Army almost on the doorstep of Cairo!

On the evening of October 29 he was waiting anxiously for news of the 395 paratroops dropped hundreds of miles behind the enemy lines. Waiting with him were Nhemia, his secretary, Itzhak Navon, and Paula, who was ill like her husband but had kept it from him. At nine o'clock the prearranged announcement was made over the Israeli radio: "An Israeli Army spokesman has announced that units have penetrated Egyptian positions at Ras el Nakb and that fighting is in progress. Other Israeli forces have occupied positions west of the Nakh'l road junction, in the neighborhood of the Suez Canal."

Now it was the turn of the British and the French. The latter arrived first. Late that night their planes dropped supplies to the Israeli paratroops—jeeps, guns and ammunition, cigarettes, jerricans of water and of gasoline, brought from the French depots established in Cyprus. During the eight days of the campaign the French never once failed to keep the Israeli advance columns supplied with fuel and munitions. The British pretended to know nothing of these air-drops.

While the paratroops were digging in on the Mitla heights, two armored columns crossed the frontier and started their dash across the desert, sweeping aside the small Egyptian detachments in their path. One column headed westward, the other made for the Mitla Pass to join up with the paratroops. The High Command expected the junction to be made in 36 hours, for it was a crack task force.

Ben-Gurion was very anxious about the paratroops dropped behind the enemy lines. However, when he had been informed that the operation was going according to plan, he soon went to sleep.

The following day, the Israeli columns advancing across the Sinai Peninsula met with strong resistance from Egyptian forces. There were several air battles—Egyptian Migs attacked the Israeli columns, and Israeli Mystères shot up Egyptian reinforcements. Meanwhile, French fighter planes were patrolling the Israeli coast, but no Egyptian bombers were sighted. Ben-Gurion's fears for the centers of population proved to be unfounded. The French fighters took off the next day to attack Egyptian convoys in the Sinai Peninsula. The Israeli forces had strict orders not to carry the fighting beyond the peninsula.

Cables were flowing in from Paris, London and Washington. In New York, the Security Council held an emergency meeting. At

225

noon, the Franco-British ultimatums were due to be sent to Israel and Egypt as arranged at Sèvres. But there were already signs of British hesitation, and the ultimatums calling upon both sides to withdraw ten miles from the Canal (again in keeping with the Sèvres arrangement), were not sent until four o'clock. Israel accepted the ultimatum, and Golda Meir sent an affirmative reply at midnight. Egypt, as expected, rejected it.

Eisenhower made an attempt to restore peace. He sent Sherman Adams to establish contact with the American Zionist leader, Abba Silver. "The President asks you to get in touch with Mr. Ben-Gurion," Adams informed the Zionist leader, "and to give him this message—that President Eisenhower proposes, in view of the fact that your objectives have been reached and the terrorist bases destroyed, that you immediately withdraw your troops into Israeli territory. If you do this, the President promises to issue immediately a declaration of deep respect and solid friendship towards Israel. The President emphasizes that despite the present, temporary interests that Israel has in common with France and Britain, you ought not to forget that the strength of Israel and her future are bound up with the United States. He expects a prompt reply."

The Israeli ambassador, Eban, was informed of the message while in New York, where he had gone to attend the Security Council meeting. The young diplomat was very much pro-American and was in favor of accepting Eisenhower's proposal. He cabled to Ben-Gurion: "I suggest a careful reexamination of our relations with the United States, especially in view of the positive developments which have occurred today . . ."

In Israel, the "positive developments" of the day were, for Ben-Gurion and Dayan, the successes in the Sinai Peninsula. The advance continued.

However, that evening, Ben-Gurion had a very difficult time. France and Britain had vetoed the United Nations resolution blaming Israel. But the air attack on the Egyptian airfields which was supposed to take place at dawn on October 31 was delayed until the evening. Ben-Gurion was both furious and anxious—he feared for the paratroops holding the Mitla bridgehead, and even thought of ordering their withdrawal. Dayan arrived to tell him that the armored column had joined up with the paratroops after a 28-hour advance across the Sinai Peninsula. Ben-Gurion spoke to him of withdrawing the spearhead, but fortunately Dayan convinced him that the force must continue to advance according to plan. Dayan's presence just then had a beneficial effect on Ben-Gurion, whose doubts about the British had been revived. The Commander-in-Chief asserted that he did not believe the French and the British would fail them, and that even if they did the Israeli forces must press on. Dayan, a bold leader who had confidence in his army's ability, was convinced that he could win the battle even without help from others. Late that night he got Ben-Gurion to agree to continue the advance. In the meantime, telephone communication had been established between Tel Aviv and Paris. Guy Mollet in person gave the assurances that the delayed air attack on Egyptian airfields would definitely begin the following evening.

At dawn that day the inhabitants of Haifa were roused from sleep by the dull roar of naval guns. An unknown cruiser was shelling the harbor. One of the French "protection" ships which was cruising off Haifa came up and at once opened fire on the intruder. She was an Egyptian ship, the *Ibrahim El Awal,* and was obviously not expecting to meet a large warship, for she turned away and made for the open sea. The French vessel alerted the Israeli High Command. Aircraft and gunboats went after the fleeing Egyptian ship and forced her to return to Haifa. This was the greatest capture by the Israelis during the Sinai Campaign.

The capture of the *Ibrahim* by Israeli forces, aided by the French, was the first news that Ben-Gurion heard on the morning of October 31, and he regarded it as proof that the French were keeping to the secret pact. Although the air attacks on Egyptian airfields had not begun, the French continued to drop supplies to the Israeli advance forces in Sinai. Moreover, at dawn the following day, the *Georges Leygues* shelled the Rafah strongpoint which was holding out against Israeli attacks. The shelling proved to be of no importance, but the French action had given a great boost to Israeli morale.

October 31 was the most important day in the Sinai Campaign. The desert became a battlefield, with thousands of men and hundreds of tanks and guns in action and scores of planes engaged in fights across the sky. News of Israeli victories led to scenes of wild enthusiasm throughout the country.

It was a different matter on the international scene. Russia declared the Israeli action to be "unworthy aggression," but was in no position to intervene. At the United Nations, however, an urgent meeting of the General Assembly was called, supported by Russia and the United States. Eisenhower continued to put pressure on Israel. Sherman Adams telephoned Silver, and then the President himself, disregarding the usual diplomatic channels, spoke to the

Zionist leader. "I want to know if you got in touch with Ben-Gurion and passed on my message yesterday," said Eisenhower. "Does he intend to withdraw his forces? You can tell him that I'm concerned for an immmediate improvement in our relations with Israel. Say to him that if I'm informed in the next few hours of his intention to evacuate Sinai, I'm prepared to make an announcement most friendly to Israel in a radio and television broadcast this evening."

Ben-Gurion was annoyed on learning of this, but the Israeli ambassador in Washington did not seem unduly offended by this unconventional approach. In veiled terms, he again advised acceptance of Eisenhower's proposition. "I ask you to examine the President's proposition very closely and to give top priority to cabling the reply" was his message to Tel Aviv. The realities of the fighting and of what was at stake seemed to escape him.

Ben-Gurion became impatient for the Franco-British action to begin, so that the world pressure being placed upon the tiny State of Israel would be distributed between all the signatories to the Sèvres pact. At seven that evening, RAF bombers began to attack Egyptian airfields. But it served little purpose, for the British had given warning of the attack by radio, and the ground staff could take shelter. This also gave Egyptian air crews ample time to take off and fly their planes out of danger. Moreover, Nasser's tanks and armored vehicles took refuge in the towns, as the British had promised not to attack civilian targets. The raids consequently had as little effect as the psychological warfare leaflets which were showered over the towns.

At least, however, some of the pressure was taken off Israel, and world attention turned to Britain and France. Eisenhower ceased urging Zionist leaders to get in touch with Ben-Gurion, and directed his anger at the French and British leaders instead, especially Eden. "But what's Anthony thinking of, then?" he exclaimed on learning of the bombing of the Egyptian airfields. "Doing a thing like that to me!"

While the debates continued at the United Nations, the Israeli forces continued to advance in Sinai. The Egyptian positions in front of Rafah were overrun and the strongpoint itself was captured soon afterwards. The Egyptian General Amer gave orders for Jordan and Syria to attack Israel, in accordance with the recently-signed agreement with Egypt. But their armies did not budge, and the Arab military pact was stillborn.

Abroad, the General Assembly called for an immediate cease-fire. The French and British were dismayed—their landings were planned for November 6 and it was only the first of the month. The French urged the British to bring the date of the attack forward, but in vain. They insisted on keeping to the original plan, and the French saw success slipping away—all because of agreeing to the British having command of the military operation.

On that day Nasser gave orders for the Canal to be blocked, and army engineers sank several ships at each end.

Dayan gave his troops no respite. And on November 2 the two large Egyptian towns of Gaza and El Arish fell to the Israelis.

The Russians were beginning to recover from the effects of the Hungarian Revolution. A recruiting office for volunteers to help the Egyptians was opened in Moscow. The timing was good. That morning, the United Nations' decision for a cease-fire had been handed to the representatives of Britain, France and Israel. Every hour mattered.

By the following day, November 3, the Israelis were in possession of the whole of the Sinai Peninsula. In the evening, Abba Eban was able to inform the General Assembly that Israel had observed the cease-fire.

It was now the turn of the French and British to act. Ben-Gurion, slowly recovering from his illness, was skeptical. He did not believe that they would resist the increasing pressure from the United States. The date for the Franco-British landings was still November 6.

Ben-Gurion was particularly anxious to preserve the different character of "his war." He gave express orders for Israeli troops to respect the ultimatum of October 30 and not to advance within ten miles of the Canal. Israel had to show that she had nothing to do with the Suez conflict. When Dayan went to see Ben-Gurion on the evening of November 3, the latter said: "We've enough problems without Suez, and we shan't gain anything by belonging to a coalition which has the whole world against it. We must concentrate on Sinai and not intervene in the Suez question."

The French had realized that the dilatory attitude of the British was leading to failure. The General Assembly was due to meet again on November 5 and would undoubtedly insist even more strongly on a cease-fire. The French wanted to be in a position to accept it—in other words, to be in possession of the Canal.

It seemed possible. A French liaison officer saw Dayan and asked if he would cooperate in a bold plan. The French were preparing to drop paratroops near Port Fouad at dawn on November 4, capture the town and advance rapidly along the Canal. They asked the Israelis to attack Qantara, on the eastern side of the Canal, with the object of drawing most of the Egyptian forces in that direction, which would facilitate the French advance.

Dayan agreed, and even proposed that the French make use of the Sinai roads. But he had to obtain Ben-Gurion's approval. This was at once forthcoming, as Ben-Gurion could not forget the help received from France. Nevertheless, he remained doubtful of the French being able to free themselves so easily of the crippling effect of British participation in the conspiracy. He proved to be right.

To the British, the Israelis were enemies to be kept away from the Suez Canal in accordance with the ultimatum. This obstinacy in adhering strictly to the Sèvres pact, even when it meant jeopardizing the whole operation, was one of the reasons for the failure of the Suez affair. While the most friendly relations existed between the French and Israelis, the British remained aloof, distrustful and distrusted.

When Abba Eban informed the General Assembly that "a cease-fire had been ordered all over the Sinai territory," he added that "Israel was ready to accept a general and immediate cease-fire on condition that Egypt did the same." The Israelis had weighed the matter thoroughly, but had overlooked one important factor—the effect of their declaration upon the Franco-British intervention. The French were dismayed, and asked Israel not to accept a general cease-fire until after their troops had landed. Ben-Gurion saw that it was not so easy to break away from "the Suez plough." But he remained loyal to his friends and sent new instructions to Abba Eban.

On November 4 the Israeli Ambassador made a statement affirming that a *de facto* but not a *de jure* cease-fire existed in the Sinai Peninsula. In order for the latter to be applied, he put five questions to the Egyptian delegate:

1. Was Egypt in agreement, clearly and unambiguously, for a general cease-fire?

2. Did Egypt consider that a state of war existed between herself and Israel?

3. Was Egypt prepared to start negotiations with Israel to establish peace between the two countries?

4. Would Egypt agree to raise her economic boycott and the blockade of Israeli shipping?

5. Did Egypt intend to withdraw her Fedayin bands in other Arab countries?

The maneuver was obvious, but the "pretext" which was of such great importance to the French had been saved just in time. There was no *de jure* cease-fire, and the French and British could still intervene to protect the international waterway. Israel had done her part. Yet the French and British reactions, far from expressing any gratitude, caused a sharp crisis between the partners to the Sèvres pact.

Through imprudence or haste, a Franco-British note was sent to the United Nations: "The two Governments still believe that the intervention of an international force is necessary in order to prevent the continuance of hostilities between Egypt and Israel, and to ensure the prompt withdrawal of the Israeli forces . . ." This paragraph, which was contrary to the agreement drawn up at Sèvres, had been included at the request of the British. Ben-Gurion at once sent a cable to Paris, asking how his French friends could have associated themselves with such a statement.

Guy Mollet was in a fix. He instructed the French representative at the United Nations to point out that the reference to the Israeli withdrawal was intended to apply only to the neighborhood of the Suez Canal. But this did not entirely convince Ben-Gurion.

The Russians were now free to concentrate on the Middle East, and the following day Israel received a strongly-worded and threatening note from Bulganin, who also sent notes to London and Paris. The latter notes were courteous and moderate in tone, but nevertheless he called the Anglo-French intervention which had at last taken place that day, November 5, an "act of aggression." "We are fully decided to crush aggressors by force," said the Russian note to the French Government. "What situation would France be in if she were the object of an aggression by other States who possess terrible, modern means of destruction?" An identical phrase appeared in the note to the British Government.

The Soviet Union was threatening to use atomic weapons for the first time. The French were skeptical, the British less so. The danger to Israel, however, was much greater even with the use of conventional weapons. Israel was not a member of NATO and could certainly not resist an attack by the Russian Army. Air raids on Tel Aviv, Haifa and Jerusalem could utterly destroy the State of Israel. Reports had been received of Russian preparations to send "volunteer units" to the Middle East.

Ben-Gurion did not panic, but instructed his aides to sound out the French on the dangers of Soviet intervention against Israel. Dayan noted with keen discernment: "If the Russian Notes had been sent to Britain, France and Israel before October 29, who can say whether there would have been a Sinai campaign?"

In any case, Israel profited from the confusion in international spheres and by the morning of November 5 had ended her own war.

The fighting around Port Said continued all that day. But even when the first paratroops were dropped, any justification for the action had already ended. The Israelis had stopped fighting, and the United Nations had decided to send an international force to police the Suez area. What pretext was there for the Anglo-French operation?

Alarming reports were reaching NATO Headquarters that the Russians were about to intervene in the conflict. By November 6 communications were being swamped by rumors of Soviet intervention. It was the greatest bluff of the postwar period, and Eden was undoubtedly the person most affected. He was a sick man, full of doubts, but at midday on November 6 he decided to abandon the Suez operation and telephoned Paris to inform Guy Mollet that he was calling a halt to the fighting. The French Premier, embarrassed by the fact that Chancellor Adenauer was on an official visit to Paris, failed to persuade Eden to continue with the operation, and he refused to carry on alone. Mollet hurriedly called a Cabinet meeting and was supported in his decision.

Ben-Gurion had been right in thinking that the French and British would not hold out for long against pressure from the United Nations.

Nasser ordered a cease-fire to take effect at midnight. A few hours earlier he had been in danger of succumbing, but now he gained a victory by doing nothing. The Suez operation turned out to be a fiasco.

But the Sinai Campaign did not. At one o'clock on the afternoon of that fateful November 6, just when Eden was telling Mollet that he was pulling out, a moving ceremony took place at Sharm El Sheikh in Sinai. Some hundreds of Israeli soldiers, exhausted but proud, stood at attention as their flag was hoisted on an Egyptian mast. On the improvised saluting platform—the chassis of two command cars—were Moshe Dayan, the handsome general with a pirate's eye patch, General Simchoni and Colonel Jaffe. Dayan read out the Order of the Day to the troops on parade and then a letter from Ben-Gurion (who was still confined to his room). This was followed by a review, and so ended the Sinai Campaign.

"A few hours ago, when I informed Ben-Gurion of the end of the campaign," wrote Dayan in his diary, "he said to me half-mockingly, 'And you can't resign yourself to it, I suppose?' I didn't reply. He knew that what worries me is not the end of the fighting but whether we can stand fast in the diplomatic campaign which is about to open."

While people in London and Paris were dismally meditating over their failure, all Israel was celebrating the successful war.

THIRTY-ONE

DISILLUSION

November 7, 1956, was a great day for Ben-Gurion. Still weak from his recent illness, he made his victory speech to the Knesset. "The armistice agreement with Egypt is dead and buried," he said, and went on to propose that peace negotiations be opened directly with Cairo.

What was to be the future of occupied Sinai? When Dayan had asked Ben-Gurion if Israel would keep the territory, he had replied: "I hope so, but I'm not sure. We shan't hang on to it with the same tenacity as we did over Jerusalem." But now he was beginning to think differently . . . "After all, Sinai never has been part of Egypt."

It is easy to understand this great war leader's intoxication with this astonishing, complete victory, though not without battles and casualties on both sides. One hundred and seventy Israeli soldiers and about one thousand Egyptians had been killed. The short war had aroused national feelings, and not long afterwards, the number of Communists in Israel dropped by fifty percent. The return to Sinai was an emotional event to every Jew, reminding him of Moses and the exodus from Egypt. When Ben-Gurion, fully recovered and wearing military uniform, was traveling across the wide expanses of the historic peninsula he met the Israeli officer who had been appointed governor-general of Sinai. "I'd willingly exchange my position for his," he exclaimed. "He can become Prime Minister, and I'll be Governor of Sinai! How wonderful!"

But would Israel be able to keep Sinai? It was too early to know for sure. However, the victory had brought immediate benefits. The approaches to Eilath were open again and ships were already using the port to discharge their cargoes for Israel. The big Egyptian guns at Sharm El Sheikh had been blown up and were useless heaps of twisted metal. The Fedayin bases in the Sinai Peninsula and the Gaza Strip had been destroyed.

But most important of all, the legend of Egyptian strength and Arab military supremacy had been shattered. In the past, the Western Powers and the United Nations had found that the simplest way of preventing a flare-up in the Middle East was to call on Israel to make concessions. They had remained silent over the Egyptian blockade of the Aqaba Gulf and refusal to allow Israeli shipping to use the Suez Canal. This attitude changed after the Sinai victory. For many years to come, the Arabs would have to forsake their idea of destroying Israel. And now that Israel had shown herself to be the stronger, concessions would not be asked of her alone as a means of keeping the peace.

But Israel had only a short time to taste the joys of victory—one day. November 7 was a day of rejoicing, but the next was one of disillusion. It began well, however. Ben-Gurion held a Cabinet meeting to decide on the text of the reply to the Soviet note, and general approval was given to a noncommittal answer. The meeting ended midday, and it was then that the wind began to turn, bringing a shower of cables and disturbing reports from abroad. Ben-Gurion's speech to the Knesset had roused the anger of the United Nations, and there was talk of energetic measures being taken against Israel. The Russian threats reached new heights. Eisenhower, who had been reelected with an overwhelming majority, spoke of taking strong action. Goldman, the president of the Jewish World Congress, informed Ben-Gurion that American Jewry had been most happy about the Sinai victory but would not stand behind Israel if she persisted in keeping the conquered territory. He added that collections for the national Jewish funds might be forbidden. And Germany too, under American pressure, might stop paying reparations.

Early in the afternoon, a message from Eisenhower was given to Ben-Gurion. Its tone was quite friendly. It referred to the cease-fire which was being observed, the resolutions to send a United Nations police force to Egypt and the withdrawal of all foreign troops from Egyptian territory. "Certain declarations attributed to your Government have been brought to my notice," the American President then went on, "and according to these it appears that Israel does not intend to withdraw her forces from Egyptian territory, despite the resolutions of the United Nations. I must frankly admit, Mr. President, that the United States views these declarations, if they are true, with the deepest anxiety . . ."

The friendly tone did not conceal the threat to the future cooperation between the two countries. And this was stated much more precisely in the message which Secretary of State Dulles sent at the same time to Golda Meir. It spoke of economic sanctions against Israel and of vigorous action towards her expulsion from the United Nations.

Meanwhile, Ben-Gurion's special envoys in Paris had been consulting the French Government on the possibility of Russian intervention. "We are on your side," Pineau replied. "France will share all she has with Israel. But our combined means are not sufficient against the Soviet menace. In the circumstances, we can only advise you to withdraw."

Ben-Gurion again had to make a grave decision. It was the hardest of all, for he capitulated. But until the last he kept trying to obtain something positive—assurances, international guarantees, American promises concerning the Eilath approaches and the Gaza Strip.

Ben-Gurion instructed his diplomatic counselor, Herzog, to contact the Israeli ambassador in Washington and to get in touch with London, Paris and New York, At least, he succeeded in obtaining American assurances of support that Israel's shipping rights in the Aqaba Gulf would be respected and that the Gaza Strip would not again become a nest of Egyptian spies and army bases.

Ben-Gurion called his ministers together and informed them of his decision to conform to the United Nations resolutions and of the terms of his reply to Eisenhower. He received their approval.

That evening, the Israeli Radio told its listeners to stand by for an extremely important announcement. It was thirty minutes past midnight before Ben-Gurion was ready to go on the air. Then, in a tired voice, he spoke of the events of the past few days and read the text of his letter to Eisenhower. "Neither I nor any spokesman for the Israeli Government has ever said that we intend to annex the Sinai peninsula. In compliance with the resolutions of the United Nations relative to the withdrawal of foreign troops from Egypt and the creation of an international force, we shall readily withdraw our troops as soon as a satisfactory agreement has been reached with the United Nations regarding the entry of an international force into the Suez Canal Zone . . ."

Ben-Gurion finished reading out the letter, then paid a glowing tribute to the soldiers who had conquered Sinai. "After the Sinai campaign, Israel will never be the same as before that glorious operation. To the fighting men, I say this—History will reward us for your action, and I believe that our whole people will have deserved it."

He spoke for nearly half an hour. He had given in, but neither definitely nor completely. The veiled terms of his reply to Eisenhower were in fact the prelude to a hard diplomatic struggle that lasted four months, during which Ben-Gurion had but one aim—to preserve a few of the fruits of his victory. It was by no means easy, and for the first and last time in his career he showed himself to be a formidable negotiator.

Meanwhile, the British and French troops had been evacuated and their places taken by the United Nations' "Blue Helmets" under General Burns. Repentant Britain lined up behind the United States again, while Eden paid the price for his Suez adventure. The French were furious, convinced that their operational plans had been right. Nasser's prestige continued to increase. Only Israel, with French support at the United Nations, was endeavoring to retain some advantage from a campaign that the world was eager to forget.

Ben-Gurion tried first to get the idea accepted that Egypt must not be allowed to recover Sinai and that the eastern bank of the Suez Canal should remain in the hands of the United Nations, which would have been equivalent to the internationalization of the Canal. But he abandoned this position at the end of November and demanded that Egypt agree to the unrestricted use of the Canal by Israeli shipping. He failed in that, too. By mid-December he was saying of the Gaza Strip: "This is a matter for negotiation. Clearly, Egypt must not return there." At the end of December he was asking for the demilitarization of the eastern part of Sinai. Under American and international pressure, he gave way yet again. But he clung to two essentials for which he was prepared to go to war again and run the risk of sanctions—the command of the Eilath approaches and the Gaza Strip. His earlier demands were probably a diplomatic smoke screen, but there was no question about his determination over the latter. At the end of January 1957 the United Nations called upon him to evacuate the whole of the Sinai Peninsula. He withdrew the Israeli forces from most of the territory, but first they dismantled all the military installations, destroyed fortifications and ploughed up the roads and airfields.

Ben-Gurion said both before and after the Suez Campaign that he did not want to keep the Gaza Strip. What mattered to him was that the Egyptians should not return there to make a springboard of it for incursions into Israel. And it was not just the freeing of the Eilath approaches and the straits of Tiran that concerned him. He was looking ahead to the time when gasoline could be brought into the country through the port of Eilath and by pipeline across the Negev, as an alternative to using the Suez Canal.

By the beginning of February, United Nations pressure was

heavy. The Secretary-General, having visited Cairo, wished to go to Israel, but Ben-Gurion refused to see him. It was at this moment, when tension was at its height, that France entered the negotiations. Mollet and Pineau arrived in the United States and, while continuing to support Israel, proposed a fresh solution—that the Gaza Strip should be administered by the United Nations with the international police force stationed there, and that detachments of Blue Helmets be sent to control the Eilath approaches.

Ben-Gurion was not at all pleased. He did not want to withdraw from Gaza without having definite assurances that Egyptian forces would never return there. For the same reason, he had no wish to abandon the land control of the straits of Tiran. And yet he gave way.

His decision was realistic. In a few days' time the General Assembly was to meet, and sanctions might be voted against Israel if she had not withdrawn her forces. But probably the more powerful argument influencing Ben-Gurion was that the French might be offended if he refused to agree to their solution, and stop their supplies of armaments to Israel. The country would then be completely alone and faced with an economic crisis, open to attack by the Arabs or the Russian "volunteers." The United States had in fact already started to apply sanctions by blocking a loan promised to Israel some time previously.

On March 1, 1957, Mrs. Meir informed the General Assembly that Israel was withdrawing her forces. At the same time, a number of maritime Powers declared, with the connivance of Israel, that the Aqaba Gulf was international waters and could be freely used by the shipping of all countries. Israel would be within her rights in using force if Egypt ever tried to prevent her shipping from reaching Eilath.

Was this a success? Ben-Gurion thought so, and explained his reasons to the High Command. The MAPAM members of the Government, the same who had been against the attack on Sinai, were now opposed to the withdrawal. But Ben-Gurion believed that the freedom of navigation in the Aqaba Gulf and the international control of the Gaza Strip were blows to Nasser's prestige and could even lead to his downfall.

The order to withdraw was given. The United Nations force took over at Gaza and Sharm El Sheikh, while the Israeli Army evacuated the last of the territory conquered four months previously.

The sea approaches to Eilath remained open to shipping until May 1967, when the closing of the straits by Nasser brought the "Six-day War." On the other hand, the Sinai Campaign did not bring about the fall of Nasser, as Ben-Gurion had hoped, and the Gaza Strip did not remain under international control. The Egyptian Army and administration returned there in greater strength than before—and only ten years later was the Six-day War to change the situation.

Was the evacuation of the Sinai Peninsula a mistake? Several observers believe the decision was a wise one. Others bitterly regret the withdrawal and the failure to root out the Gaza tumor.

Ben-Gurion the realist had prevailed over Ben-Gurion the visionary. The statesman gave way to the Powers whom the war leader had defied.

One day, at a reunion of veterans of the Sinai Campaign, Ben-Gurion said sadly and thoughtfully: "You conquered Sinai, and I withdrew from it."

THIRTY-TWO

THE TEARS OF AN IDOL

Ben-Gurion had celebrated his seventieth birthday at Sde Boker only a few days before ordering the Sinai offensive—indicating that his mental faculties and willpower were not affected by age. It has been said that the decision to withdraw from Sinai was the most agonizing he ever had to make, and that the decision to attack was the most daring.

Those hectic and anxious days ultimately had a psychological effect on him, but for the moment he was on top of his work, and immersed himself in biblical studies. However, age was beginning to affect his physical condition. In 1957, he acquired a new lease on life by following the methods prescribed by Dr. Feldenkreis, which were based upon intensive exercise. Ben-Gurion began to practice yoga, walked three or four miles a day and did exercises which left his accompanying bodyguards out of breath. He needed to be physically fit, for other than personal reasons. Soon after the end of the Suez affair he engaged in a new offensive, the greatest and most successful of the diplomatic offensives of the State of Israel.

A great change had taken place in Israel's situation. The State was no longer threatened by destruction—the Iraqis were secretly rubbing their hands at Nasser's discomfort, and King Hussein of Jordan was grateful to the Israelis for having saved him from losing his crown. Syria, however, was slipping into the wide-open arms of the men in the Kremlin.

During the Suez affair, Russia had made a spectacular entry to the Middle East scene which could not fail to alarm the United States. Ben-Gurion took full advantage of this, siding with the Western Powers against the Russians. He had no illusions as to their designs on his country, and in the following months he endeavored to draw the maximum benefit from the Cold War, to exploit the anti-Russian hysteria of the Americans. Concurrently, urged on by his colleagues, he made overtures to European countries, particularly France, which had a close and special relation with Israel following the Suez affair. Holland, too, received special attention from the Israeli leaders.

Israel was to have her greatest successes, however, on other diplomatic fronts—in Africa, where Ghana triggered off the liberation from Colonial Powers, and on the periphery of the Middle East, among the non-Arab countries which could form a counter-weight to Nasser.

It was surely something of a paradox that Israel, which one might have expected to be isolated for many years after her aggression against Egypt, should be able to engage in a successful diplomatic offensive while still being blamed and condemned at the United Nations. But Israel found her prestige had increased after the Sinai Campaign.

Relations between Paris and Jerusalem had never been as good. The Suez affair had drawn the two countries close together and created mutual confidence which was to continue for a long time. The French sent Israel some Vautour jet bombers and Super-Mystère fighters, as well as tanks and artillery. French engineers started to lay a pipeline to carry oil across the Negev from Eilath to Haifa. The French Foreign Office could say little. After Suez, its relations with the Arabs were compromised for some time to come. At the United Nations, the French firmly supported their Mid East ally.

The United States was the second objective of Israeli diplomacy, and Ben-Gurion personally directed negotiations. The experiences during the Sinai Campaign had convinced him that without the support or at least the good wishes of the Americans he would not again be able to act boldly. Fortunately there existed a means of drawing the United States nearer to Israel—by playing on the Communist danger. So Ben-Gurion endeavored to become the Middle East champion of anti-Communism in the eyes of Washington. "I feel sure," Dulles wrote to Ben-Gurion in August 1957, "that you share our consternation over recent developments in Syria. We are studying the problem closely, and we should like to proceed to an exchange of views with your Government on this subject in the near future."

Ben-Gurion jumped at the opportunity. "The transforming of Syria into a base for international Communism is one of the most dangerous events that the free world has to face up to . . . I should like to draw your attention to the disastrous consequences if international Communism should succeed in establishing itself in the heart of the Middle East. I believe the free world ought not to accept this situation. Everything depends on the firm and determined line taken by the United States as a leading Power in the free world. If you adopt this line, Syria's neighbors other than Israel would certainly take strong measures to root out the danger. This might be the last opportunity to take action. Syria has not yet been formally declared a popular democracy, and the action I refer to would not necessarily lead to international complications. You can be sure that Israel would do nothing to hinder such action . . ."

Dulles did not take up Ben-Gurion's idea of starting a war on Syria through the intermediary of Turkey and Iraq. But Ben-Gurion was not really aiming at Syria—he was looking beyond, to the integration of Israel in the defense system of the Western Powers— which would assure her security for many years.

The Americans were very worried over the state of affairs in the Middle East, but what alarmed them most was the Russian threat to Turkey. They issued a statement guaranteeing the Turkish frontiers and making it clear that the United States would not tolerate any attack on Turkey. Ben-Gurion was not long in asking Dulles to make a similar declaration in respect to Israel.

Mrs. Golda Meir had a meeting with Dulles in Washington in early October. Ben-Gurion had given her precise instructions on the discussion of his propositions, which were: (a) That the United States would issue a warning to Russia against any penetration into the Middle East; (b) That there should be coordination on Middle East policy between the United States and NATO on the one hand, and Israel on the other; (c) That the American embargo on Israel should be lifted and American war material supplied to the Israeli Army; (d) That Israeli ports and airfields be improved and enlarged with American aid, so that Israel could serve as a base in an emergency; and that the United States should promise to go to the assistance of Israel if she were attacked by Egypt or Syria.

This was the foundation of Ben-Gurion's foreign policy in 1957 —to obtain a military agreement and guarantee of Israel's frontiers from the United States or NATO. He did not confine the attempts to his own exchange of letters with Dulles and the meetings that the eloquent Abba Eban and the stately Mrs. Meir had with the American Secretary of State. He also mobilized the support of all Israel's friends at NATO. The French Foreign Minister, Pineau, agreed to present the Israeli request at the Council of Ministers due to be held in Paris in December. "Israel had asked for NATO to guarantee her frontiers," Monsieur Pineau told me in an interview later. "This request had no chance of being granted, but we put it forward nevertheless, not wishing to disappoint out Israeli friends."

Pineau was not the only one that the Israelis tried to rally to their cause. Several of Ben-Gurion's close associates left for European countries bearing private letters and messages from him. One was to Chancellor Adenauer: "On this, the fifth anniversary of the agreement on reparations," wrote Ben-Gurion, "I have pleasure in sending you, the architect and keen supporter of the agreement, this message of my respect and kind regards." Shimon Peres followed this up by going to Germany on a diplomatic mission, and Dr. Giora Josephtal, a German Jew and close collaborator of Ben-Gurion, met Adenauer and tried to persuade him to assist Israel. As envoy plenipotentiary of Ben-Gurion, Josephtal visited other European capitals, including The Hague, where he handed a personal letter from Ben-Gurion to the Dutch Prime Minister, Dr. Drees.

In Paris, two special envoys of the Israeli Prime Minister, Najar and Shiloach, had meetings with various delegates to the NATO Council of Ministers. But it became apparent that Israel's requests would not be accepted. And Dulles prudently refrained from alienating the Arab countries by making too-friendly gestures towards Israel. "NATO," he said at the opening meeting, "is an organization which depends only on itself; it cannot enter into engagements over territories that do not belong to it, except in cases where that is necessary for its own security."

This setback to Ben-Gurion's plans coincided with a personal tragedy. On October 29, 1957, a young man in the visitors' gallery of the Knesset in Jerusalem threw something down among the members. It just missed the table where the ministers were sitting and hit the floor. A few seconds later there was a terrific explosion, followed by cries of pain, shouts of alarm, panic. "Remain in your places!" cried Ben-Gurion, his leg covered with blood but in full control of himself. Several of his colleagues—Mrs. Meir, Shapiro and other ministers—were injured. But the heavy grenade would have killed many of them if it had hit the table and exploded.

The injured were swiftly taken to the hospital by ambulance. The young man had been arrested and was found to be mentally unbalanced. Doctors were soon able to assure the public that none of the injured was badly hurt, though a few—Ben-Gurion among them—had to remain in the hospital for a time.

Nhemia Argov soon arrived from Tel Aviv. His god had barely

escaped assassination, and he whose mission it was to protect and help him had not been by his side! For four days, Nhemia Argov did not leave Ben-Gurion's bedside.

On Saturday he drove back to Tel Aviv, on Ben-Gurion's instructions. He was speeding along when a wasp flew in through the open window . . . It was all over in a flash—the car swung across the road and knocked down a cyclist riding in the opposite direction. Nhemia put the bleeding, badly-injured man in his car and drove quickly to the nearest hospital. The doctor who attended to the man was quite certain that his injuries would prove fatal.

Nhemia Argov went home and locked himself in his study. The following morning he was found dead, a trickle of blood on his forehead and still clutching his revolver.

People thought that Ben-Gurion's military secretary had committed suicide either because of killing the cyclist or because he had not been with his idol when the attempt at assassination had been made. Argov had been deeply depressed for some time, and the two events coming so close together had been enough to drive him over the brink.

The Israeli newspaper editors, by general assent without precedent in journalism, decided not to publish any news of Argov's death until Ben-Gurion had recovered from his injuries and was strong enough to bear the blow. Nothing about the incident appeared in the press for three days. But the news could not be kept secret any longer, and on the fourth day several of Ben-Gurion's colleagues visited him in the hospital. It was Dayan who broke it to him. "We've got bad news for you," he said. "Nhemia is dead."

"What? What's that?" The Old Man had started up in bed. Dayan silently handed him the sealed envelope which Argov had left for him. With trembling fingers, Ben-Gurion slit it open, and the others watched him read the long letter. Then he painfully moved round in bed and turned his back to them. The only sound in the room was the strange, low noise of Ben-Gurion crying.

A fortnight later, his leg still bandaged, the Prime Minister addressed the Knesset. In a broken voice, he said a few words in memory of Nhemia Argov. "For ten years, I worked with Nhemia. I doubt if two men have ever collaborated so closely . . . What was unique about Nhemia was his gift of devotion and loyalty, which came near to perfection. That may seem devotion to a man, but it was essentially devotion to a double cause—to the State and the Army . . . Allow me, standing here alone, to observe a minute's silence in honor of his memory."

244

Then, Ben-Gurion leaned forward, and another voice, energetic and authoritative, resounded in the chamber. The fighter and the leader had taken over. He launched into a blunt political speech, provoking his opponents, criticizing supporters of neutralism, analyzing the diplomatic and military situations, attacking once again.

THIRTY-THREE

ON THE WINGS OF VICTORY

By the end of 1957 it had become obvious that NATO was not going to guarantee Israel's frontiers. The efforts to be included in the Western defense agreements had come to nothing. So Israeli diplomacy, firmly managed by Ben-Gurion, turned in other directions—to the Middle East itself, and in search of a new European ally, Germany.

The idea of forming alliances with countries on the periphery of the Middle East had originated in certain circles of the Foreign Ministry, the Defense Ministry and the Army. Its chief promoters were Shiloach and Dayan, who had left the Army.

The Middle East setup had changed suddenly once again. In January 1958 the Syrian leaders flew to Cairo and told Nasser that if Egypt and Syria did not combine forces, then the Red Flag would soon be flying over Damascus. Nasser agreed to the union, and the birth of the United Arab Republic was announced to the world. Then Jordan and Iraq, in a moment of panic, threw themselves into one another's arms—the two Kings, Faisal and Hussein, solemnly ratified the treaty. For a short time it seemed that peace had come to the Arab world. But the Syrians and Egyptians were soon looking askance at each other. Lebanon was on the verge of civil war, Turkey was uneasy in the face of Nasser's growing power, and in Jordan and Iraq there were signs of revolt against the ruling power.

It was against this explosive background that the idea of an alliance with the surrounding countries began to take shape. Ethiopia was becoming increasingly alarmed at Nasser's expansionist policy. Turkey feared the Arab enemy on her southern frontiers, and Iran was engaged in a territorial dispute with Iraq. The total population of these three countries and that of Israel was greater than all the Middle East Arab States combined. Why not try to bring about a common alliance?

Friendly relations had already been secretly established between Israel and Ethiopia, and the Shah of Iran showed himself favorably inclined. Turkey, however, had always scorned Israel. Moreover, she was a member of the Baghdad Pact as well as NATO, and felt secure. Nevertheless, it was worth trying.

Ben-Gurion's envoys flew off to the four corners of the Middle East. One after the other, their reports reached Tel Aviv. All were promising, though Turkey was showing some hesitancy.

Ben-Gurion then proceeded to the next stage, which was to sound Western opinion on the program he was pursuing. Early in May of 1958 Moshe Dayan had a long talk on the subject with Field Marshal Montgomery, who was very much in favor and promised to speak about it to President Eisenhower, whom he was going to see in Washington.

The Israeli diplomatic moves were intensified in June. Then a series of grave disorders shook the Middle East. Jordan was in revolt against its king, who called on Iraq for aid under the treaty between the two rulers. An armored column commanded by Colonel Kassem was sent to Jordan, but it never even reached the frontier. Kassem made for Baghdad instead, and he and his deputy commander, Aref, seized power. The Regent, young King Faisal and Nouri Saïd were savagely murdered. The new rulers were acclaimed by the people.

Meanwhile, King Hussein was still besieged in Amman, guarded by his faithful Bedouins. The end of him and his regime seemed a matter of hours. Civil war had broken out in Lebanon, where the pro-Nasser party was trying to seize power. Hussein appealed to the British for help, while the President of Lebanon called on the Americans.

The Western Powers reacted swiftly this time. On July 15, United States Marines went ashore at Beirut, and next day British paratroops landed on the airfield at Amman. The existing regimes were saved by these interventions.

Ben-Gurion cleverly seized the opportunity and sent long letters to De Gaulle (who had just come to power in France) and to Eisenhower, elaborating his attempts to bring about a "peripheral pact."

"Our efforts have already met with success," he wrote, "and if your Government looks upon this attempt with a favorable eye, it would be of great help and become an important factor."

He added to the French text: "This task, I feel, is of great use to France, our friend. Indeed, I should like to think that its success would contribute to a solution of the Algerian problem, as well as a tightening of the links between France and Tunisia and Morocco."

Ben-Gurion also said in his letter to Eisenhower: "I am not speaking of a distant vision. The first stages of this plan are already meeting with success. But two things are dependent upon American support: the political, financial and moral aid, and the inculcation of the feeling in Iran, Turkey and Ethiopia that our efforts have the agreement of the United States."

General De Gaulle, who had problems at home just then, merely sent a noncommittal reply. But United States reaction was favorable. Moreover, the dramatic events in the Middle East drove Turkey into the arms of Israel. The "peripheral pact" was born—without official proclamation, without ceremonies to sign it. But it was the facts, the deeds that mattered, and the alliance was to have a long life.

The events in the Middle East in July 1958 certainly strengthened Ben-Gurion's position and proved that he had been right to pursue his plan. He continued to benefit from the events by gaining allies in the West. The military *coup d'état* in Iraq and the disorders in Jordan meant that Britain had to seek new friends in the Middle East. Ben-Gurion soon realized this, and decided to make approaches. He sent for the British ambassador and pointed out to him that their countries ought to coordinate their Middle East policies and cooperate fully in all fields. He added that, in view of the reversal in Iraq, it was in the interests of Britain to supply Israel with armaments. Ben-Gurion's proposals were conveyed to Macmillan and Selwyn Lloyd, who examined them attentively. The ice was finally broken and close relations were established between Britain and Israel.

Relations with West Germany, too, took a new turn. At the time of the reparations agreement with Israel, the Federal Republic had proposed the reestablishment of diplomatic relations, but Israel had refused. The Jews had not wanted to give the impression that for 800 million dollars Adenauer's Germany had wiped out the bloodstains left by Hitler's Germany. In 1956, Israel had shown herself ready to have some official contact, but then it was the Federal Republic, flushed with economic and political successes, who had been hesitant. However, some agreement between the two countries was becoming necessary. The French were basing their policy on an alliance with Germany, and it was in the Israeli interests to follow in their wake.

Early in 1957 the General Secretary of MAPAI had gone to see

Chancellor Adenauer, and in September Ben-Gurion sent him a warm personal letter. Peres has said that it was Jean Monnet who suggested he should contact the Germans. When Peres returned to Israel he put the matter to Ben-Gurion, who told him to go ahead. Talks took place in great secrecy. Moshe Dayan was to go to Bonn to discuss the purchase of submarines and armaments. But the news leaked out, and Israeli papers gave reports of the negotiations. This led to a public scandal, for the Jews were not ready for a reconciliation with the Germans. Dayan's visit was canceled, and Ben-Gurion was obliged to drop these attempts to tighten his official relations with Bonn.

There had been difficulties on the German side too. Adenauer's Government was against selling armaments to other countries, and the Foreign Ministry was inclined to be pro-Arab. Strauss and Von Brentano had taken their troubles to Adenauer, and the Chancellor had decided the matter: "The Israelis will be supplied with armaments."

However, from a timid beginning, the relations between the two countries gradually developed, and by the end of 1958 a new stage was reached. Israel sold a large quantity of her small arms manufactures—machine guns, shells and munitions—to West Germany. This led to another public scandal, in the summer of 1959. The Left-wing parties brought down Ben-Gurion's government. He told the Knesset that the sale had been approved in the Cabinet and by the very political parties who were now so indignant. The great majority of the public supported Ben-Gurion, as it had in 1952. He formed another government with the same ministers as before, and relations with West Germany were continued in secret.

Early in 1960 Ben-Gurion felt that the time had come to take another step forward in his diplomatic offensive—he would travel abroad and have meetings "at the summit." Israeli ambassadors were instructed to make the initial inquiries, and affirmative replies were soon received. Eisenhower, Adenauer, De Gaulle and Macmillan all expressed readiness to meet Ben-Gurion during the weeks to come. The only negative reply came from the Russians, who had no wish to improve relations with Israel.

In March 1960 Ben-Gurion left Israel for a series of official visits.

THIRTY-FOUR

BEN-GURION'S TRIUMPHAL TOUR ABROAD

Although Ben-Gurion had been to Paris secretly in 1956 and had stayed on the Riviera for a short time in 1959, he had not paid an official visit abroad since going to the United States in 1951. It was a different Ben-Gurion who left Israel in 1960. Not only was he older, but during the intervening years he increased the status of his country in world affairs and obtained solid support from Western Powers. Public opinion polls placed him among the ten greatest statesmen of his day. The Israeli Army had won renown, and according to some English newspapers the Jewish state had one of the best secret services of the time. The Israeli economy, aided by West Germany and the United States, was booming. And Ben-Gurion had just won a resounding victory at home—MAPAI had gained the record number of 47 seats in the elections. So Ben-Gurion was in a very strong position when he set off on his travels. Israel held some strong trump cards. The Western Powers were impressed by the fact that she was the most stable state in the Middle East and the most loyal to the free world. The "Peripheral Alliance" had become a reality. Moreover, Israel carried considerable weight among the emerging countries of Africa. She represented an "Open Sesame" to abundance and development. Ethiopia, Liberia and the French and British ex-colonies were all turning to Israel.

Her agriculture was modern, and the different kinds of villages, varying from the egalitarian conception of the kibbutz to the cooperative settlement, could well be adapted to the African communal way of life without destroying tribal traditions. The fact that the Jews had always been victims of racism, and that the Arabs were known to have been slave traders, also created favorable feelings towards the Jewish state on the part of the African countries.

250

Ben-Gurion was ready to use Israel's strong position to obtain material aid and loans from the Americans with which to finance her activities in Africa. The Western Powers should be satisfied that Israel's action would be preventing the spread of communism in the young African States, and should support their action and give the Israeli Government a free hand.

So Ben-Gurion set off confidently to meet the heads of the Western Powers. He would have liked to have met General de Gaulle first, but for strategic reasons he had to put off this meeting—the most important of them all—until a later date. He left Israel by air for the United States in March 1960.

He was not particularly impressed by his visit to Washington. He had known Eisenhower since the Second World War and appreciated his honesty and sincerity, but did not rate his qualities as a statesman very highly. The meeting between the two was more like a monologue, with Ben-Gurion holding forth for an hour and a half. Ben-Gurion did, however, succeed in obtaining a vaguely-worded promise that the United States would supply Israel with antiaircraft missiles.

In New York, Ben-Gurion had two interviews which gave him much more satisfaction. The first was with ex-President Harry Truman, who was visibly affected by Ben-Gurion's declaration that the Jewish people would always be grateful for his help in the creation of the state. The second meeting was with Konrad Adenauer, who was staying at the same hotel as Ben-Gurion.

Ben-Gurion had never wavered from the principles that he had laid down in 1952, that the Germany of Adenauer was quite different from that of Hitler. In his conviction that any means were justified to assure Israel's security and survival, he would readily refer to the Franco-German alliance to justify his own policy with regard to West Germany. So, on March 13, 1960, braving all criticism, he was photographed shaking hands with Chancellor Adenauer at their press conference.

Adenauer was in complete agreement with Ben-Gurion, and their meeting was a friendly one. The discussions centered on a $500,000,000 loan by Germany, spread over ten years, for the development of the Negev. Other matters touched on were military cooperation and a secret, free supply of German arms to Israel. Ben-Gurion was extremely satisfied with these talks.

His meeting with Macmillan in London was the last before returning to Israel. It was formal, but little more. Macmillan did not impress Ben-Gurion as a statesman. The man he most admired in Britain was Winston Churchill—in September 1959 Ben-Gurion had written to him saying that he considered him "the greatest man of our generation."

In October 1958, when General de Gaulle had taken France in hand, Ben-Gurion had written:

"Nothing can be farther from the truth than to say that De Gaulle is a Fascist. Although I know him only through reading his memoirs, I consider him a man of integrity whose sole aim is to make France great, and in that I can see nothing wrong. This aim so fills his mind that he almost identifies himself with France, but not in the sense of *L'État, c'est moi.* He believes, and I think rightly, that he has a mission to save France and rescue her from a humiliating situation. He, and he alone, did it during the Second World War, and I hope that he will do it again. I am not sure that he will be able to solve the Algerian problem, but there are signs that he may succeed—the overwhelming vote for him, the statements he has made, the removal of the Army Commanders in Algeria and the weakening of the Arab nationalists. In my opinion, De Gaulle is a very great man, the only great statesman left after the Second World War, and I believe that he will save France and restore her greatness."

However, it was not enough to hold De Gaulle in high regard, he had to meet him and discuss the main problems between their two countries. In 1959, Franco-Israeli relations had become strained because of the French Foreign Ministry's attempts to prepare the way for friendlier relations with the Arab world after the Algerian problem had been settled. However, in 1960, General de Gaulle had said to the French Ambassador to Lebanon: "I am disappointed by the Arab world. Israel is quiet now, but if she started to hit out, I shouldn't weep any tears over it."

Friendship with France was still the cornerstone of Ben-Gurion's foreign policy. His visit to Paris was arranged for early June, but a fortnight before he was due to leave, the attention of the whole world became focused upon Israel. Eichmann had been discovered and captured by a Jewish commando.

Eichmann had been at the head of the huge, unrelenting machine that had crushed six million Jews, and Ben-Gurion wanted him to be tried in Israel by the heirs of the victims of the gas chambers.

Early in May, the world had been startled by reports that Eichmann had been kidnapped in Argentina and his Jewish captors had smuggled him out of the country, in a plane belonging to the El

Al Company. Controversy raged throughout the world and even filtered into the realms of diplomacy. Ben-Gurion confirmed the rumors that Eichmann had been kidnapped in Argentina, whereupon President Frondisi was obliged to demand that Israel return Eichmann to Argentina. The two countries recalled their ambassadors, Argentina took the matter before the Security Council, and jurists of many countries asserted that Eichmann should be tried by an international court. Meanwhile, Ben-Gurion flew to Paris as planned, arriving on June 13, 1960.

He knew that he was about to meet the greatest statesman holding the reins of office, and wondered what De Gaulle was like. He later confessed that he expected to meet a "reserved, hard and cold man." He was relieved to find him lively, pleasant, and witty. Ben-Gurion had done his homework thoroughly and had ready all the questions and opinions that he wished to put to the French President.

The guests at the official luncheon at the Elysée were, in addition to Ben-Gurion, the French Prime Minister, Michel Debré, Couve de Murville, André Malraux, Guy Mollet, Baron Rothschild, Emile Roche, General Ely and Ben-Gurion's chief assistants. At the end, De Gaulle said as he raised his glass: "We have feelings of admiration, affection and confidence towards Israel. You symbolize in your person, Monsieur Ben-Gurion, the amazing rebirth, the pride and prosperity of Israel; to me, you are one of the greatest statesmen of this century." Ben-Gurion was very moved by this tribute, and in his reply said: "It is you who are the greatest statesman of our time. I am grateful to you and your country for the splendid aid you have given us. It was the Jewish people, not I, who created the State of Israel."

While having coffee outside under the trees, De Gaulle leaned towards Ben-Gurion and asked smilingly: *"Monsieur le Président,* tell me truthfully, what are your real ambitions for the frontiers of Israel? I promise I'll keep it secret."

"If you had asked me that question fifteen years ago," Ben-Gurion replied, "I should have answered—I want the State of Israel to include the whole of Jordan and to extend as far north as the river Litani, in the Lebanon. But as you've asked me today, I'll tell you quite frankly that I am more concerned with immigration, development and peace. We will be satisfied with our present frontiers in order to avoid exposing our young people to danger. We need very many immigrants, for Israel is the land of all Jewish people."

De Gaulle called to his Foreign Minister, Couve de Murville, and Michel Debré to come over. "Imagine that!" he said to them, "Prime Minister Ben-Gurion is not a bit satisfied with two million Jews. He wants to double that number at least. Men are more important to him than territory."

Then they went into the French President's study to discuss more serious matters in private. Ben-Gurion talked at length about the emerging countries in Asia and Africa. De Gaulle interrupted him to say: "In my opinion, China presents the greatest problem, because the Negroes have more confidence in the yellow race than in the white man." Ben-Gurion told him of Israel's action in Africa and the deep understanding that existed with the young states there. "Yes, indeed," said De Gaulle, "I know that you feel that what you are undertaking in Africa is a moral mission, and I admire this activity deeply."

Ben-Gurion disclosed the existence of his "peripheral pact." But De Gaulle was more interested in Israel's fear of an Arab attack. "Do you really think that a coalition might put your existence in danger?"

"It isn't even necessary for there to be a coalition," replied Ben-Gurion. "Given certain conditions, Egypt alone could deal us a mortal blow. I told Eisenhower that, and he has made me a definite promise that the United States would not stand by and see Israel destroyed."

"Nor would France!" asserted De Gaulle.

At four o'clock Ben-Gurion was due to lay a wreath on the Tomb of the Unknown Warrior at the Arc de Triomphe. He and De Gaulle had hardly touched on the most important matters, and the French President proposed that they meet again in two days' time.

Later that day, Ben-Gurion discussed with Michel Debré the question of military cooperation between the two countries, as well as an agreement over atomic energy. Ben-Gurion broached the subject of the Common Market, and Debré promised French support.

The second meeting with De Gaulle was a great success. "Let us turn to practical matters," the General said, and expressed his satisfaction at the military agreements concluded with Debré. They discussed in more detail cooperation over nuclear research and atomic energy, and then De Gaulle again raised the subject of the dangers menacing Israel. "I think you exaggerate this threat of destruction. We would on no account allow you to be wiped out. We are not very powerful at the moment, but our strength is growing. We would come to your defense, and not let Israel down."

Ben-Gurion pointed out that by the time France or the United States intervened, there might be no Israel left to defend.

"No one will dare attack you," replied De Gaulle. "In the first place, you are stronger than the Arabs; and secondly, a war against Israel could start off another world war, and nobody wants that."

Ben-Gurion explained that Israel needed arms for her defense and to serve as a deterrent.

"You will get some good Centurion tanks from the British," said De Gaulle. "And we will supply you with our best aircraft."

De Gaulle was interested in Hitler's "final solution" and asked what possibilities there had been of saving the six million victims. He was staggered when Ben-Gurion told him that Britain could have done something to save a number of them, but had refused. Then he raised the subject of Eichmann. "Would you like me to speak to Frondisi, the President of Argentina, to try to arrange matters?" Ben-Gurion accepted this offer, although he told De Gaulle that he had already written a personal and confidential letter to Frondisi asking him to settle the matter between themselves. De Gaulle declared that Argentina had no right to ask for Eichmann's extradition. "Only Germany can do that, as he's a German citizen."

"I know Chancellor Adenauer," replied Ben-Gurion. "And I don't think he'll ask for extradition."

"I'm sure that world opinion will be on your side in this matter," said De Gaulle. "You've done a good job there."

He accompanied Ben-Gurion to his car, and in saying good-bye he told him: "I believe our talks have been of great use and importance. I am very glad to have made your acquaintance. Now that we know each other, write directly to me whenever you are worried about anything."

When Ben-Gurion had left, De Gaulle said to one of his advisers: "I think that he and Adenauer are the two great leaders on the Western side."

Ben-Gurion returned to Israel very pleased with his visit to France, and no less satisfied with the talks he had in Belgium and Holland. Well might he be pleased, for he had gotten what he wanted. Israel had never been as strong, peaceful and prosperous. Ben-Gurion had reached the peak of his dramatic ascent.

THIRTY-FIVE

BEN-GURION'S WORLD

Ben-Gurion had aged a great deal since Suez, and he could no longer forge ahead with the same drive and vigor, Yet his policy was just as clear-cut, and on the same lines as before. He changed tactics according to the circumstances, both in domestic and foreign affairs, but never swerved from his basic principles.

The men who formed the government were not always very brilliant, yet gifted men often found themselves stagnating in minor posts. This mattered little as long as Ben-Gurion concentrated power in his own hands, and was there to make the vital decisions. He overshadowed the others, and their capabilities or lack of them mattered little to him. Thus it was that Dayan remained for many years at the Ministry of Agriculture, although his talents designated him for the key position of minister of Defense or Economy. Thus, too, certain other ministries were badly run. But this passed unnoticed while Ben-Gurion was in command. When a disaster occurred, the Old Man came down from his Olympus armed with his great prestige and put out the blaze. Only when he eventually left the scene did the incapacity and weakness of some leaders become obvious to the people of Israel.

Ben-Gurion was concentrating on foreign policy, on defense problems and his broad vision for the country's development. Everything else was secondary. For him, nothing was impossible, and everything remained to be done.

He brandished his grandiose projects before the nation—the development of the Negev, the revival of the desert, the absorption of immigrants, the opening of the Gulf of Aqaba . . . Many a time he came up against skepticism or lack of enthusiasm among his colleagues. He pressed on, nevertheless. In 1953, his retirement to Sde Boker had been the biggest failure in his career, for others had not followed him to the Negev. But he did not give up then either.

Beneath this prophet's vision was a clear appraisal of facts. He fully saw that the state's continued existence depended on a deep attachment to the soil of Israel. The Negev, the largest region, had to be peopled and reclaimed. And immigration had to continue at all costs. But the fire needed to forge this nation had to be continually fanned, and without the succession of scientific, political and economic challenges that Ben-Gurion produced, the nation would have lost its pioneering spirit.

To Ben-Gurion Israel did not just belong to the inhabitants, but to the whole of world Jewry. The Jews in foreign lands could and should help Israel, but they had no right to interfere with her policies at home or abroad. The heart of Israel beat in Jerusalem, not in New York or London. This attitude had resulted in Ben-Gurion's long struggle against Zionist leaders abroad.

The Israelis were united by the Arab threat, the ever-present danger on the frontiers. Ben-Gurion feared the "next round" that was being threatened by the Arabs. Israel could not afford to lose even one battle. If the Arabs agreed to make peace, so much the better. But Israel had to be strong and powerful—so strong that the Arabs would definitely abandon their ambition of destroying her.

However, Ben-Gurion did not believe a peaceful settlement was possible in the prevailing world conditions. "Peace between us and the Arabs," he said, "will come only when the United States and the Soviet Union reach agreement on world affairs. That might happen in ten or twenty years."

Ever since the establishment of the State of Israel he had firmly taken his stand with the Western Powers, realizing that he could not draw from a neutral policy the same benefits as his Arab neighbors. Israel was too isolated and had too little to offer.

His distrust of the British had greatly diminished with the years, and he was careful to maintain good relations with the Americans. But he leaned increasingly towards France. Indeed, his foreign policy was based on Franco-Israeli friendship. This allowed him to follow a somewhat "Gaullist" policy and maintain a fairly independent attitude towards the United States—a surprisingly bold attitude on the part of such a small country. Confident of French support, he could embark on projects which did not always please the Americans.

He thus made his "peripheral pact" and only consulted Washington afterwards. He also built the nuclear reactor at Dimona without American knowledge.

De Gaulle and Ben-Gurion undoubtedly had much in common, but possibly all great men are alike in some respect. There are certain similarities between Ben-Gurion and Churchill, Lloyd George or Clemenceau, although each of these three had a distinct personality. Ben-Gurion does not possess the cynical skepticism of the Tiger, nor has he Churchill's impish smile nor the haughty disdain of De Gaulle. Ben-Gurion has climbed up to the summits of history, whereas De Gaulle has descended from the lofty heights of his mind.

Ben-Gurion's foreign policy was guided by one basic principle, the defense and survival of Israel. For this he was even prepared to hold out a hand to Germany. His attitude towards the Germans was not based on friendship—they had been guilty of the most atrocious crimes against the Jewish people, and so ought to help Israel to defend herself.

A striking feature about Ben-Gurion—this realist—is that his conception of Israel and of the world is based on the highest moral and human values. This modern prophet, brought up on the teachings of the Bible, drew on it for principles to make his small nation an example to the world. Israel is a marriage of the distant past and the near future, she is the direct heir of the ancient kingdom which has been revived after a long period—the period that she tries to forget, the Exile.

Ben-Gurion had created a nation. But the people were soon to turn against him.

THIRTY-SIX

THE NIGHTMARE

By late 1960 Ben-Gurion could rest on his laurels. He had scored a great success at the general elections, and his young disciples—Dayan, Peres and Abba Eban—were members of the Knesset. In the summer he had returned from a triumphant tour abroad. But the higher one climbs, the greater the fall. And the most tragic thing about Ben-Gurion's fall was that it resulted from an affair in which he had not played any part—the wretched Lavon Affair.

In five years much had been forgotten, many of the wounds it caused had healed—but not Lavon's, despite the important position he had been allowed to retain. The way to power, however, was barred to him, and he had become more cynical and bitter than ever. He frequently went to Switzerland for his health, and it was on his return from one of these visits, in September 1960, that he told journalists he had some new revelations to make.

Counterspy Y, who had brought about the failure of Operation Egypt in 1954, was in prison in Israel, and had admitted that much of the evidence he gave before the committee of inquiry in 1955 was false. Moreover, he declared that he had done this at the instigation of Colonel X and his assistants. Their aim had obviously been to throw the whole responsiblity for the disastrous plan onto the shoulders of Lavon.

But Agent Y was only telling part of the truth. He had said nothing about being in the pay of the Egyptians. Lavon had known of the terrorist activities of the "Egypt" group during the fortnight preceding his talk with Colonel X on July 16, 1954, but he did not know that the Egyptians were behind it all. So he was now convinced that X had persuaded him to give the order for the operation after part of it had already been put into effect and had failed. He thought that X had subsequently tried to cover himself by inventing evidence and getting Y to lie at the inquiry. And the latter had been only too happy to complicate the affair and eliminate the traces of his own treachery. While this remained unknown—and continued to be for a long time—the impression conveyed was that Lavon had been the victim of false testimony. It was only after the double role of Agent Y was discovered that the Israeli leaders realized that Colonel X had fabricated evidence to strengthen his own story— true in part—that Lavon had given the order for Operation Egypt to be carried out.

One fact at least emerged from all this imbroglio—false testimony had been given against Lavon. So he was in a position to demand his rehabilitation.

Lavon had collected testimonies some months previously and sent them to Ben-Gurion's office. The Prime Minister had at once appointed a military commission to inquire into the matter. It eventually concluded that Colonel X had been guilty, and by Ben-Gurion's order he was dismissed from the Army.

Lavon, however, did not wait for the commission's findings. He wanted to be rehabilitated at once. A few days after his return from Switzerland, on September 26, he went to Jerusalem to see Ben-Gurion. They discussed various aspects of the affair, and then Lavon put his cards on the table by asking Ben-Gurion to publish an official announcement that he was guiltless of ordering Operation Egypt. Ben-Gurion firmly refused.

"Pinhas," he said, "I've never accused you of anything. But I'm not a judge and I can't acquit you, for that would mean my condemning Colonel X. I didn't inquire into what happened in 1954, and I've no authority to do so. Even if I announced what you ask, it would have no value, for I'm not a judge."

Ben-Gurion's attitude was clear—judicial proceedings were the only means of establishing whether false testimony had been given and of clearing Lavon of blame.

An enraged Lavon left Ben-Gurion's office. He had no intention of taking the matter to the courts. Instead, he turned to the Foreign Affairs and Defense Committee of the Knesset.

During the next few days, courteous and even friendly-worded letters passed between Ben-Gurion and Lavon. But the newspapers got hold of the story and splashed it across the front page. The Opposition papers wrote of Lavon as another Dreyfus. Oddly enough, the affair as printed appeared one-sided, and attacks were being made on the Army leaders, on Peres and Dayan and even Ben-Gurion. The Old Man thought he knew the source of the leakage, and became certain when an evening paper printed a letter of which he alone had a copy. He asked Lavon to say how the paper had gotten hold of the letter, but Lavon was evasive. Ben-Gurion stopped writing to him, and soon became his greatest enemy, seeing him as Ben-Gurion's friends and colleagues had described him in 1954.

However, Ben-Gurion did not appear to realize, at first, the exact nature of Lavon's campaign against him and where it was likely to lead. He forgot that much water had flowed under the bridges of the Jordan since 1955. Although at the summit of his power, he was more than ever on his own. He failed to see that this second phase of the Lavon Affair was only a pretext to bring into the open a fight which had long been threatening—the fight for Ben-Gurion's successor.

What had happened to his companions of the past? Moshe Sharett had become chairman of the Jewish Agency Executive and lived in semiretirement. He would not have come to Ben-Gurion's aid in any case, for the aged Prime Minister aroused in him nothing but feelings of frustration, if not hatred. Eshkol had always been a faithful, close associate, but he was essentially a middle-of-the-road man and incapable of choosing one side or another. Golda Meir, on the other hand, knew her own mind, but this forceful woman, who had been among those to implore Ben-Gurion to return to power in 1955, had changed a great deal. She had come to identify herself with her ministry, was jealous of her prerogatives and authority. Her resentment at the independent foreign policy that Shimon Peres was allowed to pursue without consulting her was well known, and she had threatened to resign on several occasions. The differences between her and Sharett, which Ben-Gurion had spoken of in the past, were now revived between her and Peres. Golda Meir was not against Ben-Gurion, but against Peres. In the fight ahead, her personal feelings could carry great weight.

However, much more than personal feelings were involved. The Lavon Affair was soon to become a battlefield for the confrontation of two generations—the MAPAI Old Guard and Ben-Gurion's "fair-haired boys."

Ben-Gurion felt much closer to the young men than to his old companions. He saw his successors among the generation which had grown up with the country and had been steeled by the War of Independence, bold young men with a sense of reality, who placed the country's interests above those of party.

The Old Guard inspired little confidence in him. It was led by Lavon, Namir, Sharett and others, but its driving force was a trio of ministers—Golda Meir, Aran, the Minister for Education, and Sapir, the Minister for Industry.

The elections of November 1959 had proved Ben-Gurion was right in placing the young men—Peres, Dayan and Abba Eban—at the head of his list of candidates. All had been elected. Thanks to the young leaders, MAPAI had a great success at the polls.

However, the Old Guard had not given up hope. And the revival of the Lavon Affair provided an opportunity for revenge. But it was not just a clash between the opposing groups within MAPAI. The Opposition, too, still suffering from defeat at the elections, seized upon the affair as a means of attacking Ben-Gurion and both the MAPAI groups.

The strongest ally of the anti-Ben-Gurionites was the Old Man himself. The mistakes he made were equivalent to political suicide. This was largely due to the fact that he was very vulnerable in all matters touching the Army—*his* army. And when the barriers were down and the Army, with which he identified himself, was attacked and reviled, he could no longer control his anger or hide his hurt.

When, at the end of September, the press got hold of the story and began to use it for political ends, Ben-Gurion's aides did not know what to do. Nhemia was dead, Dayan was in Nigeria and Peres was in Paris. The headlines became more aggressive as the days passed, the Opposition papers were up in arms and the Extreme Left-wing press was crusading for Lavon. Leakages and tendentious information kept the campaign going. The accusations against Ben-Gurion and the Army filled the public's mind.

Early in October, Lavon was called before the Foreign Affairs and Defense Committee. He laid charges against the Army and the Defense organization, referring to "serious financial discrepancies" and denouncing corruption at all levels. Peres and others, when called to testify, refuted all these accusations and produced proof of their statements. But no one was interested. The Opposition was jubilant. Matters which had hitherto been secret somehow reached the press and were splashed across the front pages. Ben-Gurion was shattered; MAPAI was in a state of confusion. Old scores were revived and smoldering enmities blazed up. The leaders of the Old Guard saw no reason for helping Ben-Gurion's young string being groomed for power, against whom the accusations were chiefly directed. Lavon announced that he possessed secret documents which implicated certain well-known people, and that he would make them public if he was not rehabilitated. This was blackmail at the national level, and the MAPAI leaders were aghast and horrified. Many were prepared to do everything Lavon asked, if only the scandal could be brought to an end.

The Government made a move in that direction in late October, when it voted almost unanimously to set up a select committee of seven ministers to examine the documents relative to the Lavon Affair and to publish a report. Ben-Gurion had abstained from voting. He still believed that judicial proceedings were the only way of getting at the truth. He was against this "Committee of Seven." But no one supported him. His colleagues only wanted to see the end of this harrowing affair. And although Ben-Gurion was opposed to the setting up of the committee, he took no steps to prevent it. The fight seemed to have left him. For the first time in his career, he appeared tired and hesitant.

The Committee of Seven started work under the chairmanship of the Minster of Justice, but the guiding hand was given by Eshkol. One principle appeared to animate the inquiry—end the affair at any cost.

Meanwhile, the press campaign continued as virulent as ever. It was even said that the fateful order for Operation Egypt had not been given by either Lavon or Colonel X but by Ben-Gurion himself, that he had directed a conspiracy from Sde Boker to get rid of Lavon and return to power himself. Most exasperating of all was that the public did not have the faintest idea of the nature of Operation Egypt, for the part played by Israel was still a secret. Yet thousands of people signed petitions and appeals in favor of Lavon and which denigrated Ben-Gurion.

A disaster could still have been avoided by energetic action by Ben-Gurion, as in the past. But this time he did nothing. And on December 25, 1960, the Committee of Seven published its findings—Lavon was entirely rehabilitated.

With Lavon whitewashed and reinstated, all the accusations against the defense chiefs, Ben-Gurion and his disciples, were automatically given credence. A few days later, Ben-Gurion resigned. The most dramatic stage in the Lavon Affair was about to begin.

Ben-Gurion, roused at last, went to war against Lavon. He raged blindly against the man who had defiled the object of his pride, and against the colleagues who had committed an injustice. Only one thing could stop him, thought his friends—the elimination of Lavon. It was one man or the other.

The moment was badly chosen, for the findings of the Committee of Seven had made a popular hero of Lavon. In the movies, the appearance of Lavon on the screen was greeted with applause, that of Ben-Gurion with boos. But Ben-Gurion paid no attention to public opinion. His one real friend, Itzhak Ben Zvi, who was President of the State, tried to reason with him and to prevent a crisis, but to no effect.

Lavon had to go. Eshkol was given the task of convincing MAPAI that the only way of returning Ben-Gurion to power was by getting rid of Lavon. The Old Guard closed its ranks in opposition to this, but the party's Central Committee met in Tel Aviv on February 4, 1961, to vote on the matter. Neither Ben-Gurion, Lavon nor Golda Meir attended the meeting. Eshkol, looking haggard and pinched, proposed that Lavon be dismissed from his position at the head of *Histadrut*. Sharett argued against it, but the motion was carried by 154 votes to 96. Outside the building, demonstrators clashed with the police.

Lavon had been gotten rid of, but Ben-Gurion had never been so isolated and unpopular. He was abandoned by his friends among the Old Guard, and many of the rank and file of his own party were in revolt against him. The public saw the dismissal of Lavon as an act of revenge by the authoritarian Ben-Gurion, against a martyr of an Army conspiracy who had dared to defy him.

In 1954 the Lavon Affair had ushered in Ben-Gurion's second period of glory. But the second phase of the affair, in 1960, was the prelude to his final downfall. He would never be the same.

Another result of Lavon's dismissal, and one which gave a strong indication of the state of affairs in the country, was that the political parties refused to participate in Ben-Gurion's government. For the first time in the history of the State there was open revolt against Ben-Gurion. "The man sent by Providence" had become "the dictator." Golda Meir and Sapir both declined to belong to his government. Some members of MAPAI wanted him to resign, others thought he should become Defense Minister in a government headed by Eshkol. Ben-Gurion himself was prepared to retire.

However, the party did not want to lose him, despite having turned its back on him during the Lavon business. Although his prestige had been severely shaken, he was still the leader of the party. Even the Old Guard were against his departure from the political scene. (Sharett was one of the few in favor of his retirement.) The MAPAI leaders preferred to have a general election rather than see Ben-Gurion go. He presented his new government—it was to be his last—to the Knesset on November 2, 1961, and obtained a comfortable vote of confidence. But eighteen months later he was to resign and retire to his kibbutz. He was the real victim of that awful nightmare in 1960.

He could have perhaps prevented all the scandal, but he hesitated for too long and then made several blunders. He was old and tired, and badly hurt by Lavon's attacks on the Army and the Defense organization. He was also deeply shaken to see in his colleagues' attitudes the beginning of a moral decline which threatened to spread and corrupt the whole country. No sooner had the leader, Ben-Gurion, dropped the reins than there was a return to the old system of disregarding principles for easy settlements.

All the leading figures, without exception, had stood out against him and his young disciples, but had not been able to break him. The majority had not wanted him to leave the scene, but did not hesitate to use the Lavon Affair to break the power of the "fair-haired boys." And when Ben-Gurion ultimately retired it was the MAPAI Old Guard which took over power, and not the younger generation as the Old Man had intended. Lavon, detested by all his colleagues, served as a means to enable others to win "the war of succession."

THIRTY-SEVEN

PEACE STILL A LONG WAY OFF

The most tragic aspect of the revival of the Lavon Affair was that it came at a time when the country was calm, when the military and diplomatic situations were almost too good. If Ben-Gurion had been concentrating on some crisis he would probably have ignored the whole Lavon business. Had it broken three months later, in December, nobody would have taken notice. Israel was then in the midst of one of her most serious crises in foreign relations, and Ben-Gurion was immersed in it.

On December 9, 1960, the Israeli Ambassador in Washington was summoned by Secretary of State Herter. On the same day, the Atomic Energy Committee of Congress held an urgent meeting. Three days later, *Time* published a small item about a nuclear reactor which had been built secretly in a certain country. No name was given, it was merely stated that the country did not belong to the Communist bloc nor was it a member of NATO. But on December 16 a popular London newspaper splashed the headline "Israel making an atom bomb." These tendentious reports had been deliberately put out by the United States State Department. They gave very little of the true story.

In 1957 France had signed a secret agreement with Israel for the construction of a large nuclear reactor in the Negev. Israel's declared aim was that it should be a research station for peaceful purposes. Ben-Gurion, always mindful of Israeli sovereignty, was fiercely opposed to any foreign control over it, except of course by France.

The secret had been well kept for several years. The Franco-Israeli atomic program (which had been initiated by Shimon Peres) had the wholehearted support of Ben-Gurion, although differences arose among the handful of people in on Israel's greatest secret. But the appearance of an American U-2 spy plane over the Negev put an end to the secret, and some information had already leaked to the CIA. The aerial photographs showed quite clearly that the buildings which had sprung up in the desert were not a "textile factory."

Washington demanded explanations, and wanted to know whether this Negev reactor was intended for military purposes. Paris gave an emphatic denial. A joint communiqué issued by the French Foreign Ministry and the Commissioner for Atomic Energy admitted that the French were helping Israel with her nuclear research, but stated that it was for purely scientific and peaceful purposes. Ben-Gurion also issued a statement saying that Israel had indeed built a 24-megawatt reactor at Dimona, in the Negev, and that it was being used for scientific research and for the country's development.

But the Americans were not satisfied and put unprecedented pressure on Israel either to accept an international control or to agree to immediate inspection by American scientists

Ben-Gurion refused to comply. Despite American pressure, the sharply-worded notes and veiled threats, the allusions to measures that the United States might employ, the Israeli Prime Minister remained adamant. It was not until much later that an American scientist was allowed to visit the Dimona reactor. In May 1961, when Ben-Gurion went to see the newly-elected President Kennedy, the latter told him with a smile, "We know now that you gave us exact information on the nature of your reactor." Israel was able to continue her program of atomic research.

This affair was a reason for Ben-Gurion not resigning when the Committee of Seven was inquiring into the Lavon scandal. He did not want to give the impression abroad that he had resigned because of the crisis over the nuclear reactor, and so stayed at the helm until it was settled. He finally resigned in January 1961. The elections were not to be held until August, so Ben-Gurion made a flying visit to several foreign capitals to meet President Kennedy and British and Canadian heads of state. He also seized the opportunity for having more talks with General de Gaulle.

This foreign tour was not as triumphal as the 1960 one, but nevertheless he achieved some tangible and promising results. He had a long discussion with President Kennedy on the possibility of peace in the Middle East. Kennedy refused to supply the armaments that the Republican administration had seemed prepared to deliver to Israel. On the other hand, in London, Ben-Gurion had the great satisfaction of meeting the aged Winston Churchill, the man he admired above all. They had a long talk about Moses, and then Ben-Gurion flew to Paris to meet General de Gaulle.

This meeting, which took place on June 7, 1961, did not have the significance of that of the previous year, probably because the two men had little to say to each other. They had corresponded throughout the year and had reached agreement on a subject which occupied both their minds—China. They were of the opinion that it was time to adopt a realistic attitude towards that country and to enter into normal diplomatic and economic relations with her. France could do this, but Israel was more restricted, as the Chinese were definitely on the side of the Arabs.

De Gaulle was more reserved on this occasion, and Ben-Gurion began to fear a cooling-off in Franco-Israeli relations. They discussed Africa, and the French President repeated his approval of the Israeli efforts provided they did not include the sale of arms to the new African states. Ben-Gurion, for his part, asked for France's support in Israel's efforts to be associated with the Common Market.

The General became less aloof during the lunch which followed this meeting. In proposing the toast, he said: "It is a good thing for friends, men of goodwill, to meet again. We should like to assure you of our support and friendship, and I raise my glass to Israel, our friend and ally." The political message was clear—France and Israel were bound together not only by the existence of a common enemy but by deeper and more lasting interests.

Shimon Peres wrote in his diary that day: "One thing is certain, that personalities play a great part in the relations between countries; and I am sure that the present stage in Franco-Israeli relations is due to two men—De Gaulle and Ben-Gurion."

In November, it was a bitter, weakened and unpopular Ben-Gurion who presented his new government to the national assembly. Neither the results of his foreign tour nor the launching of the first Israeli missile in July 1961, could outweigh the disastrous effect of the Lavon Affair on public opinion. Ben-Gurion's prestige had suffered and his authority was being openly disputed. He was in good physical health, but appeared to have no interest at all in matters that did not affect the country's security. He seemed unaware of the fact that his position in the party was growing weaker every day. Only in the making of important political and military decisions did the real Ben-Gurion reappear. But such decisions were rarely needed in the Israel of 1961, and the leader of her momentous times was not an everyday leader—"secondary affairs" just did not interest him.

But even an impaired Ben-Gurion could accomplish things that were beyond any other Israeli leader. During his last months in power he secretly embarked on a new venture—to bring peace and stability to the Middle East.

In December 1961 he paid an official visit to Burma, where he was able to realize a great ambition—to spend a week in the wonderful solitude of a remote Buddhist temple, studying the religion. On his way to Burma he had made a short halt at Teheran, where the Iranian Prime Minister greeted him at the airport, and the two had a talk on matters concerning the "peripheral pact." Ben-Gurion's talks with U Nu, the Burmese Prime Minister, however, were concerned with the latter's mediation in the Israeli-Arab conflict. The proposal came from U Nu himself, a good friend of Ben-Gurion, who thought he might be able to do something during his forthcoming visit to Cairo. However, Nasser made it quite clear that a peaceful settlement with Israel was impossible. Nevertheless, the peace offensive was not affected by Nasser's refusal.

These peace moves had been suggested by President Kennedy. He had discussed Middle East problems with Ben-Gurion when the latter had visited him in May, and had promised military aid to Israel if fighting broke out in the Middle East. He had also given his complete support to the Israeli plan to divert the River Jordan in order to irrigate the Negev. In Kennedy's opinion, peace could only come to the Middle East in stages, and he had proposed that Israel should agree to separate the Arab refugee problem from the general problems of the Middle East. His idea was that once the thorny problem of the Arab refugees had been settled, the way to peace would be open.

Ben-Gurion had not rejected the idea. And three months later, even before he had formed his new government, Dr. Joseph Johnson arrived in Israel. He was a senior official of the United Nations, but in actual fact had come on behalf of the State Department to start talks with Israel and the Arab countries on the refugee problem.

Johnson's efforts lasted for a year, with many journeys between Jerusalem, Washington, New York and the Arab capitals. In the end his plan was rejected by both Arabs and Jews. His idea on a United Nations' decision giving a "free choice" to the refugees to return to Israel, was to settle some of the Arab refugees in Israel, but most of them in the Arab countries. But the second part of the UN resolution, which required the Arabs to live in peace with their Israeli neighbors, was not mentioned in Johnson's plan. In other words, Israel was being asked to absorb some of the refugees without receiving any assurances in return. In any case, the Arabs also rejected the plan. But President Kennedy held out a bait to Ben-Gurion—in August he sent his adviser on Jewish Affairs, Mike Feldmann, to tell Ben-Gurion that the United States had decided to supply the Hawk missiles that he had asked for the previous year. A few weeks later, however, the price of these missiles was disclosed—in diplomatic terms, the United States informed Israel that in return for their magnanimity in supplying the missiles, the Jewish state should look more favorably on the Johnson plan. Ben-Gurion's reaction was typical: "I don't want these 'Hawks' if the price is the Johnson plan or any other plan of that sort. As long as the Arab States won't give up their declared aim of destroying us, we won't take a single refugee."

So the Johnson plan was filed away, and Israel had her Hawks all the same.

It was not the first plan of its kind to end up in the wastepaper basket. Every American President in recent years seems to have juggled with the idea of bringing peace to the Middle East, at some time or other. Truman was the first, in 1951, when he proposed the return of a certain number of Arab refugees as a condition to good Israeli-American relations. Israel had agreed to take 100,000, provided this led to a complete settlement of the Judaeo-Arab conflict. But that condition had put an end to the plan. In 1955, the American mediator had produced a peace plan involving a "free choice" for the refugees, and Eisenhower had given it his backing. That, too, had fallen through. And now, in 1961, a third attempt had failed.

Hardly was the Johnson plan decently buried when Kennedy put forward another proposal, trying to bring peace to the Middle East by first solving the refugee problem. This plan proposed that Israel should take ten percent of the refugees and the Arab countries the remaining ninety percent. Israel could choose which refugees she would take, and the United States would guarantee her frontiers. The plan would be carried out in stages, over a period of five or ten years. Every year, Israel would absorb a certain number of Arab refugees and the Arab countries would take nine times as many. These refugees would be struck off the lists, and the Arab states would no longer raise the subject of the refugees at the United Nations or elsewhere. And in ten years, with one tenth of the total number of refugees settled in Israel, the problem would be ended.

The plan had possibilities, but was exceedingly naive. The Americans made it clear that the Arabs would not admit officially that a settlement was in process, nor would they renounce their avowed intention of wiping out Israel. Their claim that "Palestine" was the land of the Arabs, who would one day return by fire and sword, was not going to be dropped. Ben-Gurion was skeptical, and felt that in four or eight years the United States would have a different president, who might refuse to implement the clauses of the Kennedy plan. Also, while the Arab states were divided among themselves and refused to make a definite statement that the refugee problem was being solved, they might at any time trample on the secret agreement and declare that the problem still existed. And at the end of ten years, Israel would again have to face the refugee problem, having in the meantime absorbed 100,000 Arabs.

Secret negotiations between Tel Aviv, Washington and Cairo lasted about six months, but ended in failure. Jews and Arabs still suspected one another, and the plan required mutual trust. In June 1963 the Arab refugee problem was no nearer solution than in 1948.

Nevertheless, while these negotiations with Johnson or with Kennedy's special envoys had been taking place, Ben-Gurion was making tentative approaches to the Arab world.

His first attempt was in December 1962. Great changes had taken place in the Middle East situation. The United Arab Republic had disintegrated when Syria broke away. Jordan was holding out, the Yemen was in revolt against Egyptian influences and Iraq was reserved. In short, Nasser's influence was declining, and Ben-Gurion thought he might be more approachable.

He sent one of his friends on a secret mission to Belgrade, thinking that Marshal Tito, one of Nasser's best friends, might have some influence with him. Tito showed interest and asked for further details. Ben-Gurion wrote him a long letter, explaining the conflict between Israel and the Arabs and expressing his conviction that there was no hope of peace in the Middle East unless Egypt, the strongest and most influential of the Arab countries, took the first step. He explained that Israel could help in the peaceful development of Arab countries if she were not obliged to devote most of her budget to military purposes.

A few weeks later, Ben-Gurion received Tito's reply: "I do not think that the kind of action you propose is possible in the existing conditions." Tito was not inclined to risk his prestige.

However, in the meantime Ben-Gurion had found another mediator—the editor of a great European newspaper. This eminent journalist was in Cairo in January 1963, and met Hassnin Heikal, who besides being editor of the official government journal *Al Goumhouriya* was also one of Nasser's close associates. Heikal asserted that Egypt was not thinking of making war on Israel. The European editor met Nasser a few days later. They had a long conversation, in the course of which the Egyptian President let drop some very significant words. "I think that if Ben-Gurion and I were shut up in a room together for three hours we should arrive at a peaceful solution to the Judaeo-Arab conflict."

On his return to London the editor met Baron Edmond de Rothschild and told him of the conversation with President Nasser. Rothschild informed that Israeli Ambassador in London, who sent the news to Ben-Gurion. And the Old Man wrote to Rothschild in Paris:

"Dear Edmond. I have received from our Ambassador in London your letter about your meeting with the editor. In it I learn that Nasser had spoken to him of the possibility of peace if he and I were shut up together in a room for three hours. Even if he did say this, I doubt very much if he really thought so. I have met several people who have talked to Nasser, and I have discovered that he knows how to say just what people want to hear, apart from the things that Nasser himself particularly wants to say.

"However, I feel that it is my duty to suppose that he might be sincere in what he said. I know that he is the only Arab leader who could come to an understanding with Israel if he really wanted to. No other Arab leader would dare (or would even be able, in the present state of the Arab world) to make a settlement with Israel. Nasser alone has sufficient standing in Egypt and in the Arab world in general to be able to make peace with Israel, if he really wants it and thinks it would be beneficial for Egypt and the Arab world.

"I am sure you know what peace with Egypt would mean for us. Therefore, I wonder if you would kindly suggest that the editor should come and see me in Jerusalem as soon as possible—even a day or two after you receive this letter, if it can be arranged. I should like to send a personal letter to Nasser through him, saying that I am prepared to meet him in the greatest secrecy anywhere that he chooses (Switzerland, Greece, Italy—even in Cairo, if Nasser will guarantee my safety) and to confer with him for as many hours as necessary to make peace—more than that, an alliance for cultural, economic and political cooperation.

"It may be that Providence has marked you out for the historic mission of helping to bring about peace between Israel and Egypt."

The machinery was set in motion, and a few weeks later, the

mediator met Ben-Gurion in Jerusalem. Ben-Gurion was in an awkward position, being preoccupied with the grave crisis over the notorious affair of the German scientists working in Egypt. However, he repeated his desire for peace and his willingness to meet Nasser. He made no allusion to the proposed solution of the Arab refugee problem.

The editor returned to Europe and then set off for Cairo, where he saw Nasser again and explained his mission. "Since our last meeting I have seen Mr. Ben-Gurion," he said, "and I told him that you are the only statesman among the Arab leaders and the only one capable of solving the difficult problem of relations between Israel and the Arabs. Ben-Gurion is prepared to meet you anywhere—even in Cairo."

Nasser smiled. "Thank you for the compliment. But here is an article that Ben-Gurion has written. Can I trust him?" He was silent for a moment or two, then said, half to himself, "How can you tell if you can trust someone?" Then he plunged into a long discourse, the gist of which was that he had no reason at all to trust Ben-Gurion. He rehashed all of Israel's "misdeeds"—the Israeli War of Independence, when he had served as an officer in the front line, the assassination of Count Bernadotte, Israel's reprisal raids in the Gaza Strip and the Sinai War.

"Do you think it is impossible to reach a peaceful settlement with Israel?" the editor asked him.

"No," replied Nasser, explaining that he had learned a great deal since 1956 and still more from the Cuba affair in 1962. "There are some things one must learn to live with, and Israel is one of them." He was interested in Ben-Gurion's attitude to the refugee question, and admitted that most of the displaced persons should settle in Arab countries.

Nasser sidestepped any meeting with Ben-Gurion by saying that until September he would be too busy. The Arab Federation had just been formed, Kassem had fallen from power, and he would be immersed in Arab affairs for some time ahead. He was watching Jordan closly—if Hussein were to fall, Israel would in all probability occupy the Old City of Jerusalem and other strategic points. He would be in a difficult situation, but would not go to war.

There was obviously no possibility of a meeting between Nasser and Ben-Gurion. The mediator gave an account of his talks to his Israeli friends when he returned to London. It seemed clear that Nasser, having just become the leader of a federation of Egypt, Syria and Iraq, was not inclined to engage in peace talks.

It was by no means the only setback that Ben-Gurion had at this time. At home, MAPAI was going through a crisis. The Left-wing parties refused to listen when Ben-Gurion proposed that they should merge with MAPAI, and his task of governing was becoming more and more difficult. Then came the startling affair of the German scientists in Egypt.

The Swiss police had arrested two foreigners, an Austrian named Joklik and an Israeli, Joseph Ben-Gal, at Zurich on March 2, 1963, during the height of the Carnival. The two were questioned at length, but their arrest was not announced until a fortnight later. On March 15, the Swiss authorities had issued a statement that the two were being charged with making threats against the person of Heidi Goerke, a young German woman.

The press had gotten hold of the story, and published some fantastic articles. President Nasser was said to be building rockets and nuclear weapons with the help of German scientists (one of whom was Heidi Goerke's father, Paul Goerke) who were at work at secret factories in the desert outside Cairo. They had already assembled the prototype of a jet plane and two types of tactical missiles, one with a range of 350 miles. The warheads of these missiles were to be filled with strontium 90 and radioactive waste bought from India. If launched against Israel, these missiles could wipe out the whole population. This was Nasser's "final solution" to the Jewish problem.

Israel's anxiety was understandable, and it was only natural for her to protect herself by all possible means, including sending secret agents to threaten the families of the German scientists working in Egypt.

The Israeli secret service had known about the factories outside Cairo for some time. In October 1962 reports had been received that the Egyptians were preparing to use bacteriological and chemical warheads, but this information was kept secret. After the arrests in Switzerland, however, the Israelis launched a press campaign to draw world attention to the activities of the German scientists in Egypt.

The truth behind the sensational headlines was much less startling. The Egyptian jet plane was still in the experimental stages and the missiles were not yet in production. But the Israeli man on the street read, nevertheless, that he was in dire danger.

The press campaign soon produced results never intended by its instigators. The German scientists in Egypt were spoken of as Nazis (which, incidentally, they were or had been) and a wave of anti-German feeling swept through the country.

Ben-Gurion was alarmed. His policy with regard to the Federal Republic, his long and difficult efforts to bring about closer relations with Adenauer's Germany stood in danger. Relations with Bonn had recently improved still further, when Israel had received a free supply of large quantities of modern weapons, and Israeli Army personnel were being trained in their use in West Germany. Ben-Gurion had always been very careful to avoid accusing Bonn of anti-Jewish activities. The Israeli Government had acted with great discretion in 1960, when they first received reports of the presence of German scientists and technicians in Egypt.

Ben-Gurion decided that the growing Germanophobia in the country had to be stopped. It was painful for him to act, for the two people chiefly concerned were both close associates and dear to him. One was Golda Meir, whose attitude towards Germany was definitely hostile, and the other was the head of the secret service, Isser Halperin, who was devoted to Ben-Gurion. Halperin was convinced that the German scientists in Egypt constituted a deadly threat to Israel, and that a campaign against them and even against West Germany was fully justified. There had already been differences of opinion between Halperin and Ben-Gurion on this subject, and Golda Meir supported the former.

A stormy meeting between Halperin and Ben-Gurion over the question of diplomatic relations with Federal Germany brought matters to a head, and the secret service chief sent in his resignation.

Golda Meir told several of her colleagues that she too was going to resign. She did not, but Ben-Gurion found his authority badly shaken. The affair of the German scientists had affected his policy, he was becoming increasingly unpopular, he had lost his secret service chief and he and Golda Meir were completely at odds over foreign policy.

And in April 1963 Ben-Gurion suffered another blow when his old friend Ben-Zvi died. "I have had three friends in my life," he wrote later. "Yavnieli, Berl Katzenelson and Itzhak Ben-Zvi. Now they are all dead, and I feel very lonely."

He also felt let down by his colleagues. Several of them had abandoned him at the time of the Lavon Affair, others had done so later. He drew his own conclusions and thought of resigning. This idea had been slowly taking shape in his mind, and the blows he received as a result of the German scientists affair, the death of Ben-Zvi and the Lavon scandal served to hasten his decision. He decided definitely during another crisis, one which he believed—

though wrongly, as it turned out—to be among the most serious in Israel's existence. It arose from the signing of a treaty between Egypt, Syria and Iraq which brought the "Arab Federation" into being. For the first time ever, an Arab document declared that the destruction of Israel was a main objective. Ben-Gurion was deeply worried by this Arab union, which he had been dreading ever since the establishment of the State, and he decided that attack was the best form of defense. He launched an unprecedented diplomatic offensive, writing to practically every head of state. In his letters he set forth the dangers of this Arab Federation and once again repeated Israel's great desire for peace. He asked that an appeal be made to the Arab states, at the next session of the United Nations, to sign a peace treaty with Israel.

He asked Russia and the United States to make a joint declaration guaranteeing the frontiers and security of all the states in the Middle East. In his letter to President Kennedy he said that he was prepared to make a secret visit to Washington to explain the gravity of the situation.

Kennedy politely rejected Ben-Gurion's proposals. He did not believe in the panacea of a Russo-American declaration, and he was opposed to Ben-Gurion visiting Washington, saying that the secret could not be kept and that a meeting between them at such a critical time could only lead to wild speculations.

Ben-Gurion would not admit defeat. He wrote to Kennedy again, outlining another plan in which he proposed, first, a defense treaty between the United States and Israel; secondly, that great quantities of American armaments be sent to Israel, to counterbalance the Russian supplies to Egypt; and thirdly, that a disarmament plan be worked out for the whole of the Middle East.

In his letter to De Gaulle he wrote: "My chief anxiety is to avoid war with the Arabs, and only an alliance between France and Israel can prevent war."

After many years, Ben-Gurion at last adopted the idea put forward by some of his friends and political opponents alike—that a military alliance should be made with France. "I ask you, *Monsieur le Président,* if the time has now come to seal the great friendship between our two countries by a political treaty of military aid in the event of an attack on Israel by Egypt and her allies? I think we could have useful talks on this subject, when you have the time."

The replies—all disappointing—soon began to come in. No one thought that the Arab Federation presented a serious threat to

Israel. Britain considered the Arab threats mere verbiage. The United States pointed out that such threats had been made several times in the past, and the letter went on to say that, in any case, the United States would not allow any violation of Israeli sovereignty and territorial rights. France was not unduly alarmed either. De Gaulle, like Kennedy, declined to be drawn into making a military alliance. He argued that relations between the two countries and their armies were such that no military alliance was necessary. The other letters arrived at similar conclusions—there was no great danger from the Arabs and their threats need not be taken seriously.

They were right. The new Arab Federation was short-lived, and few people now remember that it ever existed.

Even before all the replies to his letters had come in, Ben-Gurion had made his final decision. On June 16, 1963, when his secretary arrived in the morning laden with papers, Ben-Gurion said, "I shan't need them. I'm resigning." His colleagues were stunned. Peres, in Paris, was informed by telephone and took the first plane home to try to dissuade the Old Man. But others had tried before him, and all their pleading was in vain. Ben-Gurion had made up his mind to quit. However impulsive his decision seemed, it had been reached only after much thought and consideration. The public was astonished when they read the news in special editions of the evening papers. Golda Meir was in tears, but the Opposition rejoiced and Ben-Gurion's opponents raised their heads again. Everyone felt that this time the decision was definite.

He did not disclose his reasons. My impression is that he was shattered by the Lavon Affair, worn out by bitterness and disappointment, and no longer had the will to govern the country. His resignation was that of a man who had been greatly hurt.

Ben-Gurion rejects this theory, and says it is "quite mistaken. I resigned for personal reasons," is all he says.

Levi Eshkol formed a new government. It was the end of an era.

THIRTY-EIGHT

THE FALL

Ben-Gurion had retired to his desert kibbutz of Sde Boker. His sudden departure was unfortunate, for he should have had the leave-taking of a glorious leader who had accomplished his mission and left the field clear for younger men. However, he did not intend to give up politics entirely. He intended to demand an inquiry into the way in which the Government had dealt with the Lavon Affair during those stormy days in November 1960. To this end, some of his aides made a thorough search of the files of the affair, going back to 1954.

Ben-Gurion believed, though wrongly, that by making a public appeal for a judicial inquiry he could right an injustice committed by the "Seven." He had forgotten that by leaving the Government he had also relinquished power. The MAPAI and public opinion backed the new leaders. As an ordinary citizen, Ben-Gurion could not force the Government to accede to his demands. The man who could face facts had made a great mistake in trying to defeat his opponents by placing himself in a weak position.

He had lost the battle before it began. And by his sudden resignation he irreparably damaged the policy and principles he himself had laid down. He had not troubled to assure the positions of his closest collaborators—either through egotism or negligence. Peres and Dayan, the two men who were thought to be his successors, were still in minor posts—Dayan was Minister of Agriculture and Peres was Chief Assistant to the Defense Minister. Ben-Gurion could have appointed them to key positions before he resigned. But it was typical of him not to have done so, for he has never rewarded services rendered.

The only people who profited by his departure were the leaders of the Old Guard and his opponents in other parties. Those who had rebelled against him, Mrs. Meir at their head, no longer had their hands tied. Some of the MAPAI leaders soon began agitating for Lavon's return. Eshkol finally agreed, in May 1964, to write to the Lavon clique saying that his dismissal had been declared invalid.

The Old Guard was successful in establishing a united front with the Left Wing, which Ben-Gurion had been trying to do for years. Then an alliance was made with the young leaders of *Ahdut Haavoda*. The latter were then regarded as the heirs apparent of the Old Guard, and so Ben-Gurion's disciples were ousted from the succession.

This battle of the generations took place within the framework of Ben-Gurion's private war over the notorious "injustice" of the Committee of Seven. The press, public opinion and the MAPAI attacked him, or called him senile and mad. He stuck obstinately to his case, but was unable to convince the public and appeared more and more like a real-life Don Quixote.

Towards the end of 1964, Ben-Gurion put before the Government the results of his personal inquiry into the "injustice of the Committee of Seven." The new facts which he had brought to light amply justified an official, judicial inquiry. The Minister of Justice was of that opinion, but Eshkol refused—a reopening of the affair could only be injurious to the Committee of Seven, over which he himself had presided when it whitewashed Lavon in 1960.

Ben-Gurion made another mistake at the 1965 MAPAI Congress. Several of his supporters begged him to declare that he would be prepared to take office again. They were sure that they could get together a majority in his favor. If he did this he would be able to achieve his aim, set up a committee of inquiry and prevent the return to old methods of government. But Ben-Gurion refused to listen to them.

There followed the painful spectacle of Ben-Gurion's ex-colleagues and associates doing all they could to break and humiliate him and destroy his legend. Even the dying Sharett was brought from his hospital bed so that he could accuse the man who had ousted him from power. On the same day, Golda Meir, dressed in black from head to foot, made a bitter attack on Ben-Gurion. The meeting was shocked into silence as she accused him of intriguing and lying, in such virulent terms as had never before been heard at a MAPAI congress. Without a word, Ben-Gurion got up and left the hall. The following day, a secret ballot gave forty percent of the votes to Ben-Gurion and sixty percent to Eshkol. MAPAI had rejected its old leader.

At the end of June 1965 Ben-Gurion decided to stand at the next elections at the head of a list of Independents. This caused a scission in MAPAI, as Peres, Dayan and Almogi resigned in order to support Ben-Gurion. Rarely has a national leader who has done so much for his country been so reviled as Ben-Gurion was in that election campaign. It is true, too, that rarely has a national leader used such harsh and vindictive language towards his opponents.

The result was humiliating. To some extent he had brought it on himself by making the election campaign an out-and-out struggle against Eshkol and MAPAI, and by revealing his obsession with the 1960 Lavon Affair. The whole country had heard more than enough of it by then. His obsession was taken as a sign of Ben-Gurion's failing mental powers. He was called a liar, a dictator, a madman.

He lost the elections, although at the great age of 79 he was returned to Parliament at the head of a tiny party of ten members.

MAPAI itself had been weakened, but with *Ahdut Haavoda* it won 48 seats, of which 37 were held by MAPAI members.

The legend of the invincible Ben-Gurion was shattered in the 1965 elections, but for him the battle continues.

Israeli President Chaim Weizmann, with Prime Minister Ben-Gurion on the right and Harry Levin on the left at the dedication of the Weizmann Institute of Science at Rehovoth on November 2, 1949.

Prime Minister Ben-Gurion in Tel Aviv signing the document proclaiming the Jewish State of Israel in 1948.

July 1946, David Ben-Gurion, Chairman of the Jewish Agency, attacks the British White Paper.

Ben-Gurion in 1961, in traditional Burmese garb donned for a garden party given in his honor by President U Win Maung of Burma, cuts a cake in the shape of the Star of David. President U Win Maung (right) and Burma's Premier U Nu (left) look on.

Ben-Gurion and Konrad Adenauer in New York in 1960.

Mrs. David Ben-Gurion, Charles De Gaulle, Madame Yvonne De Gaulle, and David Ben-Gurion in Paris in 1961.

David Ben-Gurion, Israeli Prime Minister, studies a map of the battle area and listens to a report by Major General Moshe Dayan, right, as they fly over Egypt's Sinai Peninsula on November 13, 1956. Mrs. Paula Ben-Gurion, left, the Prime Minister's wife, and his daughter, Renana, right, look on.

Mrs. Golda Meir.

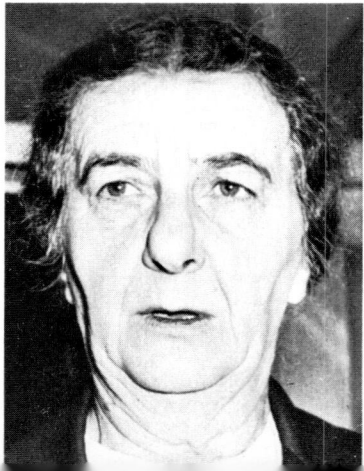

Ben-Gurion, shortly before his 1953 retirement, inspects a new road under construction in the Dead Sea area.

Premier Ben-Gurion meets with President Kennedy at the Waldorf-Astoria in May 1961.

Ben-Gurion presenting President Truman with a bronze candelabrum as a 67th birthday gift.

Eleanor Roosevelt visiting Ben-Gurion at his Waldorf Towers suite in 1961.

All photos courtesy of World Wide Photos.

EPILOGUE

He is still energetic, bright and hardworking. Whether seated at his desk in Tel Aviv or in his prefab at Sde Boker, he goes on writing numerous articles and chapters of books. "I've enough work for a score of years," this octagenarian says with a smile. He receives foreign visitors, keeps up a regular correspondence with several heads of state, including General de Gaulle, makes speeches at meetings and takes part in lively debates in the Knesset. He still charms everyone he meets, and when he bridles up in the course of a conversation or a speech, he again appears as the very spirit of a proud young nation.

His place in history is assured. The memory of the Lavon Affair and the hysterical attacks on him will soon be forgotten. Those who reviled him will one day have to examine their consciences and explain their conduct to the coming generation. When the name David Ben-Gurion is mentioned, he will be remembered as the man from Plonsk, the little immigrant who was a farm worker at Sejera, the man behind the Biltmore Program, the Father of the State and the man who won the War of Independence, the creator of a unified army and a State system of work and education, the prophet of the reclamation of the desert, the glorious leader of the Sinai Campaign and the architect of friendship with France, the developing countries and Europe.

The name of Ben-Gurion will recall the war leader who could not win the peace. Peace will come when another Ben-Gurion, with different qualities but with his strength and determination, leaves his mark on history.

Ben-Gurion's era already arouses a slight feeling of nostalgia— nostalgia for the testing times of danger and the hours of splendid successes, for the taste of the first victories, for the realization that one could be proud of being a Jew. It is true that Ben-Gurion made serious mistakes. He was so concerned with problems of defense that he neglected economic questions, did not pay enough attention to national education, and was unable to prevent corruption in his own party and certain political circles. But his successes far outweigh his faults and mistakes. And the "Ben-Gurion era" has already become legendary, purified and embellished. This is the way of the world, and one day the Israeli people will forget Ben-Gurion's defects, just as the British now overlook those of Churchill.

In David Ben-Gurion the Jewish people have found their hero of modern times, who will have his place in their gallery of immortals, with Moses, King David and the Prophets. The future will see to that. But for the moment, while passion and hatred have not yet died down, and blows just or unjust are still aimed at the old lion, the real greatness of the man escapes the common gaze. This man who, by force of will alone has accomplished, perhaps unconsciously, the finest adventure of all time.

BIBLIOGRAPHY

I made use of various sources when preparing this biography, but I must mention first of all the great assistance given me by former Prime Minister Ben-Gurion himself. In the first place, he accorded me many long interviews over a period of eighteen months, and allowed me to accompany him on his travels and be present at meetings and interviews. Secondly, he gave me access to his documents and files, especially his personal diary since 1915, notebooks, private and official correspondence and files containing papers on all his activities both before and after the creation of the State of Israel. It goes without saying that these papers and documents formed the basis of my material. I also consulted various books about Ben-Gurion or about matters of primary importance during his career. In addition I used the nineteen volumes of Ben-Gurion's complete works, as well as recently published collections of his articles which have appeared in the Israeli press, especially *On the Way to the State of Israel, In the Restored State of Israel,* and *Meetings with the Arab Leaders, An Attempt which failed.*

I found that the best biography of Ben-Gurion is Barnett Litvinoff's *Ben-Gurion of Israel* (New York: Praeger, 1954). Robert Saint-John's *Ben-Gurion* (London: Jarrolds, 1959) is more anecdotal. A Hebrew book, *Ben-Gurion and his times,* by Bracha Habas (Tel Aviv: Massada, 1952) is a study in depth of Ben-Gurion's youth (1886–1915).

I also used all the important works on the birth and life of the State of Israel, on the Lavon Affair and the Suez crisis. I was able to look through almost all the newspaper articles which appeared on all these subjects, but as they run into several thousands, I cannot name them here.

I was allowed to use documents preserved in various Israeli libraries—the Zionist archives, the *Histadrut* archives, and those of the MAPAI, the Jewish Agency, the Revisionist Party, the Knesset and the Weizmann Institute. I also studied the Palestinian and Israeli press files.

Finally, a very important source was the talks I had, not only with Ben-Gurion himself, but with dozens of his colleagues, friends and assistants, and also with his old political and ideological opponents in all walks of life. But I should like to repeat that Ben-Gurion's private papers were the most fruitful source for my research, not only because they are rich in material but because I found in Ben-Gurion's private diaries very exact descriptions and records of countless conversations, acts and happenings—the truth and exactitude of which were confirmed by reference to other sources.

1886–1915

The source material for this early period were: Bracha Habas's book mentioned above; the *Plonsk Book,* which contains childhood memories written by inhabitants of the town, including those of Ben-Gurion; the autobiography of Shlomo Lavi, *Shalom Layish,* in which this companion of Ben-Gurion writes about their youthful days. The *Letters between Ben-Gurion and his father,* at Plonsk, was also very useful; as was the *Correspondence with Fuchs.* Unfortunately, Ben-Gurion's diary up to 1915 was lost in his abrupt departure from Turkey; however, his articles in *Ahdut* and other publications, his talks with me, some letters and *Recollections of Ben-Zvi,* published in the Israeli press, proved of great use.

1915–1939

Even for these early years, a great deal of material has been preserved in Ben-Gurion's files, in the diary he kept during these years, in reports, speeches and essays collected in book form. The recollections of some contemporaries who knew him in New York have been of particular value. His relations with Weizmann are laid bare not only by the thoughts he consigned to his diary but also by the correspondence between the two men. Documents in the Zionist archives tell of the strife in the movement and of Ben-Gurion's rise to power. The *Biography of Jabotinski,* by Schechtmann, and the *Correspondence between Ben-Gurion and Jabotinski,* show up the relations between the two. Some fascinating passages in Ben-Gurion's diary, documents in his files, and the series of articles,

Meetings with Arab Leaders, tell of the attempts at negotiations between him and the Arabs in the mid-thirties.

The submissions to the Peel Commission, the partition plan, the St. James's Conference and the White Paper are fully covered in Ben-Gurion's papers and files, as well as in Weizmann's *Memoirs* and the Minutes of the Peel Commission.

1940–1947

This is not only the period of the Second World War but also that of the Biltmore Program and the final plans for the struggle to establish the State of Israel. The Zionist archives contain many factual documents on the different Zionist congresses and the positions taken up by Weizmann and Ben-Gurion. Letters to the press by Weizmann (in particular, one in April 1947, to the New York Jewish paper *Bitzaron*), and letters from Ben-Gurion to his wife and children, also give interesting sidelights.

There is much Hebrew documentation on the Jewish Brigade and the Resistance movements in Palestine. Ben-Gurion's attitude and activities are covered by his diary and writings, letters, etc. Other information was obtained from the *Private Diary* of Nhemia Argov and *A Portrait of Ben-Gurion* by David Lazar (Maariv).

1947–1948

I found *Three Glorious Days* by Zeev Sharef (Paris: Laffont, 1963) very useful for this period preceding the creation of the State, as well as a number of unpublished documents and interviews with people who played a leading part in the events.

Many books have been published in Israel on the War of Independence; one of the most complete is the *History of the War of Independence,* an Army publication. The crisis over the making of a unified army has received little attention in published works, though some details are given in Sharef's book mentioned above. I have made much use of letters between Ben-Gurion and the Army leaders at the time, the correspondence between Ben-Gurion and Galili, and Minutes of Cabinet meetings.

1949–1955

The early period of Israel's existence is covered by conventional sources. In addition, there is the correspondence between Ben-

Gurion and Weizmann, the Diplomatic Reports of Sharett and Eban, and certain anonymous letters sent to Ben-Gurion from Russia. Robert Saint-John has given a vivid picture of the German reparations question in his book on Ben-Gurion, and there is much interesting material in the archives of the Knesset.

However, the Lavon Affair was the main event of this period. Ben-Gurion refused to comment on this, or to make available any document. Indeed, this and the Suez affair, both still treated as state secrets, were the only subjects that Ben-Gurion refused to talk to me about or make available any documents. Other Israeli leaders to whom I spoke were equally silent. I therefore used only the following sources: The Report of E. A. Bayne in the *Bulletin of American Universities Field Staff* (May, 1961); an essay, based partly on this report, published in *L'Observateur du Moyen Orient et de l'Afrique,* Vol. VIII, No. 51, December 18, 1964); an essay by Hagai Eshed, "Who Gave the Order?" and the books *The Affair, The Plot* and *Things as They Are,* all of which were published in Israel. For background material, I drew upon Nhemia Argov's *Private Diary* and the correspondence between Sharett and Lavon, and Sharett and Ben-Gurion.

1955–1957

The Ben-Gurion–Sharett correspondence was also very useful for tracing the deterioration in the relations between the two men up to the time of Suez. For the proposed defense agreement with the United States, I used some of Ben-Gurion's reports and speeches and his copious correspondence with Israel Galili.

For the Suez affair, I drew upon all the new works which have appeared on this subject since the publication of my own *Suez Ultra-Secret* (Paris: Fayard, 1964), and those I found especially useful were Finer's *Dulles Over Suez,* Terrence Robertson's *Crisis,* and General Eisenhower's memoirs, *My Years At The White House.* But my main source of information came from talks I had with French personalities in 1962 and which I did not use at the time, partly because I did not want to be the first to reveal diplomatic secrets, and partly because I had not been able to check the whole of the information thus obtained. Since then, I have seen certain people several times in London and Paris, and was able to verify this information. Moreover, other writers have in the meantime published accounts of the incidents that I had chosen not to write about, so I decided that I could now incorporate some of them in this present book. This applies to the following incidents and events: the contacts made in Paris by Peres and others, just before Suez; the visit to Paris of Peres, Dayan, Carmel and Golda Meir (this was confirmed and described to me by a French minister and a senior official in 1962; but I did not decide to publish it until I saw that Dayan had alluded to it in his published *Diary*). I was able to reconstruct the Sèvres meeting by combining the information I had obtained in Paris with that given in Robertson's and Finer's books, and also by referring to some articles and chapters of books which appeared in Israel on Ben-Gurion's attitude just before his decision to attack the Egyptians in Sinai. Other material was drawn from the exchange of messages between Ben-Gurion and Eisenhower, diplomatic notes and the correspondence between Ben-Gurion and various heads of state.

1957–1960

This was the period of great diplomatic activity on the part of Ben-Gurion's Government, and I have drawn extensively upon Ben-Gurion's correspondence with Dulles, Eisenhower, Adenauer, De Gaulle, etc. The description of Nhemia Argov's tragic death is based upon Robert Saint-John's book, already mentioned, and the accounts given by several of the dead man's friends. I found Shimon Peres's book, *The Next Stage* (in Hebrew, Tel Aviv: Am Hassefer, 1965), most useful on Ben-Gurion's approaches to Federal Germany.

1960–1966

The material for the second phase of the Lavon Affair was drawn from sources already mentioned and Ben-Gurion's voluminous correspondence with Sharett, Lavon, Eshkol and others. I was helped, too, by verbal accounts given by colleagues of Ben-Gurion and by his political opponents. The Minutes of the meetings of the MAPAI Central Committee were useful.

Ben-Gurion's correspondence with Kennedy, Tito, Rothschild and U Nu was invaluable, as were the reports of his talks with Kennedy's envoys and with the editor who contacted Nasser. For the affair of the German scientists in Egypt, I referred to sources I used in my book *The Hunt For German Scientists* (Arthur Barker, 1967). Ben-Gurion's letters to nearly all heads of state, and the replies, relating to his last peace offensive in 1963, were all made available to me. His private files, letters and diary were of great help in writing of the period after his resignation.

It only remains for me to express my gratitude to Mr. Ben-Gurion for his help, and to all those men and women who gave me such wholehearted assistance and without whose help this book could not have been written.

AUTHOR'S NOTE

As this book was going to press, Paula Ben-Gurion died suddenly. On January 28, 1968, she was staying with her husband at Sde Boker, when she suddenly fell in a faint. She was rushed to the Beersheba hospital, her situation desperate. She died the next morning. She was 76.

"Paula"—as everyone called her—was no more. Her marriage to Ben-Gurion had meant the sacrifice of her own world: a middle-class way of life, the comforts of New York, her career as a nurse. But when she decided to follow the stubborn little man to a hard pioneer life on the land of Israel, she did not sacrifice her own personality. She never became a shadow beside the man she had married. She had her own opinions and she expressed them. She was frank, sincere and outspoken.

After her death the Tel-Aviv daily *Haaretz* wrote: "She never felt in awe of the great world leaders of her time. On the contrary, she always talked to them in the same frank style she used with people she knew. Many true stories describe the free way in which she told every outstanding visitor from abroad what she thought of him, of his country and his policy. Sometimes, she would have better restrained her words a little; but in most cases it was precisely this drive and frankness of hers which provoked admiration. . . .

. . . "She felt that taking care of Ben-Gurion was her mission in life. She kept her household for him, she cooked for him, she made sure that disturbing guests would not stay too long with him. . . . She followed him everywhere. . . ."

After she died, Ben-Gurion entered her room in the hospital. His eyes full of tears, he caressed her face and whispered the biblical verse: "Thou who went after me in the desert, an unsown country. . . ."

INDEX

Abdullah, King of Jordan, 121–23, 130, 155, 172
Abu Ageila, 153
Adenauer, Konrad, 173, 232, 243, 249, 255
  Ben-Gurion's meeting with, 251
Adams, Sherman, 226, 227
Africa, Israel and, 241, 250–51, 254, 268
Ahdut (periodical), 22–24
Ahdut Haavoda, 32, 40, 279, 280
Alami, Moussa, 50–52
Algerian War, 189, 196–97, 247, 252
Alon, Gen. Igal, 90, 131, 153
Altalena (ship), 132–38
Amer, Gen. Ali Ali, 228
Aqaba, Gulf of, 155, 173, 192, 235, 236, 238; *see also* Eilath
Arab Federation, 273, 276–77
Arab-Israeli war (1947–49), 95–155, 161–62
  air forces, 129, 131, 145
  arms shipments from abroad, 100, 106, 107, 110, 120, 129–30, 133–38, 145
  atrocities, 107–8
  Ben-Gurion's command difficulties, 111–15, 140–44
  Ben-Gurion's preparations for, 89–91, 94, 95
  British neutrality, 97, 100, 102
  mercenaries for Arabs, 101
  Negev operations, 150–52, 155
  peace efforts after, 172–73
  road to Jerusalem, 104–6, 120, 128, 129
  strength of Jewish forces, 98–100
  truces, 134, 139, 145, 147, 148–55
  See also Arab Legion; *specific Arab countries*
Arab-Israeli war (1956), 223–35
  capture of *Ibrahim,* 227
  Israeli plans for, 192, 194, 205–18
  Sinai campaign, 223–30, 232, 236
Arab-Israeli war (1967), iii–iv, 238–39
Arab League, 79

Arab Legion, 91
  in 1947–49 war, 120, 123, 124, 128, 130, 132, 147, 148–49, 151, 155
Arabs
  1947 armed strength of, 91
  See also Palestinian Arabs; *specific countries*
Aran, Zalman, 262
Arazi, Yehuda, 66
Aref, Abdul Salam Mohammed, 247
Argentina, Eichmann kidnapping in, 252–53, 255
Argov, Lt. Col. Nhemia, 121, 158, 183, 184, 212, 218, 225, 243–44
Arlozoroff, Haïm, 46
Arslan (Arab leader), 51
Attlee, Clement, 56, 80, 84
Auni Bey, 52
Austin, Warren, 104, 119
Avidar, Joseph, 108, 113
Avigur, Shaul, 178, 184
Ayalon, Gen. Zvi, 112, 113, 140–41
Ayzik, Simcha, 7, 11

Balfour Declaration, 29–30, 32
Beersheba, 151
Begin, Menahem, 75, 125, 133–37, 158, 174, 220
Ben Bella, Ahmed, 212, 215
Ben-Gal, Joseph, 274
Ben-Gurion, Amos (son), 35
Ben-Gurion, David (David Grin)
  attempted assassination of, 243–44
  birth of, 6
  as boy and young man in Poland, 6–13
  chooses new name, 22
  descriptions of, 13, 25, 36, 156–57
  general estimate of, 281–82
  illnesses of, 156, 191–92
    malaria, 17, 36
  Jewish religion and, 8, 159
  as Minister of Defense under Sharett, 184–90
  as modern prophet, 258

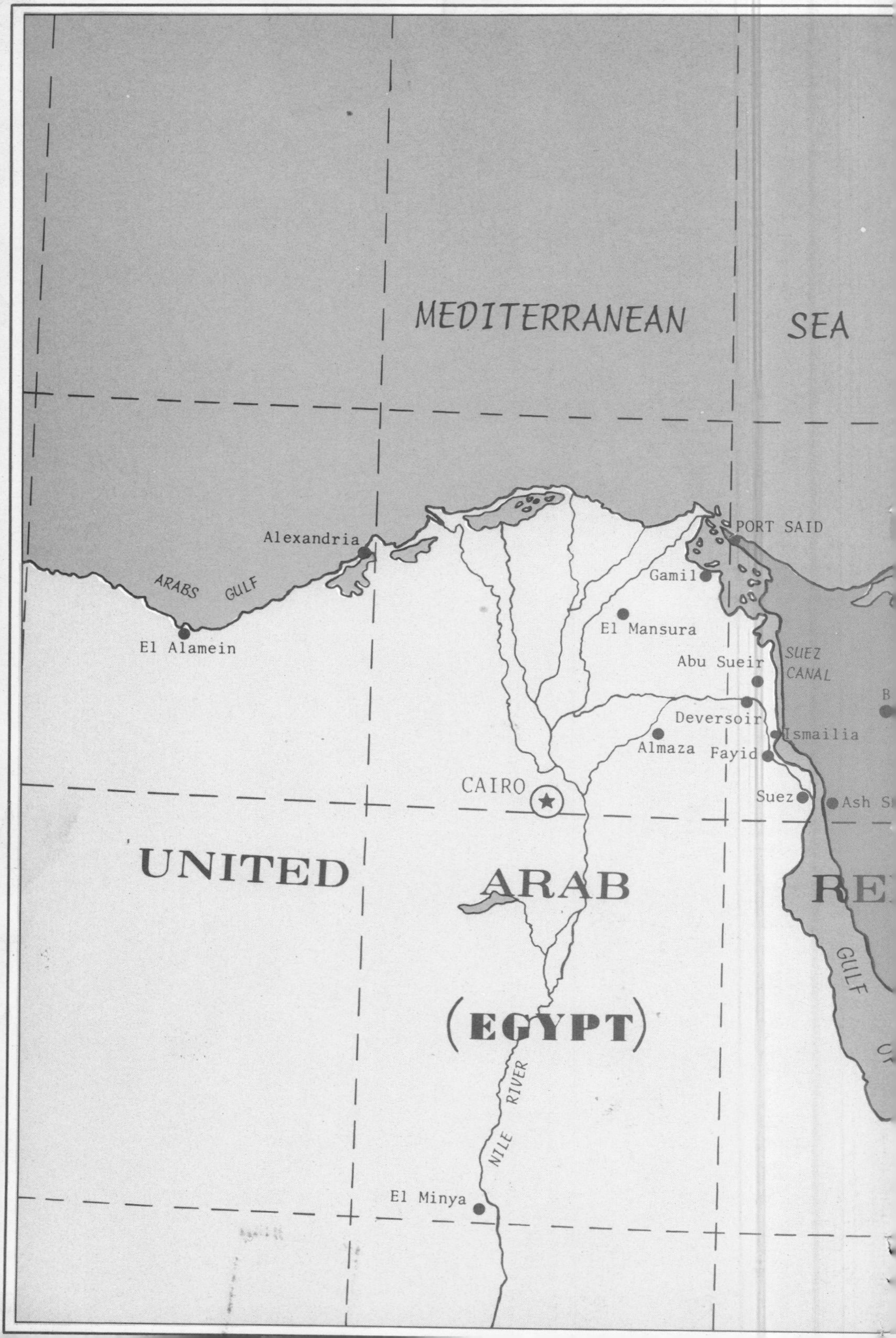
MEDITERRANEAN
SEA
Alexandria
ARABS GULF
El Alamein
PORT SAID
Gamil
El Mansura
Abu Sueir
SUEZ CANAL
Deversoir
Ismailia
Almaza
Fayid
CAIRO
Suez
UNITED
ARAB
(EGYPT)
NILE RIVER
El Minya
GULF